Popular Culture Studies
Across the Curriculum

Popular Culture Studies Across the Curriculum

Essays for Educators

Edited by
RAY B. BROWNE

McFarland & Company, Inc., Publishers
Jefferson, North Carolina, and London

ISBN 0-7864-2024-3 (softcover : 50# alkaline paper) ∞

LIBRARY OF CONGRESS CATALOGUING DATA ARE AVAILABLE

British Library cataloguing data are available

Cover image ©2005 PhotoSpin

Manufactured in the United States of America

*McFarland & Company, Inc., Publishers
Box 611, Jefferson, North Carolina 28640
www.mcfarlandpub.com*

Contents

Editor's Note

Recognition — or rerecognition — of the importance of understanding popular culture was the most significant academic and cultural development of the second half of the 20th century. Popular culture, as we are now understanding more fully, is the engine that drives culture toward more democracy, and if we are to comprehend the powers that control societies today — and have controlled them throughout history — we must understand their everyday cultures. For one reason or another, a few elites still hold out against the importance of everyday culture, but their resistance is futile. For better or worse, they are being overwhelmed.

This book is a collection of statements about the importance of popular culture studies in particular disciplines and in the overall sweep of academic and nonacademic education. I would like to thank the contributors to this volume for their thoughtful statements on the subject, and the thousands of sympathetic and like-minded thinkers who agree with us — including the thousands of members of the Popular Culture Association and the American Culture Association whose encouragement has driven and sustained my thinking through the years. For all, the sun rises higher and higher every day.

Introduction

Academic curricula are being strengthened and enriched through the enlightened realization that no discipline is an island unto itself. Instead, each is a part of the curriculum mainland, to which it feeds important nutrients and from which it draws life-giving nourishment in the form of intellectual commerce and trade. Without this cross-fertilization, eventually it will hear the death knell tolling. Interdisciplinary study is a breaking down of what Marjorie Garber in *Academic Instincts* (2003) called "Disciplinary Libido." With this breaking down, the resulting two-way flow takes the form of interdisciplinary and comparative interchange.

Sometimes this interchange of disciplines takes place on the sly. A course or two of an instructor's choice is bootlegged into a list of approved courses or daily lectures. Generally, instructors are deliberate in what they are doing — introducing relevant outside materials or related asides to make students understand better, or stay awake!

The one universal coin in these related materials, a kind of daily world currency, is popular culture. No matter how esoteric the subject we teach, we and our students live in the everyday American culture around us. We cannot shut it out no matter how hermetically tight our minds are sealed.

Throughout the disciplines, academia is rapidly coming to understand that popular culture should be admitted to and used in courses and classes on all levels. Not to do so is to deny the basic drives and lifeblood of society, especially American democracy. All academia will benefit from the open admission and use of the cultures around them. Citizens who understand the humanities, and academics who teach them, meet on the common ground of understanding the full development and possibilities of education in a rapidly developing world of powerful democratic societies. Failing to comprehend this point creates a threat to the development and stability of culture. History has demonstrated countless times that a cap on societal development is bound to explode at one time or another.

One possible educational aid in avoiding that explosion is a fuller understanding of the value and significances of the humanities. Humanities courses are designed to develop good citizens. In the study of popular culture we are advocating that students from the beginning learn to understand their culture, appreciate it, and grow up as participating members. The alternative is that they accept the notion that they should be educated *away* from their cultures, and thereby live their lives as less than full citizens of their society.

This collection of 18 essays covers the humanities, some of the social sciences, and the uses of popular culture studies in community colleges, business colleges, and high schools. Space would not allow more essays. The collection indicates the dynamics of the need for more interdisciplinary mingling, for more coffee breaks and paper bag lunches whereby the intermingling of one discipline with another can be recognized and understood. There is often some apprehension and fear among many academics about opening the door to other disciplines, what we might perhaps overemphasize as *disciplinary infatuation*, because the apprehension is that those from other disciplines take away more than they leave. Popular culture studies, however, can be like the open-hearted, legendary Johnny Appleseed (John Chapman, 1774–1845). Chapman distributed intellectual and life-enriching food in the form of literature and apple seedlings in the Ohio River Valley, and left more than he took from it. Similarly, popular culture studies enriches each understanding, threatens no other discipline, and develops understanding and growth wherever it is employed.

Popular culture studies are central to the humanities, and enhance the spirit of academia. All academics can connect over its use with the desired goal of educating students for a full appreciation of life. The earlier this obvious point is driven home to students, and employed in their education, the more life it generates. Public school students should be taught the values of the life around them and why they should understand and appreciate it. As they go on to college, they need to nurture that early realization through continued popular culture studies. Society is dominated by the hard sell of reality, both on campus and off. Popular culture studies urge us to reach out into the world around us and do a more effective job for the introduction and understanding of everyday culture. Those students who best understand and participate in their everyday cultures develop into the most useful citizens. The world should not be artificially divided into everyday and "intellectual" life. Both mix and coextend, and are part and parcel of each other.

As Garber properly said in *Academic Instincts* (2003) about academics' reluctance to admit changes in their disciplines: "Our task as scholars is to reimagine the boundaries of what we have come to believe are disciplines and to have the courage to rethink them. For as a member of any discipline comes to realize sooner or later, it's hard to know where discipline envy, like inspiration, will strike next" (96).

Popular culture studies, as a force that interpenetrates all disciplines, urges a more powerful and immediate challenge, and an opportunity to eliminate discipline envy. The larger community of shared academic inquiry waits to reward the open and outstretched mind. We hope that students who study the humanities will, as a result of their studies, settle in and develop attitudes and patterns of behavior that last a lifetime.

The essays in this book reach out to form clusters of related or seemingly related disciplines.

The first is the broad group called the humanities—English literature, American studies, folklore, and popular culture. They are already closely interwoven but need to be more openly admitted as close allies. They feed and flourish on the same drives.

The next group includes the social sciences—anthropology, history, sociology, and communications. Then come religion and philosophy, which though they come from on high have their feet on the ground and explain life to us.

The next group, geography, covers all our land and landscape. Geography offers us a look at the most immediately visible features of our world. We need to know how the many branches of those features affect our cultures.

Women's studies concerns itself with more than half the world's population in their various activities. Increasingly women are demanding their place in the sun.

Next we have two engines that influence or control nearly all aspects of culture: economics and sports. Three papers on these subjects, including how popular culture is or should be used in a business college curriculum, bring about new awareness and thinking.

Community colleges and public schools are places where the importance of popular culture courses cannot be overemphasized. Community colleges have grown like magic since the 1980s because not only are they close to the community geographically, but they serve the community's academic needs. The public schools serve the same purpose and their students have the same needs. As they progress through the grades, public school students are increasingly the products of the culture around them. They walk in out of that culture in the morning to attend classes, then merge back into it at 2 or 3 o'clock in the afternoon, to blend with cultural activities or watch on TV as cultural activities are being reenacted before them.

The final paper in this collection discusses how programs in international studies should depend on popular culture. The most American movement in the world today, popular culture is the most characteristic of the United States of America. It has the greatest impact — even surpassing in the long run the military-industrial complex of which it is an integral part.

Increasingly, educators and those who pay for education are beginning to wonder what the time and money spent on the activity bring back — what are the returns. Andrew Abbott, distinguished professor of sociology at the University of Chicago, looked at the curricula of his university, and curricula in general, and drew some conclusions that must give us pause. His thesis in a talk to incoming freshmen was that "Education has no aims," and that the University of Chicago class of 2006 should consider themselves free to graze in whatever section of the campus they chose; all ultimately would reach the same levels of achievement. His conclusions contravened those of most other educators who believe that college teaches not so much particular subject matter as training in general skills that can be applied through life. Abbot said he could not accept "another variant of the cognitive argument for college education — the notion that there is a particular body of material that constitutes cultural literacy and it is the duty of the liberal education to teach you some large fraction of that material. I call this the *lingua franca* argument," he continued, "for the canon so taught is meant to be a *lingua franca* between 'educated' people no matter what they currently do. A canon works only if everybody who is supposed to have it agrees on what it is." He concluded emphatically, "But the situation of our educational system is that since nobody agrees on what the canon is, the system definitely does not have a canon" (55).

In other words, Abbott advocated the nearest thing we have to an educational method, tool, and purpose found in the humanities. It may fall short of creating well-educated people, but they will be able to look to the future and the challenges it brings. Sometimes students are ahead of their professors in understanding the role of education. For example, at the conclusion of Abbott's hour-long talk the students all rose in a standing ovation.

Abbott's survey of what happens to University of Chicago graduates is interesting: 24 percent go into banking and finance; 15 percent into business consulting; 14 percent into law; 10 percent business administration or sales; 7 percent into computers. Of historians, 24 percent become lawyers. For students in English, 11 percent go into teaching; 10 percent into business; 9 percent communications and law; 5 percent into advertising.

Education, as Abbott's survey demonstrated consists of more than stimulating individuals to think in their own narrow interests. Education is meant to develop people's self-interest and produce the best citizens possible. To become such citizens they must develop knowledge of two potentials—their own and that of society. To know themselves they must open the doors to all possibilities, see which they prefer, and in which they can develop. That is, as Shakespeare called it, being true to oneself:

> To thine own self be true,
> And it must follow as the night the day,
> Thou cans't not then be false to any man [*Hamlet* I. iii. 75].

Shakespeare's caution about being false to any man, that is, society, tells us that developing individuals likewise owe something for their development. It is a naturally occurring opportunity, especially in a democracy, where the culture allows the individual considerable, though perhaps not full, growth, and he or she in return provides opportunities for others. To make the fullest contribution to self and society the individual needs to comprehend all its resources, in other words to be a participant in them and know as much as possible about them. The humanities are the best key with which to unlock all facets of society. In other words, society is or should be the humanities and the humanities should be society. To paraphrase baseball's famous philosopher, Yogi Berra: we have seen the humanities and they are what we should be.

But growing into full appreciation of the humanities is sometimes slow and difficult for both established and young cultures. Youth tends to drive individuals into small groups, for assertion of one's rights, development of individuals through competition, and for self-recognition. For established groups, age tends to modify separation. As people grow older and develop more sense of the need for community, realization of one's dependence on others and what is to be gained from the sense of community, the influence of the humanities deepens. Until then, however, it seems that the humanities run counter to human nature. It is therefore the duty of the formal humanities to draw forth the sense of community in students and citizens alike. In the future, despite the seeming explosion of demand for specialists, society will need generalists who for their own satisfaction and the needs of society will be trained in generalities and therefore capable of moving in several directions. Consequently, they can make a richer contribution to their own lives and to society than they might acting as specialists.

The value of intermingling disciplines is being increasingly acknowledged, especially in those areas that demand the solo work of individuals, such as authors of books. Authors in all walks of life constantly acknowledge the debt owed to others. No better example can be found than in *Mark Twain and Medicine* (2003). In the acknowledgments, the author, K. Patrick Ober, a medical doctor, paid tribute to his patients for his success as a physician and author: "No one deserves more recognition than my patients, though. They have taught me more about medicine, and more about the joys and challenges of being a human being than I could ever explain in words. It is an honor to be allowed to be a part of their lives" (xii).

All aspects of culture coalesce in its popular culture. It is the key to what makes up the individual, and national and international societies. Individual curricula in all their drives toward education should understand as a part of their obligation the teaching of theories of popular culture studies in order to deepen and enrich their own areas of specialization and their students' appreciation of education.

Works Cited

Abbott, Andrew. "The Zen of Education." *University of Chicago Magazine*, 96/1 (2003): 52–58.

Browne, Ray B., and Marshall Fishwick. *Symbiosis: Popular Culture and Other Fields.* Bowling Green, OH: Popular Press, 1988.

Garber, Marjorie. *Academic Instincts.* Princeton, NJ: Princeton University Press, 2003.

Ober, K. Patrick. *Mark Twain and Medicine.* Columbia: University of Missouri Press, 2003.

1

English Literature Departments as Centers of the Humanities

RAY B. BROWNE

English literature departments in the United States are generally the leaders in expanding their offerings to include any new approach to keeping up with the diverging and growing interests of society. This is because usually those faculties are more wide-ranging than other faculties in their interests and reading. They take greater liberty in introducing into their assignments and reading materials they find interesting, though their subject matter might be on the periphery of the assigned texts.

This has been especially true of the expanding interests, ever since the early 1920s, when, under the leadership of the Harvard faculty, it was recognized that American authors were writing "literature" comparable in interest and value to the canonical English literature of the past and present. It became obvious through the leadership of the American studies programs that many of the leading authors of American literature demonstrated the power and influence on American society of its popular writing. A relatively late example of the genre would be Harriet Beecher Stowe's *Uncle Tom's Cabin* (1852).

To a large extent the concept of what constitutes literature has undergone a radical change since the 1970s, fired by the political and social energies that forced academics and critics to open their minds to the writings of new — sometimes minority, sometimes previously ignored — groups and genres. Despite the security of so-called canonical literature, English literature departments like to sail in the giant battleship called the humanities and to mix their literature courses with other humanities offerings across campus, which not only brings in more students but also mixes the various disciplines into a better rounded educational package.

But academia has a glacierlike movement for changes, and changes come only as the ideas about genre integrity — what Garber in *Academic Instincts* (2003) called "disciplinary libido" — melt slowly and merge into the surrounding society.

Sometimes the changes are incremental, led by authors and instructors who "bootleg" changes; wide trails are blazed sometimes by powerful professors and authors, sometimes by demanding students. Sometimes it is a leading academic organization such as the Modern Language Association, which for its own reasons leads the way in implementing the mixing of educational subjects. For example, in 2003, the outgoing president of the Modern Language Association, Mary Louise Pratt, in her final message in the MLA *Newsletter*, proudly outlined how departments of literature nationwide were reaching out to bring in what are now recognized as new branches of the humanities, such as philosophy, history, journalism, media studies, rhetoric, religious studies, gender studies, and others to "prepare students to be ethical, creative, and critical thinkers and doers in a culturally diverse society and an increasingly interconnected world" (3). Commercial and university presses, always eager to participate in a profitable market, are encouraging wider-ranging studies of literature in order to expand their markets and sales.

There is nothing new in this drive. In the early 1950s, The American Studies Association, with many influential antecedents, dedicated itself to having the effective curricula on all campuses expanded from the regular mix of philosophy, history, and literature into other recognized (and often unrecognized) departments.

To a certain extent the American studies programs have succeeded, as demonstrated by their presence in one strength or another on many campuses across the nation. They reached out and brought in new subjects and new instructors who realized the value of what President Pratt had acclaimed as the central function of education. Some instructors in English literature departments have been dedicated from the beginning to this goal. I myself, in my Ph.D. training at UCLA, thought I recognized the urgency of the American studies point of view and in my work majored in folklore, literature, and history (the nearest I could get to a regular American studies program). From that platform I have kept reaching out throughout my career.

Outreach and growth should be a constant in academic development. The folklore of the inviolability of the canon is just that, folklore. Old ideas and practices, especially when professors still look back at the wonders of their graduate school training and the professors who led them down the path to wisdom and truth, lead many new budding faculty into stagnant ideas and practices. We used to joke that their transmission of ideas was straining old ideas through old filters and pouring them into old bottles. But these old liquids could still draw high prices on the antique market and were therefore in circulation. Now that antique market has virtually closed its doors.

In defining the humanities that should be included in the present-day ideal educational program offered to students, President Pratt outlined the pleasure of teaching the humanities: "The last thirty-five years or so have been an extraordinary time to be a humanities scholar," she said, then mentioned the "methodological changes and parameters, and by the information technology revolution that has been enabling in so many ways." She concluded her essay with the statement that the rebels in the information field call themselves and their materials "the new humanities."

Two academic organizations—the Popular Culture Association and the American Culture Association, along with the hundreds of academics interested in everyday culture—have been working under the rubric of the "new humanities" since the 1980s, when I coined and popularized the term *popular culture* in print. Even then the realization of its aptness was probably overdue.

So that we know precisely what we are talking about, perhaps reiteration of the definition of popular culture will be useful. The definition I have been advocating for 35 years still holds true, as the paraphrase of one version indicates: By the term *popular culture*, despite many scholars' and lay people's efforts to divide and restrict it, we generally mean all aspects of the society we inhabit: the way of life we inherit, practice, and pass on to our descendants; what we do while we are awake and how we do it, the dreams we dream while asleep. It is the world around us: the mass media, the small groups, the individual controls and directors of our life, the entertainments, diversions, heroes, icons, rituals, psychology, religion, irreligion—the total life picture. It is disseminated by the mass media, the small group community, individuals, all means of communication.

Most important, the popular culture of a country is the voice of the people—for better or worse, their likes and dislikes, the lifeblood of their daily existence, their individual and national way of life. In America presumably popular culture is the voice of democracy—what makes America the country she is. It is America's greatest export and influence on the world at large. We should admit to ourselves that such immediately accessible aspects of American democracy as the fast food industry and Hollywood movies are the most powerful ambassadors of the American dream and the American way of life.

American popular culture in its many manifestations is increasingly being equated with the humanities because they include all aspects of existence that make people human everywhere. Robert Coles, psychologist and Pulitzer Prize winner, years ago recognized that the humanities include all kinds of culture. "The humanities," he said, "belong to no one kind of person; they are part of the lives of ordinary people, who have their own various ways of struggling for coherence, for a compelling faith, for social vision, for an ethical position, for a sense of historical perspective, for a meaning — a *raison d'etre in life.*"

T.S. Eliot recognized in his *Essays Ancient and Modern* the importance of everyday culture in society: "I incline to come to the alarming conclusion that it is just the literature that we read for 'amusement' or 'purely for pleasure' that may have the greatest ... least suspected ... earliest ... influence upon us. Hence it is that the influence of popular novelists, and of popular plays of contemporary life, require to be scrutinized." Richard Hoggart, one of the most influential literary and cultural English critics of the 1980s and 1990s, commented on the same subject: "Literature at all levels has the unique capacity to increase our understanding of a culture." It is a growing attitude expressed by "movers and shakers" throughout the elite world. For example, Thomas Hoving, former executive director of the New York Metropolitan Museum of Art and chief editor of *Connoisseur Magazine,* said in 1984: "There's a role for it [popular culture] no question. It's not the culture I care much about. But if we had examples of it from Pericles' Athens, we certainly would be better off."

Leslie Fiedler, one of the more articulate advocates of popular culture studies, drives this logic to its reasonable conclusion. He believed that popular culture — or popular humanities — could reunite us into a community which existed before people became separated by class, education, interests, and desires. In other words, the popular culture is the basic, unvarnished democratic culture that makes us, at the same time, very similar and fundamentally human.

One of the more explicit academic points of view was expressed by Ernest L. Boyer (1975), former U.S. Commissioner of Education, in "Toward a New Core Curriculum" (published in NEA *Advocate,* April/May 1978). He had no patience with those educationists who tried to distinguish between "liberal" and "vocational" education, to the disparagement of the latter. "Education," he insisted, "has always been a blend of inspiration and utility, but because of tradition, lethargy, ignorance and snobbery, mindless distinctions are made between what is vocationally legitimate and illegitimate." Boyer insisted that the work ethic plays a strong role in the true meaning of liberal education.

Historians too are increasingly recognizing the indispensability of the popular culture of the past, of Pericles' Athens if you will. In their new realization they are cutting closer to the bone of the association of the historian and the humanist. "Popular culture is a mainstream in American history now," said David Thelen, editor of the *Journal of American History*. "It's at the center of a lot of interpretive issues in the humanities." The *American Historical Review*, for example, had a forum on history and literature, "Storytelling Has Returned to Claim a Prominent Place in History," which had a preface by the editor. The return has "rekindled controversies about the virtues and vices of recovering the past through the methods of historians and novelists, the pages of histories and historical fictions" (1502). But history, at least to many people, is the investigation and recording of human nature and action. Novelist Margaret Atwood, whose historical novel *Alias Grace* served as stimulation for the examination of history and literature, itemized the passions that drive, impede, unite, and divide humankind, interests common to both novelists and historians, as "pride, envy, avarice, lust, sloth, gluttony, and anger." Then she listed the subjects of historical novels, which are similar to those of all novels: "They are about truth and lies, and disguises and revelations; they are about crime [violence] and punishment; they are about love and forgiveness and long suffering and charity; they are about sin and retribution and sometimes even redemption" (1516).

Other historians and authors are increasingly recognizing the value of the author in historical subjects and the value and place of historical fiction in their research and teaching. Yale professor Robin Winks came to a parting of the ways from his former point of view about the weakness of using the popular culture of the past. "Historians moved too far away from their origins, as storytellers; now storytellers may bring historians back to those roots, to the benefit of both ways of exploring the past." Popular culture is becoming the center of efforts for authors to develop their desires in such fields as historical crime fiction, Indian crime fiction, regional fiction of all types, poetry, essays, and other mixed genres of writing. Though most are motivated by the desire to make money, they also write what society demands, that is, "serious" or successful fiction. Barbara Mertz, for example, under the name Elizabeth Peters has written about a Victorian Egyptologist-detective, and has written two straight history books under her own name. She once stated, "When people ask 'When are you going to write a serious book?' my response is 'Every book I have written is a serious book. Especially the mysteries'" (xv).

As the bounds of fiction reach out to include peoples and cultures hitherto largely ignored, new ideas about them are presented and new interpretations are made. Louis Owens, one of the more powerful Indian scholar–fiction authors working today, has written with power and conviction about the injustices he feels have been dealt to Indians in the past and are still being dealt at this time. In so doing he has revealed unique characteristics not found elsewhere in American culture but which in the long run tie in. Owens has had perceptions that are not intellectual or rational and "in communications that might be termed extra-rational, in spirit, in dreams, etc." He has had "direct contact with what people might term 'ghosts' and so on. That's simply a part of a larger reality that figures in my fiction. Either a reader crosses that threshold or he doesn't but if he doesn't then the fiction probably does not work."

In further explaining the psychology of his fiction, Owens said:

> In addition to writing about reality as I have always perceived it, including dream reality, I always want to extend my readers' consciousness and challenge them by urging them to see beyond ordinary limitations.... I cross boundaries as much as possible, with characters who are of more than one culture and ethnic heritage and with characters who inhabit more than one kind of reality. I think you will find a lot of ... mysticism in writing by and about Native Americans in large part because Indian people tend to see the world in this way, tend to believe in realities beyond "perceptual or intellectual apprehension but central to being." I don't personally know any Indian people, for example, who do not take dreams very, very seriously. And I have immediate, personal evidence that Indian people share experiences and communicate through dreams.

Not to understand the Indian world and psychology is to be ignorant of a long, broad, and rich American and human culture, which can only enrich the humanities. In part Owens's drives are partly those of the professor trying to explain a culture to his students, but more important are the compulsions of a novelist opening the book on the soul of a people.

On all campuses the English literature departments are likely to be the largest and most diverse of the humanities departments. Usually one of the heavy loads is the teaching of composition, and now a large shift is being made to rhetoric. But the active love of many is still literature and its place in the development of the humanities.

What is needed on campus is a large stream of invigorating water circulating through all the departments, from architecture to zoology, to bring fresh oxygen and life-giving nourishment. The freshest and most comprehensive campuswide nutrient is popular culture studies. The English literature departments can then return to their leading role of making literature the flagship of the campus. But the popular cultural aspects of the offerings should be emphasized. While in school, most students, regardless of their place of residence, spend most of their lives off campus. They therefore need to be taught about life in the world they inhabit off campus. Academia is a shrinking haven that coddles fewer students every year, and all of us should recognize this reality.

English departments already offer many courses in popular culture that are the choice of both professors and students: crime fiction, science fiction, pulp fiction, best sellers, soap operas, daytime TV, folklore, women's studies, gay literature, music, food, fashion, icons, heroes, Western studies, movies, sports, travel, Latino, and Indian literature.

Professors try to teach the subjects they like, and become something like professors of English and (say) folklore and women's studies, and music. The English department as a whole could help itself by stretching its umbrella in name to something like professor of English and popular culture, or lengthening its shadow to department of English and popular culture, or incorporating a major in popular culture studies, as some schools are now doing.

Professor Pratt was certainly correct when she warned against paranoid shrinkage: "Defending against downsizing easily leads us to add bricks and mortar to departmental and disciplinary walls at a time when intellectual and pedagogical momentum would take us the other way." Examination of the program of the 119th annual convention of the Modern Language Association demonstrated that the organization was struggling to keep abreast of the interests of ever-shifting academic demands. Of some 2888 named participants in some 763 sessions of one length or another, at least 54 were on unconventional fields such as "Electric Technology (Teaching, Research and Theory, No. 12), "Cultural Studies, Folklore and Popular Culture" (No. 13), "Film, Television and Other Media" (No. 30), and at least 121 others on what is described as "other than conventional literature." This aggregate is in addition to some 113 "Allied and Affiliate Organizations," of which some 24 comprehend popular culture subjects in their 45 sessions.

In addition there are numerous presentations on popular subjects sprinkled throughout the other sessions. For example, "Popular(izing) Law (No. 252), where there is a paper on "Who Needs the NAACP When You Have John Grisham?" "Rape, Race, and the Romance of Legal Injustices" (No. 252), three papers in the section "Milton and Popular Culture" (No. 64), arranged by the Milton Society of America: "Helen Keller and the John Milton Society for the Blind," "Popularizing Pandemonium: Milton and the Horror Films," and "*National Lampoon's Animal House* and the Fraternity of Milton," and "Daily Life in the Golden Age" (No. 728), with papers on "Finding the Traces of Women's Everyday Lives," "The Quotidian and the Exotic," and "Indoors and Out: Women's Everyday Life in Golden Age Spain."

Everything is to be gained by this outreach by the MLA, the individual faculty members, and the individual campuses at large: more attractive and useful classes, students, faculty, and greater participation in the worlds off campus. Taxpayers ante up our salaries, so perhaps their world should be allowed on campus. Community and junior colleges are finding it very beneficial, both in finances and curricula, to move back and forth across the invisible dividing line. At a time when budgets continue to shrink and must be explained and justified, if justification can be kept out of the hands of the politicians, time may have come to cast a dispassionate eye on curricula and see where we are, what we are doing, and whither we tend. English literature departments enjoy the greatest opportunity to take advantage of the circumstances. They walk lightly and can read many literatures. The opportunity should be seized.

2

American Studies and Popular Culture

RAY B. BROWNE

Academia is generally peopled with a few professors who are prepared to use their training not as the basis to tie them down to repeating the canon, but as stimulation for thinking for themselves and exploring the unknown. Knowledge grows not from repetition but from stimulation. Occasionally, pioneering movements that work in new combinations of thinking develop and prosper, and such have been the beginning and growth of the American studies movement and the Popular Culture Association/American Culture Association. The former began formally in 1951 when a group under the joint leadership of the professors at the universities of Pennsylvania, Maryland and Minnesota suggested that the study of the humanities should expand beyond the conventional fields of literature, philosophy and history and cover allied fields. To a certain degree, because it is worthy and widely encompassing, the American studies movement has prospered.

Through the years, however, many have felt itchy over the restrictions the American studies movement has imposed on disciplines and subjects recognized as legitimate. Even under this expanded view, many subjects were felt to be desirable or undesirable, acceptable or unacceptable, sufficiently "elite" to be worthy of study or too insignificant to be noticed. Such a restrictive attitude did not reflect the fire of rebellious development of the 1970s and the demands for more acceptance and legitimization. In that period, the demands came from many of the more imaginative and productive of the American studies scholars. In the 1979 bibliographic issue of the journal *American Quarterly*, 14 scholars in the field were asked to respond to the general question, "Suppose there had never been an

17

American studies movement, no *American Quarterly*, no American Studies Association. What would have been lost to American higher education, and to our understanding of American culture, by their absence?" My response, like that of the others, was more of hope than satisfaction (see Chapter 1 for a note on my background).

After graduation, working for the American Studies Association, I organized sessions and panels for the American studies section at annual conferences of the Modern Language Association and published in the *American Quarterly*. Most important, perhaps, concerned over the wide rift that lay between the American Studies Association and the American Folklore Society, I organized two conferences at Purdue University in 1965 and 1966 on the role that the study of everyday culture(popular culture) could play in bringing the two disciplines together. I was particularly disturbed at the second of these conferences when Richard M. Dorson, the second Ph.D. at Harvard in American studies and one of the prime movers worldwide in urging American studies, head of the Folklore Institute at Indiana University, was not taken seriously when he urged that folklore be given a respectable role in the development of American studies. Seeing the success of these two conferences, I however, determined to develop the popular culture movement by establishing a *Journal of Popular Culture* (1967) and a Popular Culture Association. Russel B. Nye, Marshall Fishwick, John Cawelti, Carl Bode, and others shared my enthusiasm and offered unrestricted support.

At the first annual national meeting of the American Studies Association (ASA) in Kansas City, Missouri, in 1969, I proposed to Robert F. Lucid, Executive Secretary of the ASA, that I would sponsor the second national meeting in Toledo, Ohio, if the officers would cooperate by allowing me the time slot to establish a Popular Culture Association (PCA). They agreed. So in 1970 in the annual meeting at Toledo, the Popular Culture Association was born. I always thought the situation was propitious: we met in the Crystal Room of the Commodore Perry Hotel, the finest in Toledo, and just across the street on the corner was a typical White Castle hamburger joint, with space to serve up to a dozen hungry street people (and academics), a dozen hamburgers for a dollar.

Over 200 people attended the organizational meeting, discussed the establishment of the PCA, its purposes, and future. Filled with enthusiasm and hope I trumpeted the establishment among my friends at the conference and was surprised to see that many were less than enthusiastic. As had been my hope all along, I felt that the PCA and the Journal would broaden and enrich the ASA and make it more useful to humanities scholarship in general. But many conventional scholars in the ASA, who had been sufficiently rebellious to break away from the old-line subjects and approaches to form the ASA, saw the new breakaway as a threat to what they had achieved and hoped to continue to develop in their own way. What has since been called "discipline libido," which so often drives academics as well as others, spread its protective umbrella over the ASA and tried to keep new changes out. This fear continued for almost the first 10 years of the existence of the PCA and the Journal.

To a certain extent this fear resulted from a misunderstanding of the mission of the PCA and perhaps the unfortunately named "Popular Culture Association." *Popular culture* is, in the historic use of the term, the culture of the people. In a democracy it is the culture of all or virtually all the people. In 1782, the French commentator Hector St. Jean de Crèvecouer, in his *Letters from an American Farmer*, asked, "What is an American?" He answered that such a person is the creation of America and in turn is the author of the country's culture. Indeed, notions of the American dream and the American way of life have long been grounded in the dream of democracy; that is, culture, "by the people, of the people and for the people." Popular culture, democratic culture, is linked fundamentally to America and people's dreams and realities.

Academically, the word *popular* has generally meant *mass*, a political term, and *entertainment* to scholars who take scholarship and knowledge solemnly. Popular culture is aspects of life that are not to be taken seriously and are indulged in by "the people," and therefore must be "entertainment," and as such, though it is the subject of most of the culture of most of us it is not to be taken seriously. Academic society despises popular culture while luxuriating in it. It is as though humanities scholars, even those in American studies, donned the rags of monks when they went into their offices and looked backward to the past instead out of the window at the students and society that supported them.

Ever since its formation, the American Studies Association has been a mixture of new elements, and to a certain degree new attitudes, of old subjects in search of a new and comforting methodology. Perhaps the search for *the* proper methodology has been without fruitful conclusion. Educator and author Henry Nash Smith in 1957 suggested conservatively that the strength of American studies lay in the fact that it could not find and did not need a methodology. To him the strength of the movement lay in its reexamination of old materials using whatever methodology was desired. But the methodologies can provide strength and comfort only to a certain extent, after which they provide barriers for further development. As it is with the new electronic developments dazzling us today, a particular methodology must be improved when new materials and improvements in the existing product become evident. New inventions demand new materials developed in different ways.

American studies, however, seem to be developmentally static, or they backtrail, looking for the way back to the golden spring, the fountain of knowledge. In his seminal and often cited article "'Paradigm Dramas' in American Studies: A Cultural and Institutional History of the Movement" (1979) Gene Wise cut close to the bone of purpose and need in his suggestions: "As culture critics of American Studies, we should ask, '*What imperatives are there in the larger American culture and social structure, and in the culture and social structure of academe, which have made possible the question for an integrating 'American studies'*" and "*How have these imperatives changed over time?*" He demonstrated the futility of the search for *the* methodology in citing perhaps a hundred fellow workers feeling around in the cave of uncertainty and so far coming up with no jewels. With such gloom, Wise felt that "Intellectually, American Studies has never recovered from the earthquake jolts of the sixties, and the consciousness those events forced upon the culture" (314). To his eye, "American Studies has been in decline ever since" (314).

Perhaps Wise's evaluation of ASA's health and impending demise was a little premature. Correct or too early, he realized that popular culture studies might be the medicine to reinvigorate the patient. Because the ASA is still a mass of disciplines trying to find itself, the general harbor of popular culture studies will provide a haven until the storm dies down. Many American studies scholars are already mooring their ships at least for a time in such harbors. Although full programs in popular culture studies are limited to those at Bowling Green State University with a sprinkling of courses elsewhere, there are many professors who come out of the closet to teach such subjects as sports, crime fiction, pulp fiction, sci-fi, comics, women's studies, popular culture in law, TV, movies, and many others. It's as though the professors come out of the closet for special occasions, though they might still display the sign "Conventional American Studies Only" above their degree sign.

Popular culture studies proudly display the sign "All Studies Welcome." They are interested in present-day cultures of all stripes and countries, the history of all, even the archaeology and paleontology which must be studied via the methods of the discipline, and then used to bring depth and breadth to the background and development of our cultures. American studies often still stick to what conservative historian Gertrude Himmelfarb called "elitist" studies. American studies scholars agree with Himmelfarb who holds "history from below" in contempt and despair:

If ordinary people are being "rescued from oblivion," as has been said, by the new "history from below," they are also being demeaned and deprived of that aspect of their lives which elevated them above the ordinary, which brought them into relationship with something larger than their daily lives, which made them feel part of the polity even when they were not represented in it, and which made them fight so hard for representation precisely because they themselves attached so much importance to their political status [23].

It is difficult to imagine the humanities so far removed from humanity, but some American studies scholars do float on Cloud Nine and think of themselves as seeing beyond the vision of the world.

Popular culture studies, on the contrary, insist that "footnote culture" past and present, in all forms, is of some consequence and interest. It assumes that the voters and taxpayers, purchasers and sellers, workers and consumers move society along in the culture they inhabit. What seems of importance today may be transitory and gone tomorrow, but some elements leave their indestructible monuments and graffiti for all today and in the future to see.

Popular culture's field of study and understanding is the full culture, that of the more than 350 ethnic groups in America and the greater cultural force that impacts on the totality of ethnic cultures. Its classroom therefore is the total world — inside academia, politics, the public at large. Popular culture is the study of America, warts and all, the American dream and the American nightmare, the American way of life, and those who have achieved it, America as a country in the world, without the blind self-congratulatory impulses that make the outside world both envy and hate America.

American studies programs, though begun for the purpose of expanding the study of the humanities both inside and outside the United States, have centered largely on America. Academics outside America, through American studies and American civilization programs have generally been more concerned with American elite affairs than their own. Thus they have been like their American counterparts in that they approach new subjects but in conventional ways; in other words, they plow new fields with conventional plows. What both groups need is a searching eye and, as it were, modern approaches, a new philosophy, sociology, dynamics, and above all a new respect for the everyday aspects of a people wishing for and exercising some degree of democracy and hoping to spread it throughout the world.

Popular culture studies has succeeded somewhat in this broad goal, though the field must remain ever vigilant and continue to push against the restraints of academia and human nature. In addition to particulars, popular culture studies in their comparative and broader range of subjects have widened and enriched the canon of the humanities both in the United States and abroad. The movement has provided several new elements:

1. Greater respect for the countless aspects, of society, both large and small;

2. Release from academic restraints that insisted that the old canon, though augmented in some ways, should continue to be the sole or main province of interest and research in the humanities;

3. Courage to encourage and allow closet interests of scholars to develop;

4. Recognition that American popular culture is the major force and export of America today, as it has been for over 200 years, and is therefore the heart of interdisciplinary and international study;

5. Graduation to a new way of learning and teaching. Our participants feel they have graduated from graduate school and therefore are no longer bound by the star system, which makes us sit at the feet of former professors. With popular culture, each learner is also a teacher and each teacher a learner. All sit at the same table eating the same bread because we believe that active contributions make for active learning.

The route popular culture studies has chosen is not the perfect one and may not even be the ideal choice. But it has demonstrated the possibilities to be gained from the open academic mind and all-inclusive imagination.

Popular culture studies and American studies actually have their eyes on the same stars and often hold hands as they walk the same path. Both have the same ideals and hopes. On some campuses and in many scholarly endeavors they might be engaging in unnecessary and costly competition and duplication of efforts, which is perhaps the wrong course of action. "Disciplinary libido," withers growth and development. Courses in popular culture studies already include materials included in American studies programs. Both fields would benefit from a free flow of attitude and materials from one to the other. In other words, such a program as American popular culture studies would enrich both fields and drain off no energy. The two should walk toward the academic altar and live together for happiness and family enrichment.

References

Browne, Ray B. "The ASA and Its Friends," *American Quarterly*, 31 (1979), pp. 354–8.

Himmelfarb, Gertrude. *The New History and the Old.* Cambridge, MA: Harvard Univ. Press, 1987.
Wise, Gene. "Paradigm Dramas in American Studies: A Cultural and Institutional History of the Movement." *American Quarterly,* 31 (1979): 293–337.

3

Folklore to Populore

RAY B. BROWNE

Writing a brief chapter on the role popular culture studies should play in a folklore program is in most ways stating the obvious. It is a three-way sermon — preaching to the choir; haranguing the audience in the front row; and pleading with the scoffers who came to doubt and sneer.

Folklore studies are well established in the public mind and in academia. The Library of Congress has a magnificent collection, recognized worldwide, and each year holds a festival attended by tens of thousands. Government money, procured largely through the tireless energies of folklorist Archie Green, provide funding for various activities. Society at large approves the study, and academics, especially those with proven track records, teach various thrusts in numerous kinds of folklore. Yet courses are being phased out and students in the field constantly ask questions about their future. To a certain extent historically, folklorists have been too narrow in their approaches and have vociferously engaged in what might be called discipline defense; that is, raising the walls of self-assurance of their purpose too high and being too exclusive. Perhaps the walls should now be lowered or at least penetrated.

To a large extent the task before us is to make definitions clear. Historically, folklore has been thought to be the life culture of the mass who made up the majority of any population's present or past. Folklore is the manifestation of some element of historical development, generally presented in an artistic form. It is nostalgia to some degree, a desire to revisit the time and place in which the culture occurred. People in any culture other than their own, wish for the imagined good old days, places, and societies. Folklore is a yearning to return to yesteryear, yesterplace, and yesterculture. People may or may not feel a stirring in their blood for the beauty and magic of some element of folklore but they feel they can hold onto

24

the past through the reenactment of its lore. It is especially appealing when the society one finds oneself in is a polyglot of hundreds or thousands of bits of cultures congregated from all over the world.

One may not be able or even desire to leave the lore of one's environment, and the physical trip is not necessary. We can use the magic wings of folklore to travel from the present, and go to a more desired location of our real world. In the new land we still feel the throb of the home country blood, and can return at will. In the United States, we maintain nominal linkage with the pasts through linking ourselves to the points of origin of our ancestors. We are German Americans, English Americans, Latin Americans, Japanese Americans, Native Americans, African Americans. We enrich our emotional lives through reenactment of the human, daily practices and arts of the country and people of the "old" country.

As time has compressed the boundaries of mixed countries and cultures, folklorists have increasingly looked upon folklore as the magic heritage of a people, which defined them, and was to be used by scholars as a cultural pantry from which old ways of life could be extracted. This trip down memory lane has been a kind of cultural security blanket from which old ways of life, which we have raised to the level of ideal, have become the practice of dealing in antiques, a practice which actually bled the life from the lore and left skeletons from which DNA had to be extracted to provide paleontological evidence of the locale and tribe of the past.

This attitude involved tunnel vision and putting blinders on us that directed scholars and the populace at large to make false readings. Looking toward the past has given us a false sense of reality. We don't have folk anymore in this country; they probably disappeared in Europe in the 15th century and never were alive in the United States. Instead of folk we have a general population. The members of the population at large or of groups do have, to be sure, traditions and memories of earlier days and societal groups. To a certain extent these traditions and memories influence our attitudes and patterns of behavior and are the groupings of an earlier national and cultural identity.

But the past is past though not dead, and cultures have been modified or changed. That means folklore is surviving in and being influenced by different dynamics—the mass media, new cultural concepts, different ways of life. This changed world forces a modified folklore. Culture is broader and deeper, civilizations march to different drums, the "lore" of culture, whatever that is, has changed. American society is now the result of, and ruled by, its popular culture. Popular culture consists of the aspects of attitudes, behaviors, beliefs, customs, and tastes that define the people of any society. Popular culture is, in the historic use of the term, the *culture of the people*.

Popular culture and folklore are twin bodies joined at the heart and head, popular culture looking to the present and past, folklore viewing reality from the past to the present. Folklorists are beginning to recognize the attachment. Linda Degh (1996), called by Alan Dundes "our most distinguished folklorist," had led the way in the new thinking on folkloristics, especially vis-à-vis the mass media:

> The mass media liberate folklore from its earlier confinement to the so-called lower layers of society and from the prejudice — both pro and con — that stigmatized it. Folklore belongs to everyone, not only to the under-privileged, uneducated masses. It is a common cultural property characterizing our ways of thinking, believing, and dreaming, and our modes of defining our identity. The observer of emergent folklore may be able to decipher the interpretations through the accessibility of modern media. We are eyewitnesses to a new era in which folklore gains power and prestige as an authoritative dream, and hope; the voice of all humanity alienated and fractured by electronic efficiency. The task of folklorists is to read these meanings of folklore, and this task makes folkloristics an important interdisciplinary science, now more than ever before [2].

Numerous other folklorists are advocating the use of a wider umbrella to cover the subject. Alan Dundes, one of the more learned and amusing folklorists working today, has the Freudian approach to humor and folklore, especially published in several books on the folklore of present-day duplicating machines. Roger D. Abrahams broadens the study in *Singing the Master; The Emergence of African American Culture in the Plantation South* (1992) in a whole geographical region's culture. Archie Green (1993), one of the fiercest exponents of folklore studies, recognized the influence of everyday culture on folklore and was willing to subdivide the term into "folk, popular, plebeian" (*Wobblies, Pile Butts, and Other Heroes*, 238).

Other scholars have turned to value what are considered the most threatening media of all — TV and movies. Bruce Jackson wanted to clutch the movies to his bosom:

> Film is the dominant narrative mode of our time. Film and television provide much of the sense of community in a mobile and electronic world; the verbal and imaginative referents we utilize in ordinary face-to-face encounters are as likely to come from our separate — but shared — media experience as anywhere else. Film and television are far too important to be left to the media studies and literature scholars [JAF 102, 388–389].

The suggestion is carried into somewhat greater detail by Mikel J. Koven:

Folklore studies have examined or at least recognized the importance of examining, popular cinema from a number of perspectives. At one level folklorists are able to observe and trace the process of homogenizing cultural expressions through the mass media. On the other hand, a great deal of folklore scholarship has explored those traditional narrative types and motifs when they appear in popular film and television. Yet, still other folklorists have noted further areas for fruitful exploration of popular culture texts, such as how popular culture texts reflect contemporary belief traditions, ethnographies of fan culture, the rituals involved with popular cultural consumption, narratives about technology and technological industries, and the existence of multiple versions of seemingly fixed texts [JAF 116, 176–195].

Shakespeare's question, "What's in a name?" should be answered, "Quite a lot," especially when the name is the flag that a whole academic and public community has been serving under for a hundred years. The word directs and limits a group's direction and vision. Notice how closely Degh's new definition of folklore, quoted above, parallels my definition of popular culture (see chapter 1, p. 11). She and I have carried on our thinking independently but have arrived at the same conclusions.

If therefore folklore and popular culture are but two tracks for the same train to run on, why shouldn't the name be modernized and brought up to date? I believe the word *folklore* should be changed to *populore,* since it is no longer the lore of the past but the living, vibrant culture around us, past and present, that we are concerned with. If I were naming a folklore program today I would call it *populore.* Blending popular culture and folklore courses can only be logical and beneficial, no matter what the name might be. Nothing would be lost and a great deal gained by both the instructors and the students. The latter will flock to the classes and the faculty will have to grow with more staff. The education the students get will be richer and broader and more useful. Not bad for a program that has much to offer a campuswide curriculum.

References

Abrahams, Roger D. *Singing the Master: The Emergence of African American Culture in the Plantation South.* New York: Pantheon Books, 1992.

Degh, Linda. *American Folklore and the Mass Media.* Bloomington: Indiana University Press, 1994.

Green, Archie. *Wobblies, Pile Butts, and Other Heroes.* Urbana: University of Illinois Press, 1993.

4

Snap, Crackle, Pop Culture and Communication Curricula

Carlnita Greene

If we operate from the understanding, as Stuart Hall (1997) asserted, that it is impossible to study culture, especially from a contemporary perspective, without studying media — then it is reasonable to argue the reverse (Jhally, 1997; *Representation and the Media*). If one is to examine media or other communicative practices, it is essential that one also look to culture. Perhaps the most common form to which we are exposed is that which is deemed popular culture. Despite its numerous definitions, we can best define popular culture as being rooted in "the ordinary" or everyday experiences of groups of people within any given society. As Ray Browne (1996) revealed, popular culture is "the everyday world around us: the mass media, entertainments, diversions; it is our heroes, icons, rituals, everyday actions, psychology and religion — our total life picture"(22). Popular culture, regarded from this perspective, infuses the very essence of human communication. Yet, many communication scholars still do not consider it a part of their erudition. Nevertheless, it is imperative that we begin to understand popular culture's relationship to the field of communication and view it as a preeminent communicative aspect within society. As such, departments of communication must incorporate popular culture as a part of their curricula. In doing so, they will provide a number of benefits to students, themselves, and their universities that may, in turn, benefit the greater society.

James Carey's (1988) seminal text, *Communication as Culture: Essays on Media and Society*, presented the argument that we need to move away from the model of communication as a transmission or a transaction in which senders pass messages to receivers (15). From this perspective, he explained that many communication scholars view our discipline in terms of the perceived effects that particular forms of communication have on audiences (15). Instead, he advocated that we begin to view communication from a ritualistic perspective in which we focus on how communities are formed and maintained (18). He believed that we must view communication as symbolic. That is to say, we need to understand how we use communication to create and maintain our relationships, our communities, and how we describe our world (23).

Carey revealed, "To study communication is to examine the actual social process wherein significant symbolic forms are created, apprehended, and used" (30). Further, he explained that our models of communication do not simply describe our world, but also work to create it so that they are a form of culture, stating: "We not only describe behavior; we create a particular corner of culture—culture that determines, in part, the kind of communicative world we inhabit" (32). It would be remiss, therefore, to examine communicative practices and not regard them as cultural. Perhaps even more importantly, we need to consider other cultural practices, particularly those that are popular, and how they work to shape and create our society.

If we generally define culture as the way in which human beings make sense of the world and how we explain that world to others, then ultimately popular culture is the purest expression of that process. Popular culture, viewed from within the perspective of human communication, opens up this sense-making process, therefore providing us with increased understanding of it. Both culture and communication are so ingrained in the fabrics of our daily lives that we often take them for granted. However, these subjects have definite importance to us precisely because we experience them daily.

Communication is one lens, if you will, with which we can grasp how popular culture functions. However, this is not to say that a communication perspective is the only way to analyze popular culture. Yet, it seems likely that including popular culture in the curricula of communication departments will also serve a dual role of illuminating both subjects individually as well as increasing our understandings of ourselves. Therefore, we will now discuss how popular culture relates directly to specializations within the field of communication.

As a discipline, communication by nature is interdisciplinary as well as having diversified subcategories in which scholars focus their research. In *Communication Research: Strategies and Sources,* Rubin, Rubin, and Piele (1996) explained:

Communication researchers examine the processes by which meanings are managed — in other words, how people structure and interpret messages and use language and other symbol systems in a variety of contexts: interpersonal, group, organizational, public, and mass. Thus, the focus of communication inquiry is broad, and the contexts in which the communication process is examined are diverse and interrelated [7].

Because communication scholarship is varied in its scope, popular culture fits directly into each specialization within the field.

Interpersonal and Group Communication

The most common kind of communication that comes to mind when people think about the discipline is that which occurs between two or more people, or interpersonal communication. In other words, within interpersonal communication, scholars study how people communicate verbally and nonverbally to create and maintain relationships with others. One way we can comprehend interpersonal communication is to consider it as focusing on the *how* aspects of communication. Some of these aspects are as follows: (1) How do people understand each other? (2) How do relationships form? and (3) How does conflict occur?

For the purposes of this chapter, we will collapse the category of group communication into the area of interpersonal communication, although some scholars would argue that they are separate specializations. We are doing so because group communication is interrelated to interpersonal communication in its focus. Group communication involves the study of three or more people and how they interact, as well as how groups emerge and form. If we consider the fact that groups also create and maintain relationships, although on a larger scale than one-to-one, then it is logical that we can consider group communication within the realm of the interpersonal. For example, a person may decide to join or leave a group due to the interpersonal dynamics between that person and the other members of the group.

Although there are a number of ways that popular culture links to interpersonal communication, we will explore the ones that demonstrate the closest connections. Popular culture is used as a form of expression to manage interpersonal relations. In particular, there are times when we may want to express a certain sentiment to someone, yet we have a difficult time demonstrating these emotions. To reveal our love for someone, for example, we might turn to popular culture in the form of music, poetry, or even greeting cards to communicate this feeling. In other words, we may use popular culture to express ourselves instead of speaking with the person face to face.

Popular culture itself is the topic of many conversations, which speaks to its importance or the preoccupation that people have with it. However, this still leaves the interpersonal communication researcher with a number of questions. How does popular culture aid interpersonal communication? What qualities might it have as a topic of conversation that would cause people to discuss it widely? Does it serve a purpose of helping to create or maintain relationships? Does it act as an enabler to starting conversation? Or, is it because popular culture is readily available as a topic that people draw upon it in their interactions?

As both creator of and reflector of culture, popular culture may serve as a model for how some groups communicate or interact interpersonally. For example, television shows may offer us insight into how teenagers communicate with their parents. Similarly, popular culture phenomena might reveal how we are socialized to act in certain ways according to our home or work environments. They might demonstrate those issues that are most important to various people because these subjects emerge regularly within popular culture. It also may be possible to use popular culture as a reference point for demonstrating models of communication used by individuals and within groups.

Finally, popular culture may bring people together through the process of identification within groups. These groups may emerge because of shared interests in particular forms of popular culture. In his (1997) book, *Dancing in Spite of Myself: Essays on Popular Culture*, Lawrence Grossberg traces the development of various groups of fans based upon their musical interests, although he warns us that the categories he uses are not static (45). If someone were interested in how these groups form, resolve conflict, or communicate interpersonally, we may discover that the popular culture artifacts themselves influence group dynamics and interactions. These issues with regard to groups may be found within some aspects of organizational communication as well.

Organizational Communication

Authors Rubin et al. (1996) explained, "organizational communication is concerned with the processing and use of messages between and within organizations" (9). Instead of the informal relationships between people, organizational communication scholars analyze "complexities of communication in formal structures where many of the interpersonal and group relationships already occur" (9). Scholars in organizational communication study several aspects of organizations such as how they emerge and maintain their systematic networks. They also analyze the ways in which people identify with organizations, meaning the impact that individuals have on organizations, and vice versa.

If we delve further, we can begin to realize that organizations themselves are represented within popular culture. The ways in which people consider themselves members or workers within organizations may depend on how popular culture represents them. For example, many of the professions derive part of their reputations from how people perceive them based upon their representations in popular culture. Frequently, much of our knowledge about professions, aside from being in them, comes from how they are represented. Recently, for instance, people may begin to gain an understanding of the culinary field and how chefs work due to their rise in popularity in books and television shows.

Popular culture affects how people within organizations work and how organizations regulate people's uses of it. If we consider the Internet as an example, we can begin to see how it has changed the ways in which many people perform their job functions and how they interact at home. It allows some people to complete many of their job responsibilities from home causing a rise in telecommuting as an alternative to being in the office. It allows people within organizations to send information faster and over greater distances. Further, issues of whether people are using the Internet for job-related or personal purposes at work arise providing a challenge for how organizations manage its use internally.

Some organizations themselves influence popular culture directly, such as the marketing, advertising, television, and film industries. Various organizations such as these help to shape popular culture and how it is disseminated. They also act as creators of culture or catalysts for new popular culture trends. Organizations such as these may have techniques for communicating both internally and externally that may be of interest to communication scholars exploring how these kinds of networks function.

However, these networks within any type of organization are comprised of individuals. The means by which these individuals collaborate may shape how the organization as a whole functions. Organizational members' individual experiences with popular culture may have an effect on the organization overall. In other words, within any organization, you have individuals with different tastes, ideas, politics, and viewpoints (some of which may be shaped by popular culture) who come together in order for the whole organization to function. Conflicts may arise when these differences come together as well. Similarly, people also may find that they have common interests with regard to popular culture. These commonalties might serve to strengthen the bonds that people have in working inside the same organization because they are able to relate to each other professionally and socially. Therefore, we may begin to understand how popular culture functions on a larger scale than in organizations by turning our focus to mass communication.

Mass Communication (Radio, Television, Film, Advertising, Public Relations, Marketing, Journalism)

Perhaps more than any other division of the communication discipline, mass communication has embraced the study of popular culture as a part of its curricula. Grossberg, Wartella, and Whitney (1998) stated: "the discipline of mass communication (sometimes called media studies), attempts to understand the significance, not only of particular communications media, but of the general processes of media communication in contemporary society" (xi). In fact, popular media has been an area in which mass communication departments have had an ever-increasing interest. However, most of the research within mass communication has focused on media from an effects tradition, as James Carey (1998) explained in his work (42–43). In other words, most people research how popular media affects audiences from a stimulus-response perspective in which viewing media causes their actions or reactions. We, need to dig deeper, therefore, into the creative human structures that underlie popular media than we have in the past by more forcefully integrating culture into the research that we undertake.

Furthermore, popular media play a significant role in the dissemination of various cultures. As our world increasingly becomes a global one, much of our information about how other people live and their everyday lives comes from representations of those groups within popular media. Whether those representations may be considered positive or negative, they nevertheless exist and do have major social, political, and cultural implications. As John Fiske explained in his (1994) work *Media Matters: Everyday Culture and Political Change*, various texts of popular culture and particularly the media can be sites of struggle (4). In other words, various concepts and policies are communicated in and out of the media.

Popular media impact us locally, nationally, and globally. It is for this reason that they spark a number of debates between scholars in the field as to their actual function. Some see popular media as detrimental whereas others are more optimistic about their role. Therefore, there is a need for further investigation from a mass communication perspective about the roles of various media within American society.

Since much of mass communication is concerned with the implications of mediated communication, it is no surprise that other forms of popular culture are explored within this division. Let us not forget, as James Carey suggests, that the battle over the study of mass communication links with the struggle over popular culture (37–40). Correspondingly, the mass communication division also produces many students who themselves work in "the culture industry" and directly shape popular culture. For example, many advertising campaigns, not only sell products, but also actually help shape what people think about society and how they view themselves as members of particular groups. Mass communication scholars, therefore, are at the forefront of the integration of popular culture into their scholarship.

Rhetoric

Having numerous definitions within the field, rhetoric has its roots in ancient Greek oratory. Plato defined rhetoric as "an art of influencing the soul through words..." in his famous work *Phaedrus* (48). Aristotle, on the other hand, maintained: "Let rhetoric be [defined as] an ability, in each [particular] case, to see the available means of persuasion" (36). Since that time, rhetorical scholars have continually debated rhetoric's definition and its purposes. Some scholars define rhetoric as the art of oratory in which they examine speeches, debates, or other speaking engagements. Other scholars define rhetoric as the art of persuasion. Still others focus more on the political implications of rhetoric. In *Modern Rhetorical Criticism*, Roderick Hart (1997) explained that rhetoric is "the art of using language to help people narrow their choices among specifiable, if not specified policy options" (2). Nevertheless, perhaps the most useful definition for purposes of this chapter is the one that Barry Brummett (1991) provided in his text *Rhetorical Dimensions of Popular Culture* in which he revealed that rhetoric is "the social function that influences and manages meaning"(xii).

Although some rhetorical scholars are hesitant to integrate the two within their scholarship, they need to remember that popular culture is rhetorical in that it can be a form of persuasion with policy implications and is rooted within the social realm. Popular culture texts as discourses create and maintain how we view our society. They may call into question or challenge existing social relations, or in contrast, they may maintain the status quo within our society. For example, we may consider a car simply as an object of transportation that moves us from point A to point B. However, it is a form of rhetoric in the sense that we are trying to encourage or persuade others to view us in certain ways based upon the kinds of vehicles that we drive, their colors and decorations, and even through the use of bumper stickers that we place upon them. Otherwise, we all would drive cars that have no aesthetic variants.

Rhetoric, as rooted in the art of oratory, still parallels popular culture in the sense that popular culture is one of the ways in which contemporary society expresses its viewpoints, represents groups of people, and affects public policy. Furthermore, in contemporary society, we do not usually go out into public arenas to debate political matters as was once the norm. Rather, we turn on our televisions where politicians, pundits, and at times ordinary citizens debate issues. Along these lines, we read newspapers and books or we purchase items that reflect who we are as individuals or members of groups to signify our various genders, ethnicities, classes, and cultural backgrounds. It is precisely in this way that contemporary American society is characterized by the increasing presence of politics within the realm of popular culture.

In *The Practice of Everyday Life*, Micheal DeCerteau suggested that scholars also look to those aspects of our lives that we consider ordinary because they are also a form of politics or tactics that people utilize to contend with living in contemporary societies (cited in Highmore, 2001, 68–71, 73). Rooted in the everyday experiences, popular culture has several rhetorical dimensions as Barry Brummett explicitly demonstrated throughout his scholarship. Rhetorical scholars need to move beyond (although not disregard) their ties to ancient Greece and move forward into the 21st century, which means that scholars need to further study the everyday and the ramifications of popular culture, because these facets directly affect how society functions. Rhetorical scholars need to integrate popular culture more actively within their erudition and the communication field as a whole. As such, we now will consider some of the benefits that studying popular culture in the context of communication provides to students, departments, and universities.

Before discussing the benefits of integrating the two subjects, we must remember popular culture and communication already are joined in the sense that each one of them occurs within the experiences of our lives that we usually deem "ordinary" or "mundane." In other words, both are located in the "everyday" which makes them topics that are even more significant. As Raymond Williams (1958) explained: "Culture is ordinary:

that is the first fact. Every human society has its own shape, its own purposes and meanings. Every human society expresses these, in institutions, and in arts and learning" (4).

One cannot consider oneself a contemporary scholar of communication without being involved within the realm of popular culture. If we closely consider our academic roles, we also are educators within the field of communication, and utilizing current popular culture studies allows us to maintain a connection with our students. Along these lines, the field of communication is rare in the sense that we teach students using both theory and praxis. Often students utilize the information they have learned, about interpersonal relationships, for example, and try to apply these to their ordinary lives. Popular culture resonates with students in a similar manner because they may be influenced by it. By making the connections to popular culture, students may be better able to comprehend and relate to our scholarship. Often in teaching, we find that students have a lack of focus if they feel that the course does not pertain to them. Many of them ultimately want to know the class's value and how it will aid them in their lives. Utilizing popular culture may be the key to unlocking the answer to this question because it is, in fact, an aspect that many students consider central. We will need to find a means of reaching these students, aside from relying solely upon our models or theories of communication, and popular culture may be one of the ways that we can help them understand communication more clearly.

Following Kenneth Burke (1973), we need to consider that people use various art forms as "equipment for living" or guides for how to manage our lives and our problems (296). Although Burke referred to literature, others such as Barry Brummett have extended Burke to include popular culture (112). If this is the case, then it is probable that this "equipment for living" also will provide us with information about how and why people communicate in various ways. This includes our students and even how our own departments function.

Departments will benefit from including popular culture in the curricula by maintaining a sense of being on the cutting edge of contemporary culture. The university as a whole is considered a place for new ideas and delving into unexplored areas of research. Too often, popular culture as everyday culture has been ignored and now more than ever, we need to welcome it into the Academy. We should consider it, not just for its newness or trendiness, but because it provides us with insight into how our society functions. Furthermore, as a field, communication should be at the forefront of this endeavor because of the close ties it has to popular culture.

In a 1994 article, Ellen Wartella challenged communication scholars to make their presence better known on campuses and worldwide (54). What better way to do so than by incorporating popular culture into their curricula? Popular culture by its very definition is that form of culture rooted in the everyday lives of individuals, whether it is widespread or local. Therefore, it seems likely that by incorporating popular culture, communication scholars will remain on the cutting edge of occurrences within our communities, American society, and the world. We, therefore, could refute our reputations for being removed from the larger society.

Too often people accuse academics of being distant from the "real world" or only focused on their research within "ivory towers." Studying popular culture is one of the ways that we can remain connected to what is happening outside of our classrooms and our campuses. Far too often, when programs on television appear in which individuals are being interviewed about how well a politician sounded or how well a message was communicated, the expert usually is not a communication scholar. We should ask ourselves the question of why this is the case. It seems likely if we are experts in communication, then we should be able to comment on these issues. However, unfortunately, some communication scholars are hesitant to study popular culture because it supposedly is not as serious as other kinds of erudition.

Studying popular culture allows us as scholars the ability to generate stronger and more complex scholarship due to the fusion of materials from both areas. It also makes people more creative by helping to spark new ideas from older ideas or from drawing connections between communication and popular culture. Some may already engage in this kind of scholarship; however, we need to do so on a broader scale. If the purpose of studying communication includes all areas of communicating, then surely popular culture should be included. Furthermore, as a field that fuses theory and praxis, we should incorporate more aspects of the everyday within our curricula.

We need to bring our study of popular culture to the forefront more and not simply focus on those areas that are more "traditional" while dismissing others as trivial. Too often scholars try to link popular culture solely to entertainment, and it is much more than that. We need to consider its communicative aspects and what it tells us about how we communicate. For instance, if we view it specifically as a discourse, we can understand how popular culture expresses various facets of our society. We could try to reveal why and how people discuss it. Correspondingly, we could ask questions regarding how it influences the way that people communicate or messages that they express. Finally, as educators in communication we need to ask ourselves two important questions: What are we offering our students with an education in communication? Are we simply teaching them models about communication or are we trying to encourage them to learn how to think critically, become better communicators, well-rounded individuals, and active citizens?

Part of our function as educators is to try to help students understand how subjects, like popular culture and communication, influence each other and intertwine in daily life. This leads to more interdisciplinary study, which is a more holistic approach to teaching and learning. Instead of viewing concepts separately, we should consider how these areas shape and interact with each other in daily life. One bleeds into the other, if you will, so that these things are not mutually exclusive from each other. Therefore, we can encourage students to grasp macrocommunicative aspects of society by fusing popular culture and communication. We can use popular culture as a bridge to understanding how our students think and how they become more engaged. In turn, we can learn from them in the process, as the relationship between educators and students is an exchange of ideas and learning on both sides.

Finally, we must remember the benefits that studying popular culture and communication in conjunction can provide. They each might aid us in recognizing how societies and cultures generally are created, how they are maintained, and how they are transformed. Both are shaped by societies as well as being shapers of societies, or what we may consider the elasticity of the world; it shapes us while we also shape it. The relationship between popular culture and communication is even more complex and the connection between the two is more widespread than people may have previously considered it. Thus, it is of utmost necessity that communication scholars not only integrate popular culture studies into their curricula, but also advocate for its study within our departments, universities, and society overall.

Works Cited

Aristotle. *On Rhetoric: A Theory of Civil Discourse.* George Kennedy, Trans. New York: Oxford University Press, 1991.

Browne, Ray. "Internationalizing Popular Culture Studies." *Journal of Popular Culture* 30.1 (1996): 21–38.

Brummett, Barry. *Rhetorical Dimensions of Popular Culture.* Tuscaloosa, AL: University of Alabama Press, 1991.

Burke, Kenneth. *The Philosophy of Literary Form: Studies in Symbolic Action,* 3rd ed. Berkeley, CA: University of California Press, 1973.

Carey, James. *Communication as Culture: Essays on Media and Society*. New York: Unwin, Hyman, 1988.

Fiske, John. *Media Matters: Everyday Culture and Political Change*. Minnesota, MN: University of Minnesota Press, 1994.

Grossberg, Lawrence. *Dancing in Spite of Myself: Essays on Popular Culture*. Durham, NC: Duke University Press, 1997.

Grossberg, Lawrence, Ellen Wartella, and D. Charles Whitney. *MediaMaking: Mass Media in a Popular Culture*. London: Sage, 1998.

Hart, Roderick. *Modern Rhetorical Criticism*, 2nd ed. Needham Heights, MA: Allyn & Bacon, 1997.

Highmore, Ben, Editor. *The Everyday Life Reader*. London: Routledge, 2002.

Parenti, Michael. *Make-Believe Media: The Politics of Entertainment*. New York: St. Martin's Press, 1992.

Plato. *Phaedrus*. W.C. Hembold and W.G. Rabinowitz, Trans. New York: Macmillan, 1989.

Jhally, Sut, Dir. and Prod. *Representation and the Media*. Videocassette. Media Education Foundation, 1997.

Rubin, Rebecca, Alan Rubin, and Linda Piele. *Communication Research: Strategies and Sources*. 4th ed. London: Wadsworth, 1996.

Wartella, Ellen. "Challenge to the Profession." *Communication Education*, 43.1 (1994): 54–64.

Williams, Raymond. *Resources of Hope: Culture, Democracy, Socialism*. London: Verso, 1958.

5

Is the Anthropological Study of Popular Culture Still at a Distance?

BENJAMIN K. URISH

"We were mugged!" my colleague Tom Patterson shouted as I began a presentation on anthropology, culture studies, and popular culture. He was expressing a common belief among anthropologists that sees the fields as rivals encroaching on anthropology's cultural turf rather than as complimentary approaches. (It happens on the "other side" as well. A different colleague argued that a work I termed *an anthropological study* wasn't really anthropology, merely because it dealt with popular culture.) At best, most anthropologists have seen the situation as being promoted by academics, untrained in the virtues of anthropological fieldwork, who are doing low-quality cultural analysis, and giving "real" anthropology a bad name.

Well, yes, sometimes. But much of the *blame* (if that is the right word) can be laid with anthropology itself for being first at the train station — in fact, building it — but then missing the train when it arrived. The future of all approaches lies in constructive cross-pollinating. This essay is not about culture studies, but it does deal with anthropology and the study of popular culture, and it contends that both can give a lot to each other. That can happen most productively when the study of popular culture becomes an integrated and essential part of anthropology's core curriculum, taught at all levels in a variety of courses and classes.

The study and use of popular culture has achieved a certain measure of hard-won respectability and legitimacy within most quarters of the academy as an arena of research. However, it still remains for the trans-discipline to fully legitimate itself in the officially recognized curricula.

Certainly one fairly successful thrust toward academic sanctioning has been for various departments and programs to become the campus center for oriented topics and courses that are oriented toward popular culture. It may be an English department at one location, a mass communications program at another, or the sociology department at a third. But in any location, popular culture courses, so construed and so labeled, are becoming much less of an academic rarity.

Additionally, it is clear that individual scholars are using their research and expertise in popular culture studies in the classroom with increasing regularity. As a result, popular culture studies are more firmly entrenched in academic circles than a mere survey of departments, programs, and courses might indicate.

Yet the field of popular culture studies is too fundamental a resource and endeavor to remain so limited. At its core, it is a comparative and inclusive study, which requires application beyond the dictates of disciplinary boundaries and methodologies. Yet somewhat paradoxically, popular culture studies are most relevant when applied with specificity to a particular case or instance. As a result, the strength of such work would be increased in its overt incorporation as a regularly sanctioned and codified aspect of the curriculum.

There is, of course, an already existing discipline, which, like popular culture studies, requires a holistic approach while looking at specific events: the field of anthropology. In fact, anthropology, at least as practiced in U.S. academia, would seem the prime candidate for incorporating popular culture studies into its basic curriculum.

Anthropology is the study of cultures (as phenomena) and cultures (as specific delineated entities). Culture is all that is learned and shared by humans as members of a society, usually passed on from generation to generation. It encompasses all of the aspects of humanity that are not directly a result of biology. All culture is based on symbols, of which language is the primary example.

American anthropology is known as the "four-field approach" and those fields are sociocultural anthropology; biological/physical anthropology, which studies humans as biocultural creatures; linguistic anthropology, which studies the relationships between language and culture; and archaeology, which studies the pasts of cultures. There are many subfields and topics within the unified four fields.

While a wide range of theories infuses anthropology, there are shared "philosophies" and methods that unite the subfields. All branches of the discipline strive to be holistic and espouse cultural relativism and see culture as largely historically particulate. Anthropology relies on cross-cultural comparison based on information obtained by in-person fieldwork, usually participant-observation, and interviews.

Each subfield adjusts methods to fit its unique needs, and clearly some aspects of anthropological analysis and research are more amenable to popular culture studies than others. Yet each major subfield can and has engaged in popular culture investigations. Popular culture studies would seem particularly useful when engaging with anthropology's ongoing interests in cultural change and continuity, while considering cultural forces that unify social networks and those that separate social networks.

While individual scholars and occasional courses have dealt explicitly with popular culture studies, the field, to its detriment, has been slow to officially accept popular culture studies as a regular aspect of itself. At first glance, this is puzzling. Most would agree that anthropology is the study of culture and cultures, so it would seem to follow that popular culture, as a particular subset of cultural phenomena, would assuredly be included in anthropology's subject matter. But such practice has been far from commonplace.

Aside from the academy's institutional biases toward popular culture itself, the major explanation seems to have been the erroneous concept that anthropology was solely concerned with nonindustrial, pristine, indigenous, and "exotic" or "primitive" culture systems, and that popular culture was largely a function of industrial and postindustrial "modern" culture systems. These presuppositions are not surprising because institutions and practitioners of both fields perpetuated them. It was not until alternate definitions freed "popular culture" from its early synonymous definition with "mass culture," coupled with a reinvigorated anthropology, that the mutual biases began to dissipate.

Before then, though, there were a few notable exceptions, and they warrant review. One of anthropology's antecedents was the study of folklore. What anthropology brought to folkloristics was, among other things, an emphasis on cultural context. To some, popular culture studies are really the inclusive and contextualized "folklore" studies of the industrial and postindustrial "folk," forming a continuum between folklore and popular culture. In that sense, popular culture studies would have a base in the anthropological study of folklore!

There are more specific examples of the anthropological study of popular culture. Ralph Linton's (1953) landmark article "One-Hundred Percent American" was a sly attack on U.S. ethnocentrism by detailing the common habits and actions of a "typical" middle-class U.S. male as he rises and prepares to go to work. In doing so, Linton gave information on the culture of origin, which for many is almost everything man does or utilizes. Since popular culture is sometimes defined as the everyday activities and beliefs of average ordinary citizens, Linton's essay would easily qualify as a pioneering effort in the polemics of popular culture studies.

Linton's work explicitly influenced Horace Miner's famed "Body Ritual among the Nacirema" article (Miner cites Linton) in which Miner satirized the anthropological texts of his time while furthering both of Linton's points. The popularity of this still much anthologized article spurred a whole body of "Nacirema studies," much of which can be seen as an unintentional anthropological study of U.S. popular culture.

Perhaps one of the most significant anthropological popular culture studies (little known outside of the field) is Hortense Powdermaker's masterful institutional analysis *Hollywood: The Dream Factory.* This groundbreaking work was the first detailed application of traditional anthropological methodologies to an aspect of a "nonprimitive" culture.

The work demonstrated the powerful insights that an anthropological study could bring to questions of corporate decision making and commercial influence, as well as the production of popular entertainments, and several other issues. Powdermaker's wary agitation at the effects totalitarian institutions might have on popular democracy remain fresh and vivid more than half a century after her research ended.

In retrospect, it would seem that Margaret Mead's and Rhoda Metraux's (1953) *The Study of Culture at a Distance* should have both legitimated and started the anthropological study of popular culture in earnest. While the volume had an influence on some aspects of the then current mass culture debate, it failed to fully connect in anthropological circles, despite being termed a *manual* for future research by its editors (Mead and Metraux, 1953, 6).

The volume called for anthropological methods and precepts to inform research into cultures and cultural phenomena when the subject of the study is "at a distance," meaning temporally or physically unavailable to be studied by traditional anthropological fieldwork (Mead and Metraux, 3). The editors suggest that "books, newspapers, periodicals, films, works of popular and fine art, diaries, [and] letters" be utilized to create a new sort of "culturally oriented literary criticism" (3, 5). Further they warn, "major dangers in this field are facile imitation and pat and inappropriate applications of theory," a warning still relevant to popular culture studies (6).

The studies included encompass a variety of parent disciplines and topics, united by varying degrees of anthropological methodology and attempting to draw inferences and conclusions regarding "national or cultural character." Though such studies have fallen into theoretical disfavor, the tools and much of the results of their applications often remain laudable.

Aside from exploring and justifying certain research methods, scholars of popular culture could find much of interest in two key sections of the book, one on film analysis, and another that links oral and folk literature to popular literature (Mead and Metraux, 219–343). The intriguing volume even included an analysis of "The Soviet Style of Chess" (Mead and Metraux, 426–431).

Another significant article was Laura Bohannan's "Shakespeare in the Bush." It told of an anthropologist telling African tribal elders the story of Hamlet. The elders "made meaning" of Hamlet on their own cultural terms and the article demonstrated that cultural context and audience response are paramount concerns.

The shake-up of the American academy in the 1960s and 1970s impacted anthropology as well. A watershed of sorts was reached with Dell Hymes' *Reinventing Anthropology*, which included articles calling for the recognition that anthropology need not limit itself to the study of the stereotypical "primitive tribes." Instead it was time for the self-proclaimed cultural relativistic anthropology to live up to its own dictates as a holistic, uniquely positioned humanistic social science which investigated any and all cultural manifestations of humanity. This could of course include popular culture studies.

The impact of cultural studies and other constructs was also soon felt. By the mid–1980s, anthropology was negotiating its academic space alongside departments and programs of ethnic studies, and Native American studies, in addition to growing interest from several fronts which overlapped — and sometimes usurped — areas of inquiry where anthropology had previously held sway. Anthropology was harshly critiqued for being insular, passe, and even a mere manifestation of imperial colonialism; ironically some of the very topics it had been addressing while reinventing itself.

Two aspects of anthropology at this time had a big impact beyond the field, including an impact on popular culture studies. They were the structuralism of Claude Lévi-Strauss and the theories regarding ritual and performance of Victor Turner. Lévi-Strauss's functional-structural approach to "primitive myth" fused well with semiotics and gained large favor. Eventually, structuralism was applied to any cultural phenomenon that could be construed as a narrative, regardless of whether or not it should be so constructed. One of the better applications to popular culture while firmly grounded in anthropology was Ellen Rhodes Holmes's "Little Orphan Annie and Claude Lévi-Strauss."

Turner built upon the work of Victor Van Genep in codifying the stages and attributes of rites of passage and celebrations. Turner and others broadened their investigations into the individual performance of social roles as well as social performance in festivals. Turner's concept of the liminal state in ceremony was applied to a variety of cultural situations, including modern Western culture as a whole. Into the mix came Clifford Geertz's "thick description" interpretive ethnography, and a combination of both theoretical approaches has been applied to ideas of reading cultural texts and interpreting them as significant aspects of cultural discourse. Furthermore, audience-centered reader response theories have come fairly close to what one type of an anthropological approach to a popular culture studies methodology might look like (for a more comprehensive discussion, see Mukerji and Schudson, 1991, 3, 18–26).

There is then, a long, though erratic, and fractured legacy of anthropology and anthropologists actively engaging in popular culture studies, and in more recent times that legacy has been furthered. As the field deals more and more with popular culture as an arena of research, it is reasonable to assume that individuals will bring their interests to the classroom and departments will bring it to the curriculum. Knowing that students can readily engage with the material, both for itself and as an entryway to other materials, is certainly an additional incentive to pursue the formalization of such courses.

Evidence that popular culture studies are on the increase in anthropology is easily seen. Past programs of national meetings list many presentations of popular culture studies. Also, a look at *Anthropology News*, the newsletter of the leading academic anthropological organization, the American Anthropological Association (AAA) is instructive. The organization is divided into 28 subsections, with 24 of them publishing a journal in addition to the organization's flagship journal *American Anthropologist* ("Section News," 38–54). Clearly the field is varied, and the sections are said to "represent the rich diversity of the discipline's subfields" ("Section News," 38). The diversity is expressed in region (such as a section for the central states, or one for the anthropology of Europe), topic (such as the section for anthropology and the environment), and collegiality (such as the section of the Society for Lesbian and Gay Anthropologists).

But while there is no section that focuses on popular culture studies, such studies are definitely not absent. The cultural anthropology section is where anthropology directly engages culture studies, and is therefore also frequently in the arena of popular culture studies. For example, an article from May 2003 dealt with "Musical Community on the Internet" (*Cultural*

Anthropology 233–263). *American Anthropologist* also regularly features articles on popular culture topics.

A quick survey of the "Section News" shows attention being paid to popular culture studies. The Association of Senior Anthropologists discusses e-mail spam ("Section News," 40–41). The section on Culture and Agriculture discusses farmer's daughter/traveling salesman jokes ("Section News," 43–44). Both the Society for the Anthropology of Work and the Society for Linguistic Anthropology examine films ("Section News," 49–50, 51–52). The Society for Humanistic Anthropology looks at television ("Section News," 50).

To be sure, the "Section News" is an informal information column and more likely to reference aspects of popular culture than the more formal parts of AAA. But the evidence shows that anthropologists are thinking, researching, and writing about popular culture.

However, this has yet to transfer into a disciplinewide commitment to the inclusion of popular culture studies into anthropology's core curriculum. As mentioned, certain individual scholars bring up the subject in many classes, and there are occasional anthropology courses devoted to popular culture as a topic-at-large, or even more narrowly defined. But until popular culture is taught at the introductory level in anthropology classes, it will lack the codification it needs to fully integrate into the field.

Regrettably, such is largely still the case. A survey of the five best-selling anthropology introductory texts reveals that popular culture, as a topic is not considered as part of the anthropological canon. While popular culture studies are mentioned and used for examples, they are not featured, with one tenuous exception.

Conrad Kottak's *Cultural Anthropology* (2002) is that exception, tenuous because in it popular culture is not given its own regular chapter, but instead discussed in an abbreviated appendix. Popular culture first gets a brief but key section in the book's chapter on "Cultural Exchange and Survival" (Kottak, *Cultural*, 412–433). It is used to discuss both the culture of consumption and how cultures take images and texts and use and interpret them in ways that "fit" their own cultural needs (Kottak *Cultural* 422–424).

The appendix itself concentrates on American popular culture and is about a third of the length of the true chapters. The appendix also lacks their supplemental materials, which include a summary, a list of terms and definitions, questions for critical thinking, and a bibliography for further study.

However, it does exist, and discusses popular culture as a shared experience that in the United States at least, helps to unify a disparate plurality.

Kottak exemplifies his ideas by looking at going to McDonald's as a ritual practice, *Star Trek* as a cultural discourse, and football as replicating key American cultural values (2002, 463–468). Elsewhere in the textbook, the films *Star Wars* and *The Wizard of Oz* are given a Lévi-Sraussian analysis (Kottak, 2002, 348–350).

Kottak's inclusion of popular culture sources and studies throughout his text, as well as the appendix highlighting approaches to the anthropological study of American popular culture, are strengths that other anthropology texts would do well to emulate. Assuredly, the appendix ought to be developed and given full chapter status.

It is not surprising that Kottak's text is at the forefront on this topic. He has written that, "It is axiomatic in anthropology that the most significant cultural forces are those that affect us every day of our lives" (Kottak, 1990, 8). He also chides forays into popular culture studies as being too interpretive and lacking in-depth field research (Kottak, *Prime-Time*, 12). Kottak further contends that it is the bias of the academic intellectual subculture that has hampered the acceptance of popular culture studies (2002, 463).

The future bodes well for an increasing emphasis on popular culture studies in anthropology as a move to sanction such work in the academy by adding it to the curriculum. In an address to anthropologists, Ray Browne (1995) stated that, "The trouble with the study of popular culture is that it's largely American." The cross-cultural approach of anthropology is an obvious method to counter that "trouble." In the same presentation, Browne called for a "comparative, freewheeling, nonparameter, humanistic [...] kind of anthropological methodology" to infuse the study of popular culture. For the study of popular culture to broaden itself in academia — including the classroom — it needs to develop as a relevant field for international and transglobal issues and investigations, an arena dealt with successfully by anthropology for over a century.

The field of anthropology, with its holistic approach, traditional four-field structure, case-study methodology, plus numerous fluctuating subfields, is an obvious arena for the overt and officially sanctioned inclusion of popular culture studies into its core curriculum. In fact, a modern anthropology, which seeks to study such things as multicultural systems, corporate entities, imagined communities, and transglobal culture, requires it.

It is not sufficient for anthropological scholars to expect that students will learn all they need to know about popular cultural phenomena from other departments, any more than that they would abandon the study of race and ethnicity. The expectation is similarly insufficient that haphazard exposure to an anthropological educator who chooses to use popular culture studies in the course of other work will adequately prepare the student or advance the field.

For anthropology to retain its relevance as a vital and useful social science it must continue to engage with cultural issues and problems. Turning its back on popular culture studies as a primary part of its curriculum ignores a key aspect of cultural systems and undercuts the stated goals the discipline has had since its inception, and is a detrimental oversight. The incorporation of popular culture studies into the pantheon of anthropology's subfields and core curriculum is long overdue and can only benefit all involved, from the introductory student, through the department and parent institution, to the discipline and even the academy itself.

Works Cited

American Anthropologist: Journal of the American Anthropological Association. 105.2 (2003).

Bohannan, Laura. "Shakespeare in the Bush."

Browne, Ray. "Anthropology and All the Cultures: Adventures and Misadventures with Anthropologists." Paper presented at Temple University, Philadelphia, April 1995.

Holmes, Ellen Rhodes. "Little Orphan Annie and Claude Lévi-Strauss." In Dell Hymes, Ed. *Reinventing Anthropology.* Ann Arbor, Michigan: University of Michigan, 1999 (1972).

Kottak, Conrad Phillip. *Cultural Anthropology* 9th ed. Boston: McGraw-Hill, 2002.

Kottak, Conrad Phillip. *Prime-Time Society: An Anthropological Analysis of Television and Culture.* Belmont, CA: Wadsworth, 1990.

Linton, Ralph. "One Hundred Percent American," Marcus and James Clifford.

Mead, Margaret, and Rhoda Metraux, Editors. *The Study of Culture at a Distance.* Chicago: University of Chicago, 1953.

Miner, Horace. "Body Ritual Among the Nacirema."

Mukerji, Chandra, and Michael Schudson, Editors. *Rethinking Popular Culture: Contemporary Perspectives in Cultural Studies.* Berkeley: University of California Press, 1991.

Powdermaker, Hortense. *Hollywood: The Dream Factory,* 1950.

"Section News." *Anthropology News* ,44.5 (2003): 38–54.

Works Consulted

Allen, Susan L. (ed.) (1994.) *Media Anthropology: Informing Global Citizens.* Westport, CT: Greenwood.

Alvermann, Donna E., Jennifer S. Moon, & Margaret C. Hagood, (1999). *Popular*

Culture in the Classroom: Teaching and Researching Critical Media Literacy. Newark, DE: International Reading.

Berger, Arthur Asa. (1976). *"Bloom's Morning: Coffee, Comforters.*

Bigsby, C.W.E., ed. *Approaches to Popular Culture.* Bowling Green, Ohio: Bowling Green University Popular Press.

Browne, Ray B., and Marshall W. Fishwick, Editors. *Rejuvenating the Humanities.* Bowling Green, Ohio: Bowling Green State University Popular Press, 1992.

Browne, Ray B., and Marshall W. Fishwick, Editors. *Symbiosis: Popular Culture and Other Fields.* Bowling Green, OH: Bowling Green State University Popular Press, 1988.

Browne, Ray B., and Pat Browne, Editors. *Digging into Popular Culture: Theories and Methodologies in Archaeology and Other Fields.* Bowling Green, OH: Bowling Green State University Popular Press, 1991.

Buckingham, David, Editor. *Teaching Popular Culture: Beyond Radical Pedagogy.* London: UCL, 1998.

Canaan, Joyce E., and Debbie Epstein, Editors. *A Question of Discipline: Pedagogy, Power, and the Teaching of Cultural Studies.* Boulder, CO: Westview, 1997.

During, Simon, Editor. *The Cultural Studies Reader.* New York: Routledge, 1993.

Grossberg, Lawrence, Cary Nelson, and Paula Treichler, Editors. *Cultural Studies.* New York: Routledge, 1992.

McRobbie, Angela. *Postmodernism and Popular Culture.* New York: Routledge, 1994.

Motz, Marilyn, and Michael T. Marsden, Editors. *Eye on the Future: Popular Culture Scholarship into the Twenty-First Century in Honor of Ray Browne.* Bowling Green, Ohio: Bowling Green State University Popular Press, 1994.

Nye, Russel B. *Notes on a Rationale for Popular Culture.* Popular Culture Association, 1970.

Ruby, Jay, Editor. *A Crack in the Mirror: Reflexive Perspectives in Anthropology.* Philadelphia: University of Pennsylvania, 1982.

Storey, John. *Cultural Studies and the Study of Popular Culture: Theories and Methods.* Athens, GA: University of Georgia, 1996.

Strinati, Dominic. *An Introduction of Theories of Popular Culture.* New York: Routledge, 1995.

White, Leslie. *The Concept of Cultural Systems: A Key to Understanding Tribes and Nations.* New York: Columbia University Press, 1975.

6

History

A River Both Wide and Deep

RAY B. BROWNE

History, or more properly histories, is like a river both wide and deep. History records the creation (development) consequences of all existence. Interpreters of this history should therefore try to know the complete makeup of the effects of development of all forms of life on all other forms. Just as in Imperial Rome's heyday all roads led to and from that capital, perhaps it is proper now to conclude that history is the mother of academic disciplines, encompassing in one way or another and to one degree or the next the sciences, social sciences, and humanities. History draws its lifeblood from the flood plains that feed it, as the Nile enriches Egypt, flows out and brings life-giving nutrients to all cultures.

Generally this attitude has been reflected to one degree, and on one level, or another, in the interpretations of the past by historians. But there has usually been a fault line between the conservatives and the modernists, those who thought themselves carriers of the golden torch of truth and those who wanted to let all levels of facts speak for themselves. The conservative historian Gertrude Himmelfarb was discussed in chapter 2.

Clearly conservative historians such as Himmelfarb have never thought of Benjamin Franklin, Abraham Lincoln, the 25,000 Confederate and 23,000 Union dead and wounded at Gettysburg, of Lincoln's immortal words commemorating them, and the nation for which they suffered. This conservative view also ignores the struggles of the labor movements, King's "I Have a Dream" speech, and women's assertions of their rights, which have made the United States the envy of the world.

The rift between the old-school historians and the new has continued to widen as the younger group have freed themselves from slavish imitation of the elders. The "new historians" have realized that they cannot, and should not, rule by Ph.D. authority alone, with an assumed professor's right, but must make themselves useful in a dynamic world rattled by the noise of daily life and threatened by ignorance and nuclear weapons. History has demonstrated time and again that if a people are not satisfied with their leaders they themselves, or their neighbors, will topple them.

Increasingly, historians are recognizing the importance of everyday (popular) culture in their work and teaching. Books on different aspects of popular culture flow from commercial and university presses almost weekly, and almost no issue of the *American Historical Review*, the leading publication for professional historians, fails to have some article about some aspect of popular culture, sometimes with full development, sometimes only with background.

The fields covered in the stretch of popular culture studies extend from the most ancient to the more current. As noted in chapter 1, historical crime fiction, reaches into the distant past, but the history of everyday life, celebrations, rituals, and rites intrigue us and help explain the past. An excellent example of the way historians mine popular culture, sometimes against the grain of established opinion, is an account by Robert C. Davis in the acknowledgments to his *The War of the Fists; Popular Culture and Public Violence in Late Renaissance Italy*:

> A few years ago, shortly after I had discovered the pleasures and challenges of the Chronicle of the *Pugni* in Venice's Museo Correr, I mentioned to a more experienced colleague how much I would enjoy the chance to write my own history of the city's Battagliole. His immediate response was, in so many words, Why? Who would ever want to read about such a tasteless topic? Happily, as I explored and worked out the principal themes of the *War of the Fists*, I discovered that my colleagues in Venetian history, and indeed in social history generally, were as likely to be as fascinated and attracted as I was by this cult of popular violence and public disorder that flourished for so many centuries in the heart of the world's Most Serene Republic. It is largely due to their constant encouragement, support and criticism — their understanding of the central role of popular culture in an absolutist society — that this book has been possible [vi].

History is a search-and-reveal exercise, an account of growth and development, and studies in it in popular culture are just as serious and revealing as those of conventional subjects. As noted in Chapter 1, historian Robin Winks, long a reader of historical crime fiction, always felt that the facts in such writing are often wrong, therefore it was more amusing than informative. Now he has changed his mind. Historical novelists often take their subject seriously and research clearly and thoroughly. As noted earlier, Barbara Mertz and Elizabeth Peters writes both historical detective novels and straight history. Sharon Newman, author of a series of books about 12th-century Europe, in her novel *Strong as Death* about the pilgrimage from Le Puy in the 12th century, took the pilgrimage herself, studied the geography and climate, and tried to relive the psychology and trials of the pilgrims 800 years ago. When she began she thought the trip a "research journey," but because the story had to be a credible novel she had to reshape the trip and the history to suit her purposes.

The new popular culture approach to history in many instances requires a thorough rewriting of the whole canon on the subject. It's like opening a door to a new part of a house and discovering where the majority of the household lived and their culture.

One of the new interests among both male and female historians is the history of prostitution. Despite the fact that in 1870 New York City there was a prostitute for every seven men, the subject with its ramifications has not received the attention it deserves. In "Prostitutes in History: From Parables of Pornography to Metaphors of Modernity," Timothy J. Gilfoyle (AHR, 104, No. 1, Feb. 1999, 117–141) suggested that previous studies of prostitution, in scores of scholarly monographs and countless articles, had rescued prostitution from the school of "rotten flesh" and "commercial sex" and placed it "in larger historical and national narratives." Gilfoyle insisted that prostitution was "now correctly being studied as a vehicle not only to explore sexuality and gender but also on the evolution of state power and modernity in the nineteenth and twentieth centuries."

Another scholar of prostitution, Mary Louise Roberts, in "Gender, Consumption and Commodity Culture" (AHR 103, No. 3, June 1998, 817–818) believed that prostitutes and kleptomaniacs "dominate the nineteenth century landscape of female depravity." The "prostitute represented woman as commodity, the kleptomaniac was both her antithesis and evil twin: woman as consumer." Both "served as projections for a particular set of nineteenth-century anxieties concerning the growth of consumerism, the commodification of modern life, and the impact of these processes on the social relations of gender, race, and class."

Authors of crime fiction involving the murder of women have come to recognize the value of their craft in turning back the layers of society to read the blood of those hideous crimes. Two publications by history professors, *Murder Most Foul: The Killer and American Gothic*, by Karen Halttunen (1998) and *The Murder of Helen Jewett: Life and Death of a Prostitute in Nineteenth-Century New York*, by Patricia Cline Cohen (1998), created quite a stir in newspapers and the popular profession press, with reviews in such publications as *The New Republic* and *Chronicle of Higher Education.*

Both authors realized that they were using historical crime fiction (or faction, as the combination of fact and fiction is called), for new outreaches in the study of human nature and behavior: "Mine is a study of the oral imagination," Halttunen said, calling it "the pornography of violence." The reviewer of Cohen's book for *The New Republic* said, "By reproducing her evidence in colorful detail, and by assessing its strengths and weaknesses frankly, Cohen draws readers into the excitement of the historian as detective" (47). Of her book, Halttunen explained, "Our intense interest implicates us, if only as voyeurs, in the crime, however much we assert the inhumanity of murder," and, according to Scott Heller, of the *Chronicle of Higher Education,* her book "should provide fodder for other historians to more fully comprehend individual lives and individual deaths of the past" (A13).

"By looking at crimes that are way out there, you begin to open a window on a culture in a particular time," argued Amy Gilman Srbnick, author of *The Mysterious Death of Mary Rogers* (1995), a study of the murder case in New York City that triggered one of Edgar Allan Poe's tales of ratiocination. "What the press did with the case tells us a lot about journalism. How the police handled the case tells us a lot about policing at the time," she said. But even more important in the long run, opening the case tells us about the desires, needs, and feelings of the public of the time, a public which, intrigued by the power of logic, accepted Poe's short story on the same subject, which he called "The Mystery of Marie Roget" (1842–1843), transferring it to Paris, and solving it by means of ratiocination, his name for logic, (Poe's term has been consistently used in crime fiction ever since).

The study of women in history as entertainers (sometimes with suggestions of sex on the side) are being recognized as revealing new threads, some illustrative but all revelatory. In her study of dancer Maud Allan, the interpretive dancer of Salome's Dance, Judith Wilkowitz pointed out the many movements in the public's feeling about the arts and sexuality. Cosmopolitan London, where Allan danced, was fascinated but somewhat frightened by her and the way in which she expressed her art. "By the late nineteenth century, theatrical dance, including the spectacular form of ballet on display in London music halls, tended to be denigrated as a foreign practice associated with commercialized sex and the demi-monde" (359). In her detailed study of Allan's career on the European continent and in London, Walkowitz outlined how the female dancer had changed women's attitude toward themselves and the display of the female body (2003, 337–376).

In recent years both professional and amateur historians have given increased thought to the place and value of historical fiction in their research and teaching. As noted earlier, a 1998 issue of the *American Historical Review* contained a Forum prefaced by the remarks of the editor that "storytelling has returned to claim a prominent place in history." I assume that in the term *storytelling* was including all kinds of narrative, especially that in movies and on television. The return has not been without debate, for renewed interest in the narrative "has also rekindled controversies about the virtues and vices of recovering the past through the methods of historians, the pages of histories and historical fiction" (1998, p. 1502).

As noted earlier, the Canadian novelist Margaret Atwood's work *Alias Grace* (1996) served as a point of discussion for the AHR members. In outlining the drives in her novel, Atwood itemized the passions that drive, impede, unite, and divide mankind: (see chapter 1, p. 13). She quite properly highlighted "sin and retribution" and "crime and punishment" and mentioned how these songs of the heart and flesh are particularly described in canonical historical fiction. "What does the past tell us?" she asked. "In and of itself, it tells nothing. We have to be listening first, before it will say a word, and, even so, listening means telling, and then retelling. It's we ourselves who must do such telling, about the past, if anything is to be said about it; and our audience is one another." She concluded with an urgency and immediacy: "The past belongs to us, because we are the ones who need it" (1516).

The historians who responded to Atwood's statements generally agreed with her, though one had a slightly differing interpretation: Lynn Hunt, author of several books about the place of history, believes that history and fiction both flow from the same well dug in the 17th and 18th centuries and perhaps need to be separated as two separate but parallel streams, but she agreed with Atwood that her statement "the past [Time] belongs to us, because we are the ones who need it." "Time consciousness," in the slight variation Hunt would give it, "like Atwood's past, has to be infused with 'meaning for those alive today.'"

Developing from the new approach to the study, the rumblings of the historical mountain, like Mount St. Helens in 1988, are rattling beliefs throughout institutions of academia. Kristin Noganson, in "Cosmopolitan Domesticity: Importing the American Dream, 1865–1920" (AHR 107, No, 1, Feb. 2002, p. 57), for example, awakened to a new dawn and professed that historians of international relations:

[T]ired of being dismissed as the methodological troglodytes of the historical profession and conscious of cultural and social historians' encroachments on their field ... have started to add new topics, including human migration, transnational non-governmental organizations, tourism, cultural expansion, borderlands contacts, and intellectual and imaginative engagement with other peoples and nations, to their traditional interest in diplomacy, war, and trade [57].

But as she properly pointed out, *domesticity* is a term applicable to the inside of the house and to the outside as well. As she glanced out her window she must have seen numerous—almost countless—new fields: smuggling, illegal border crossing, American retirement cities in foreign countries, international crime, eco-degradation, animal mistreatment, use of foreign TV programs and movies in different cultures, slavery in its manifold manifestations. If fear of her area of study being overwhelmed drives her, then she needs to add fear of fear to her areas of study.

A casual survey of recent issues of history publications demonstrates the range of fascinating and useful fields of research helpful in enriching and vivifying not only the study of history but also its "truth." In the very stimulating essay, "Smelling like a Market" (AHR 106, No. 1, pp. 119–129) Fernanco Coronil took us through his memory into the significance of the smell of markets. From this beginning he led us into what he wanted as a map of history. "A map of history," he concluded "is not simply its model but its figuration. Our journey's desired destiny also defines he way we depict its trajectory."

Also in 2001, a perhaps more revealing and material study was "Sleep We Have Lost: Pre-Industrial Slumber in the British Isles," by A. Roger Ekirch (AHR 106, No. 2, 2001), in which he recounted how people on all social levels have had to forego sleep. He revealed that "Sleep has remained among the most neglected topics primarily because the relative tranquility of modern slumber has dulled our perceptions of its past importance."

In the same issue of AHR was the article, "The Great Bophuthawswana Donkey Massacre: Discourse on the Ass and the Politics of Class and Grass," by Nancy J. Jacobs, whose purpose was to outline another instance of the power of the ruling class over the weak. She described how some 20,000 donkeys were slaughtered in 1983 when the elite class, who owned cattle, decided that they would rid the country of the donkeys that were eating the grass that "belonged" to the cattle of the upper class. Her conclusion: "Although it targeted animals, it was a violent demonstration of the power of the state over poor and disenfranchised people" (AHR 106, No. 2, 2001, p. 485).

The shape of the human body and the clothes that cover it, a common subject in popular culture studies, constituted two historical articles that reveal a great deal about the American and the way he or she appears. In "Sartorial Ideologies: From Homespun to Ready-Made " (AHR 106, No. 5, Dec. 2001), Michael Zakim traced how Indians, early Americans, the working man, the pioneer, and the city gentleman all donned and wore out their clothes despite that fact that they all looked alike, and Nathaniel Willis, of New York City, was told by a British friend of his that in the city all people looked like "a procession of undertakers." Despite the fact that they all wore the same kind of clothes, most wanted something different and new, especially women. Though they were all "democratized" by their common clothing, it was the invention of the sewing machine that really democratized the populace by making clothes inexpensive and available in one's own choice.

With the concept of the importance of clothes might well go an interest in the importance of body posture. In the 19th century, posture was thought to signal character, family, and upbringing, as well as health. But in America all things change if there is comfort or capital in the change. The 20th century brought those changes in posture — despite the cautions of doctors. It is difficult to tell whether furniture, parks, sitting positions, radio and movie houses, and dancing styles brought the changes or the changes in posture dictated the change. But Americans in the 20th century did not look like their ancestors (David Yoksifon and Peter N. Stearns, "The Rise and Fall of American Posture," AHR 103, No. 4. 1063).

These several articles— and scores of others and numerous books on all aspects of the past — indicate that historians are recognizing the importance of popular culture in their investigations and interpretations. Pouring old wine into new bottles, even with new tasters, adds little of value to the study of history. What is needed is new wine in new bottles. Obviously, historians need to include new materials from popular culture, the everyday lives of cultures and peoples: folklore, toys, games, music, fashions, sports, literature, movies and their interpretations, TV, radio, domesticity, rural life and life ways, crime, Wall Street–Main Street, pioneering, inventions (great and small) fresh and saltwater life, and the impact of interacting cultures from and to the United States, and small cultural groups in the United States and abroad. All have impacted American and world cultures in one way or another and to one degree or another in the long chain of interwoven and sequential events, and all demand their place on the pages of history.

Realization of the need for radical changes in the "new" history is being increasingly theorized and examined in numerous places, sometimes in the open, sometimes covertly. A good example, perhaps, is that outlined by David Brion Davis and answered by three eminent historians (AHR 105, vol. 2, 2000, pp. 452–469) Davis argued in "Looking at Slavery from Broader Perspectives," that the need was to cover slavery in breadth and depth, who in history had practiced it, and why. To study slavery in this range and depth, Davis admitted, a course would need to be taught by several instructors who specialize in the several movements. Stanley L. Engerman enriched Davis's suggestions with his own observation that general acts like abolition and emancipation might provide insights "concerning what can feasibly be done to bring about social improvement."

As interesting as Davis's and Engerman's observations are, they must be recognized as official historians' points of view directed to official historians. They are a whole shower of old wine rained over those traditional umbrellas and are not likely to cause a stir outside the pages of the AHR or the classrooms of the professors who teach history in the conventional way.

Instead of grand and sweeping theory, history needs to get down to the nitty-gritty, the details that provide the materials on which the historians base and from which they draw their generalizations. The old-fashioned historians represented by Gertrude Himmelfarb are certainly correct in seeing the turn to reading history as a continuum of footnotes. History may be an account of social and time movements but its value to the individual is its revelation of the power of those movements in and from the individual and thence to society, in a constant renewal of life. "Nothing in education," said Henry Brooks Adams, "is so astonishing as the amount of ignorance it accumulates in the form of inert facts." And facts adhere to all things, sometimes for the good, sometimes for the bad, of cultures. "They say everything in the world is good for something," wrote 17th-century poet John Dryden (1631–1700) but he offered no proof.

In other words, the movements of history move in the flow of the tide in and out, and its importance lies in its outflow rather than its inflow, its generalization from example to mainstream rather than generalization to example. If properly envisioned, perhaps history is strung on the truth of storytelling.

Just as disciplines across campus need to weave history into the courses they teach, historians should enrich their courses with the indispensable elements of the history of all courses. Then history will return, in the words of the 5th century B.C. historian Thucydides to a useful and "everlasting possession, not a prize composition which is heard and forgotten" (Book I, 22).

References

American Historical Review, Vol. 103, No. 3, June 1998, pp. 817–844.
Ibid., Vol. 103, No. 4, Oct. 1998, pp. 1057–1095.
Ibid., Vol. 103, No. 5, Dec. 1998, pp. 1503–1552.
Ibid., Vol. 104, No. 1, Feb. 1999, pp. 117–141.
Ibid., Vol. 106, No. 1, Feb. 2001, pp. 119–129; 343–386; 485–507.
Ibid., Vol. 106, No. 5, Dec. 2001, pp. 1553–1586.
Ibid., Vol. 107, No. 1, Feb. 2002, pp. 55–83.
Ibid., Vol. 108, No. 2, Apr. 2003, pp. 337–76.
Himmelfarb, Gertrude. *The New History and the Old*. Cambridge, MA: Harvard University Press, 1987.
University of Chicago Magazine.
Ibid.,
Ibid., Vol.

7

On the Linkages Between Sociology and Popular Culture

Arthur G. Neal

Both sociology and the systematic study of popular culture are products of the modern world. During the early part of the 20th century, sociology was introduced into the curriculum of most colleges and universities. Initially, sociology was defined as the science of society, emphasizing the importance of the scientific method and the quest for scientific objectivity. Subsequently, sociologists shifted attention to subjective reality with the focus on subjective meanings and perceptions of reality. It is this later concern that promotes an overlap between the fields of sociology and popular culture.

The origins of sociology and popular culture were built on subject matter left out, or ignored, by the more fully organized and institutionalized disciplines. The success of both as academic disciplines was due primarily to their innovative character. Each carved out new areas for systematic study and investigation that did not exist previously. The world increased in complexity as a result of vast changes, and it became evident that something more was required beyond the subject matter of traditional disciplines.

Both popular culture and sociology take the mundane things in everyday life and find sources of meaning and significance in them. Frequently, this is achieved by concentrating on origins, or by examining functions served that are not a part of the awareness of the people involved. Such topics as graveyards, popular music, detective fiction, circuses, slapstick comedy, and soap operas serve as mirrors for providing insights into the world in which we live.

Both popular culture and sociology place a special emphasis on the modernity of cultural developments. As such, each reflects sensitivity to the trends and changes that are in process. The modern world is here-and-now, the contemporary time period that differs in significant ways from anything that existed previously. Instead of placing a premium on traditional knowledge or the classics, emphasis is on the cultural developments that are in process.

Both fields thus place a value on studies of the many phases and aspects of everyday life. It is through going about the business of everyday living that novel cultural forms emerge and are elaborated. The innovations spring especially from the life cycle that is implicit in the human condition. Each generation puts its stamp on the social heritage and on the historical events that are transpiring in their time and place.

The process of creating social meaning will be illustrated by drawing upon the symbolism of money, traffic signals, and time clocks. The objective of this paper is to take these self-evident realities of everyday life and examine some of their basic functions in the creation and maintenance of order. The increased complexity of the modern world has generated a primary need for coordinating and calibrating the activities of an extremely large number of individuals. Deriving satisfactory solutions to the problem of order were necessary prerequisites for the development of the modern world.

Master Symbols of Modern Culture

In response to the complexity, confusion, and chaos of everyday life, there are several sources of order that have been created to make modern social life workable. Foremost among these are the creation of money, time clocks, and traffic signals as universal symbols. These symbols stem from the need to coordinate the activities of a large number of people and to have common denominators of value. From a cultural standpoint, these symbols are socially constructed forms of reality. They are selective, arbitrary, and based on conventional understandings. But once created, they become the evident attributes of what is currently experienced as normal, natural, and inevitable. Money, the time of day, and traffic signals are among "the solid facts" that permit everyday life to proceed in an orderly fashion.

TIME

The way in which social meanings enter into thinking and the organization of our everyday experiences may be illustrated by examining our conception of time. The measurement of time by the ticking of a clock is representative of the mechanical worldview that is built into modern society. It is a notion of time as successive events moving in a linear direction through fixed and identifiable intervals. Time does not have an existence of its own but is a social creation for the purpose of establishing intervals, organizing events, and coordinating the schedules and activities of an extremely large number of people.

While we agree to conceptualize time as the ticking of a clock, we have experiences with time that contradict our notion of time as a fixed set of intervals. "Time flies," "time moves on," or we do not have "enough time" when we are engaged in activities rewarding to us. On the other hand, "time drags" when we are required to endure a boring lecture, and we have "time on our hands" while waiting to catch a bus or a plane. Our ideas about "saving time," "wasting time," or "doing time" are purely artifacts of our own creation. We utilize symbols as a way of imposing order on the world around us and then respond to these symbols as though they had a reality all of their own.

The scheduling of activities is essential for large, complex, and interdependent metropolitan areas. As Georg Simmel (1950) noted about a hundred years ago, the city of Berlin would grind to a halt if the hands on all the clocks and watches were to start running in chance and random directions. Economic life would be disrupted, appointments would be missed, workers would not be able to report to their jobs at the appropriate time, and the transportation system would be in a state of chaos. If the clocks failed for only an hour, a great deal of confusion would result. The organization of urban life is unimaginable without the punctionality and coordination that a uniform method of measuring time provides.

The failure to adequately coordinate activities frequently results in a great deal of "waiting time" in our society. We frequently are required to wait in lines for obtaining tickets to a sports event, a music concert, or a stage play. We frequently are required to wait in airports for the departure of a scheduled flight, to wait for a connecting flight, or to wait for the arrival of our luggage. We frequently are required to wait in lines at the supermarket and in lines of traffic during the congested business hours, The discomfort of being required to wait stem from "a nonproductive use of time" and a feeling that one's energies could be directed more effectively toward some other activity.

The clients of a physician are required to wait not only in getting an appointment, but also during the time scheduled for the appointment itself. Many physicians apparently schedule more than one appointment for the same time, or several appointments in close succession, in order to assure that no time will lapse from the failure of a patient to show (Schwartz, 1974). Waiting time in obtaining the services of a expert remind the person who waits of his or her subordination and insignificance as compared to the person for whom he or she is required to wait. Deference to a power holder is expressed by a willingness to wait and by feelings of gratitude once the service has been performed (Emerson, 1962).

While the time clock is a central organizing feature of modern society, the ancient method of using critical events as a means of gauging time is still employed. For example, most people have little difficulty in recalling their activities when they were interrupted by some major event of societal importance. Most people who were adults at the time can describe where they were and what they were doing when they heard about the Japanese attack on Pearl Harbor, the assassination of President Kennedy, the landing of a man on the moon, or the terrorist attack on 9/11.

We tend to draw on news events as benchmarks for linking the past with the present in our personal lives. Important occurrences are useful in marking social time in pretty much the same way that birthdays, anniversaries, getting a job, being promoted, changing place of residence, and attending funerals are used by individuals as reference points for assessing the general qualities of their life circumstances. Such events are used creatively for constructing the meaningfulness of past experiences and anticipating the future.

MONEY

Let us now consider the second of our major symbols of modern culture. In his classical writings, Georg Simmel (1978) emphasized the importance of money for exchange relationships. Money does not have an "intrinsic" value of its own. As a matter of fact, if it were not for its value in exchange relationships, money would be worthless. Yet as a socially constructed reality, money frequently becomes very important to most of us because we work to get it, and once we have it we may exchange it for a wide variety of goods and services.

Imagine the difficulties we would have in getting stereos, television sets, radios, refrigerators, automobiles, and telephones if we had to obtain these items without the use of money. In the absence of money as a common denominator of value, exchange relationships would necessarily be based on a system of barter. A great deal of time and effort would be required to establish the equivalency of the goods or services offered and those received. Having money as a common denominator of value facilitates exchanges among strangers and symbolizes many of the qualities of interaction in urban areas. These qualities include social interactions of short duration, impersonality, and a rational calculation of self-interests.

Agreements on the use of money as a medium of exchange permits reducing objects and services that are qualitatively different to a common quantitative basis. Such qualitatively unrelated things as a music concert, a meal in a restaurant, a new wheel for a bicycle, or the services of a prostitute can be reduced to a common standard of value. The basic questions in any given case are, "How much does it cost?" and, "What is it worth to me?" Objects for exchange are thus transformed into arithmetic problems; values are set on a numerical scale; and mathematical formulas undergird such diverse activities as wage negotiations, retail sales, and bank transactions. The calculating attitude in monetary transactions adds greatly to the direct approach and matter-of-factness in modern social life.

Richard Easterlin (1973) examined the paradox that what is true at the individual level may not be true for the society as a whole. He identified this paradox in response to the question, "Does Money Buy Happiness?" Gains in income may increase life satisfaction at the individual level, while increasing prosperity does not increase the overall sense of well-being within a nation. For example, in the United States between the late 1940s and 1970s, the purchasing power of the American family increased by about 60 percent. Yet, there is no evidence to indicate that Americans were any happier in 1970 than they were in the late 1940s. Instead, survey research indicated a linear increase in levels of alienation at the same time that income levels were improving.

Easterlin noted that for many Americans the pursuit of happiness is equated with the pursuit of money, and that materialistic values play an important part in definitions of the good life. The results of national surveys do indicate a modest correlation between level of income and reported level of life satisfaction; yet increases in the overall standard of living within the general population have not contributed to a corresponding level of happiness.

The basic reason for the gap between happiness and material well being, according to Easterlin, lies in the vast changes that have occurred in the scale by which material well-being is judged. What concern people the most are matters of everyday experiences rather than long range historical advances. Standards for evaluation have moved upward, and living conditions defined positively in our grandparents' day would be regarded by many as unacceptable today. People now think they need more, and such thinking is encouraged both by peer pressure and commercial advertising. The result is that perceived needs at the individual level have grown, and this upward shift has offset the effects of income growth on the sense of well-being for people in general.

The steady increase in per capita income since World War II has provided more leeway in personal choices and decisions for people in general. Having money is a source of freedom that permits individuals to generalize their purchasing power and to calculate the relative amounts of enjoyments from the many goods and services that are available. In this sense, money permits reflection on what one wants to get out of life, on how to maximize pleasures and satisfactions, and how to assert control over people.

But perhaps more importantly, having control over desired resources greatly enhances the individual's capacity to cope with psychological stress. Such occurrences as illness in the family, troubles on the job, traffic tickets, or difficulties with one's sex life produce some degree of psychological distress for everyone. Yet, the emotional impact of these events and the coping capacities of individuals tend to vary by social class level (Myers, Lilenthal, and Pepper, 1975). People with only limited resources tend to respond more intensely to the crises of life. In contrast, the more privileged have greater resources for coping with the stresses growing out social living; they have a greater sense of effectiveness; and they have higher tolerance for conditions of uncertainty and complexity.

One of the peculiar characteristics of money is the extent to which it becomes a measure of the social worth of individuals. People who have high incomes are accorded high levels of esteem, and they enjoy lifestyles that others envy and seek to emulate. Such advantages become reflected in a greater sense of well-being and self-esteem among the rich as compared to the poor. National surveys consistently indicate that level of life satisfaction increases with increasing income (Campbell, 1981). A high level of income confers a valued status on the individual, providing an advantage in terms of social comparison with others. Appraisals of self-worth are validated through the responses of others, and income attainment is regarded as one of the major life accomplishments. The income level achieved through personal effort provides proof of an individual's effectiveness in achieving desired goals.

The relationship between income and life satisfaction, however, requires several qualifications. Having a relatively high income is not the same as being satisfied with one's income or with one's lifestyle. Many people with only modest incomes report being satisfied with their financial situation, while several of the affluent fail to reflect a generalized sense of well-being. The wretched lives of celebrities as reported in the supermarket tabloids clearly reflect the lack of a correspondence between wealth and life satisfaction. Further, the brain strain on how to use money to increase happiness is often pretty great among those who suddenly win the state lottery or inherit unexpected wealth. The well-being of humans is to some degree dependent upon living in a predictable world (Durkheim, 1951). If all things suddenly appear to be possible, individuals become disoriented and encounter a great deal of confusion and chaos.

TRAFFIC SIGNALS

The traffic signal is another of the social inventions that grew out of the need to coordinate the activities of a large number of people. The crisscrossing of a large volume of traffic as people move from one part of the city to another is a distinctly modern and highly complicated type of activity. Yet, the control of traffic flow has become such a self-evident part of urban living that it is now regarded as a normal and natural attribute of modern social life. Without the traffic signal, urban dwellers would be confused, disoriented, and incapacitated.

Our dependency on an orderly flow of traffic became evident a few years ago with the electrical blackout in the northeastern part of the United States. In New York City, the streetlights went out, and a massive traffic jam developed when the traffic lights failed to work. An estimated 800,000 people were trapped in subways, and many people were stuck in elevators (Burke, 1978). A small malfunction in the power transmission system at Niagara Falls had temporarily crippled a vast population area. Such an episode is a dramatic reminder of the interdependent character of modern social life and the imperative of coordinating the activities of a large number of people. If the traffic lights fail to work, a sense of entrapment is likely to develop for many people in congested urban areas.

The lights signaling "stop," "go," and "caution" capture the disjointed and fragmented character of urban living. The automobile driver is required "to be alert," "to pay attention," and "to be defensive" in aligning his or her behavior with that of other people. A large number of people are in close proximity, and negotiations are required for the use of public space. Knowing "who has the right of way" and "who is required to wait" are essential for events to proceed in an orderly fashion. The extent to which nearly all adults in our society share such knowledge is a remarkable accomplishment in social control.

The traffic signal is a major symbol of governmental authority in modern society. The regulation of automobile traffic is a major variable in the expansion of such agencies of government as police departments, courts, urban planning commission, and licensing bureaus. Governmental control of the flow of traffic is made possible through the use of standardized rules and regulations that must be known and understood by those allowed to use our highways and city streets. A failure to follow rules and regulations in driving an automobile is a source of irritation to other drivers. The term *road rage* crept into our everyday vocabulary in the late 1980s. Just notice the mouth movement among drivers in other cars when someone makes an improper left turn or fails to relinquish the right of way. Insurance companies and law enforcement personnel express a more consequential form of irritation.

The movement of people and the flow of automobile traffic are symbolic of the urban dominance of our personal lives. In observing the flow of traffic on a typical work day, we may note that there is a congested flow of traffic toward the centers of our metropolitan areas during the beginning of a typical workday and a congested flow of traffic out of the central city when the workday is over. These patterns of traffic flow reflect the degree to which we have separated the places where we work from the places where we live. Such a separation is symptomatic of the fragmentation of modern social life. The work sphere is not very well integrated with the nonwork sphere. The two are separated both psychologically and geographically. The self becomes fragmented in the sense that individuals are pulled in many different directions all at the same time. The many activities in which people are engaged are carried out in spheres that are socially and psychologically unrelated to each other.

Discussion

Why study time clocks, money, and traffic signals? Some might say these are such self-evident aspects of the modern world that they do not merit study or investigation. But if we probe beneath the surface of everyday events, these qualities are far from being self-evident. Each of these features of the modern world has symbolic meanings that are not generally recognized and each has mysterious qualities about it (Langone, 2000).

While our method of measuring time is necessarily based on consensus, its mysterious qualities derive from its representations in the physical world. The time dimension of the human life span suggests that time is a one-way street as we move from birth through adulthood to death. Our experiences with certain aspects of time as irreversible are stressful and disturbing. To deal with this aspect of time as irreversible, human cultures have elaborated several forms of denial of the reality of death as final. An extension of the life span in a linear direction is achieved through postulating that the spirits of the dead live on in the community or that the soul travels to some remote place far removed from the world of the living.

According to Edmund Leach (1979), the human experience with time takes several forms. Time is experienced as cyclical if we observe the movement of the seasons from spring to summer to autumn to winter to spring in an ongoing pattern.

By viewing time as cyclical in nature, conceptions of reincarnation offer the promise of an opportunity for starting over and perhaps doing a better job of it the next time around. We hope that the recycled product will be better than the original.

Time is also experienced as a movement up to a certain point and then a sharp reversal, as with a pendulum swing. Experiences with the alterations between night and day appear to be of this order. The swing from night to day in an endless progression appears to be of this order. Throughout most of the human past, the night was a time for sleeping. In the modern world, the uses of electricity and the light bulb have greatly extended the range of night activities. As a result, sleep deprivation is more of a problem today than it was in the past. While nightlife is typically associated with leisure and recreation, it also has nefarious connotations. The theme of "take back the night" has become an important slogan for those concerned with increased freedom of movement for women.

The alteration between night and day is one of the predictable aspects of the human experience and has been so elaborated within cultures. In Northern Europe the ratio of nighttime to daytime was greatly influenced by seasonal variations. As the days grew shorter and the nights grew longer with the approach of winter, the levels of fear and anxiety intensified among the Druids.

Apocalyptic religious beliefs in the far north held that humans were doomed in the long run: If the trend toward shorter days continued, the world would eventually be engulfed in darkness. Only the performance of sacred, religious rituals, such as those performed at Stonehenge at the peak of the winter solstice could alter the direction of the sun. The remarkable feature of this ceremony is that it was performed precisely on the shortest day of the year. Just through the performance of the sacred ceremony, the days automatically started getting longer. Scheduling celebrations of the birth of Christ with the winter solstice greatly increased the acceptability of Christianity in Northern Europe.

In addition to subjective meanings, the creations of time, money, and traffic signals also have objective referents that are clearly understood in conventional ways by the members of a given society. These shared meanings are important solutions to the problems of complexity and coordination in highly urbanized areas. Such forms of order in a modern society stand in contrast to the seeming chaos and disorder in the more rural and less urbanized parts of the world.

References

Burke, James. *Connections*. Boston: Little, Brown, 1978.

Campbell, Angus. *The Sense of Well-Being in America*. New York: McGraw-Hill, 1981.

Durkheim, Emile. *Suicide*. Glencoe, IL: Free Press, 1951.

Easterlin, Richard A. "Does Money Buy Happiness?" *The Public Interest*, 30, (1973): 3–10.

Emerson, Richard. "Power-Dependence Relations." *American Sociological Review* 22 (1962): 31–41.

Langone, John. *The Mystery of Time: Humanity's Quest for Order and Measure*. Washington, DC: National Geographic, 2000.

Leach, Edmund R. "Two Essays Concerning the Symbolic Representation of Time." In W. A. Lessa and E. Z. Vogt, Editors, *Reader in Comparative Religion: An Anthropological Approach*. New York: Harper and Row, pp. 221–229.

Myers, Jerome K., Jacob L. Lindenthal, and Max P. Pepper. "Life Events, Social Integration, and Psychosomatic Sympotomatology." *Journal of Health and Social Behavior*, 16 (1975): 421–427.

Schwartz, Barry. "Waiting, Exchange, and Power: The Distribution of Time in Social Systems." *American Sociological Review*, 79 (1974): 841–870.

Simmel, Georg. *The Sociology of Georg Simmel*. Glencoe, IL: Free Press, 1950.

Simmel, Georg. *The Philosophy of Money*. Boston: Routledge and Kegan Paul, 1978.

8

Popular Culture and Philosophy

RAYMOND RUBLE

When major news events such as 9/11, the war in Iraq, or the *Columbia* space shuttle disaster happen, why are no philosophers seen on TV news programming such as CNBC, CNN, *Larry King*, *Meet the Press*, or *Nightline*? These are programs whose bread and butter involve the discussion and analysis of culturally important topics. Again, why are philosophers never consulted in talk shows such as Oprah? Why is there a Doctor Phil, but no Professor Phil? Religious figures, psychologists, scientists, military figures, political figures, and economists regularly fill these time slots, but seldom, if ever, philosophers. Why are there no philosophers who regularly write editorials in newspapers or news magazines? It is because philosophy is not seen by our culture as having anything meaningful to contribute to the discussion. Philosophy is not even on the radarscope, so to speak. Philosophy, the love of wisdom, has a minimized cultural status in America. Even our existence as an academic discipline is seldom acknowledged by our culture, and to the extent that it is "acknowledged" it is treated as a quintessential ivory tower subject having no relevance to the "real world."

Indeed, we philosophers are some of the major perpetrators of this image of philosophy. As professional teachers of philosophy we have adopted a strategy toward our own students akin to that of the U.S. Marines. We are "looking for a few good [students]." The vast majority of our students simply cannot measure up to this status, and like the chaff that they are, they are left behind on the threshing floor. Indeed, we philosophers act as if it is better that the many (what Hume refers to as the rabble or the vulgar) be left on the threshing room floor. Thus we ourselves create the very ivory tower we find ourselves trapped in. But we should know better. We know that philosophy applies to everything both inside and outside of the so-called real world. This essay is a small step in consciousness-raising for professional philosophers. Let us more readily apply our skills to even more of the events that occur outside of the professional classroom. Let us treat our students more like U.S. Army recruits and help them to "be all that they can be." To do so, let us apply our skills to the analysis of popular culture. Philosophers have much to contribute.

What defines culture? Isn't popular culture an oxymoron? This negative attitude toward the academic study of popular culture is common in academics itself, both inside and outside of philosophy circles. But it is a mistake in that it willfully eliminates the application of philosophical analysis from an area much in need of it. For purposes of this essay, "culture" can be defined in at least two separate ways: (1) as the customs and civilization of a particular group of people ("common culture"), and (2) as the appreciation and understanding of literature, the arts, music, etc. ("high culture"). These two definitions are related in that the *high culture is actually a subset of common culture*. The position that popular culture is an oxymoron rests on the intentional elimination of common culture as culture in favor of high culture as the only real culture. Indeed, the very labels *common culture* and *high culture* are value laden in that under the guise of describing a phenomenon they equally prescribe value-laden status to the phenomenon. And the values that they ascribe equate "common" with vulgar and unworthy and "high" with worthwhile and (innately) desirable.

Furthermore, according to the received position, philosophy itself is part and parcel of high culture. As such, it is to be automatically segregated from common culture. Indeed, in the minds of many its segregation is so complete that it should not have anything to do with common culture. It should certainly not dare to elevate the status of common cultural practices by treating them as worthy of serious academic discussion. To do so would be to lower philosophy itself to the status of the common. How plebian! Should we philosophers reduce ourselves to this oxymoron?

Such an attitude is a mistake. As influential as this negative attitude is toward popular culture, it isn't the only possible attitude. And it is an attitude that comes at a price. It cuts philosophy off from a wealth of material ripe for philosophical analysis. It cuts us off from most of the students we are trying to teach. It cuts us off from common culture itself. Popular culture is a subject worthy of serious academic and philosophical analysis. We have taken to heart only part of Plato's message found in the Myth of the Cave (514ff). We have torn ourselves out of captivity and struggled (upwards!) to the light of the sun. But Plato's message compels more than personal liberation. It compels us to go back into the cave to free our fellow citizens (516e). In our elitism, we professional philosophers have been slow to do just that. We have been slow to recognize the rich possibilities common culture (the cave) makes available for our analytic skills. The two sections that follow focus on separate concerns that impact the willingness of professional philosophers to see popular culture as a subject worthy of philosophical analysis.

Pedagogy, a Means to an End

Many university students who are first introduced to philosophy come to it with either a blank incomprehension or the assumption that philosophy is about deep and spooky stuff that certainly has no relevance for their own lives. And frequently, the way philosophy is taught only adds to that misconception. Most university students who take philosophy courses do so in order to satisfy humanities requirements. As such, they constitute an unwilling but captive audience. At worst, they hide behind a front of bored disinterest; at best, they display a polite willingness to be enlightened. Few have a ghost of an idea before hand of what philosophy is all about. They are all largely clueless. As philosophy teachers it is our job to supply the enlightenment. But all too often what do we do? We choose topics and texts that are far away from our students' experiences and capabilities and we dare them, so to speak, to make sense out of these topics and texts. We fall victim to the worst in the Socratic *elenchus*, the capacity to tie our intellectual inferiors into puzzled knots, to reduce them to silence so that we may be seen by all to "win" the argument. They are just too dumb, and they are better off if they know it. In short, we act like latter-day Sophists who frequently win all the battles, but lose the war.

To win the war, to better reach average university undergraduates, we must begin with what they already know. This is how any effective teaching works. As Aristotle acknowledged, knowledge begins with what is "prior and better known to man..." (72a2). And Kant says, "There can be no doubt that all our knowledge begins with experience" (B1). This position was intended by Aristotle and Kant to apply to specific perceptual claims, but it applies to far more than this. It applies to the bits and pieces of our knowledge as well as the common ways we fit these pieces together. We philosophers know that even synthesized experience, however, is only the beginning of knowledge; it is not the be all and end all of knowledge. We then proceed in the usual manner to show our students that there are other components to knowledge claims, ethical claims, social ideas, and so forth. This is all to the good. We go wrong in our teaching process, however, when we too easily rocket beyond our students' actual experiences by applying complex ideas to what many of them regard as weird and crazy thought experiments to which they have a difficult time relating. We call these ideas and thought experiments "possible worlds." ("Suppose we were all brains in a vat." Or "Suppose there were an evil genius." Or "Suppose that we were all in the original position in a state of nature.") These scenarios do not work very well with many of our students. Supposing these things is too far away from their own experience. Why not call them movies, TV programs, songs, sport contests, Internet searches, family dynamics, and whatnot and adopt current examples from those with which they are familiar? Thus we may easily and profitably integrate popular culture studies and examples within our traditional curriculum.

Nor do our problems end with our failure to reach average undergraduates. Consider those who are considering majoring in philosophy. What gives them pause? Two things. The first thing is social incomprehension or scorn. It is not a good pick-up line at home or socially. "You're majoring in what!?" Couple this with dirty looks and a defensive posture and we have a rerun of our own announcements when we decided to major in philosophy. The second thing is the common question university students who are thinking of majoring in philosophy ask of their advisors. "What can I do with it?" In effect this question means, "What careers or jobs does philosophy prepare me for?" Our traditional answer, teaching philosophy to other university undergraduates, has for some time been disingenuous given the job market. But what else can you do with it? The correct answer is anything and everything that requires sustained intellectual reflection, analysis, synthesis, and emphasis. Most undergraduate majors in philosophy do not go on to graduate studies in this area. If they go on to graduate school at all, it is usually in an area outside of philosophy. And those studies include popular culture. Certainly they all go and live within popular culture. Why on earth would their very own existential environment be out of bounds as a suitable subject of philosophical reflection?

How often have we academic philosophers perpetuated this unfortunate stereotypical perspective of philosophy in our culture by saying to our students: "However, in the real world..." as if what we did in the classroom was not part of, related to, of significance for the "real world." What is this "real world" such that philosophy stands aloof from it? And what sort of "reality" are philosophers thereby endorsing? We offer to them the cornerstone of a liberal education. It is about time we acknowledged that.

Nay, it is about time we *insisted* on that! Accordingly, the very arguments we can make for encouraging students to major in philosophy are the ones we can use for applying philosophical analysis to popular culture.

An End in Itself

The study of popular culture is more than a means of introducing students to philosophy. It has intrinsic philosophical interests it its own right. Professional philosophy covers a wide range of topics, and that range increases with every passing century. The core areas of metaphysics, epistemology, and value theory never exclusively defined the issues of concern to philosophers even among the ancient Greeks. There were always other areas (e.g., rhetoric, medicine, magic) that overlapped philosophy. Over time, concerns about the boundaries of philosophy and other subject areas raised issues about the development and growth of the discipline of philosophy, issues that were never resolved, but evolved into structural concerns within the profession thanks to two 19th-century phenomena — the subsumption of professional philosophers into university teachers and the development of professional societies of philosophers (as opposed to mere schools of thought) with the rise of the American Philosophical Association (APA) and the like. With these two developments, the domain of philosophy could now be established by the fiat of which conferences, papers, and publications these professional societies endorsed as well as what was taught by professional philosophers to graduates and undergraduates alike. And these professionals were interested in the canon. Does this make the historical canon of intrinsic interest? Yes, but only because it so viewed by its proponents. Does this prevent the augmentation of the canon by the addition of new areas of interests that some philosophers find intrinsically interesting? No, but only if it is so viewed by its proponents. John Stuart Mill maintained, "the sole evidence it is possible to produce that anything is [intrinsically] desirable is that people actually desire it" (44). Ultimately, the sole evidence it is possible to produce that metaphysics, epistemology, value theory, or the philosophy of popular culture are intrinsically interesting, is that philosophers themselves desire to explore these issues. If we did not, no utility argument will carry sufficient weight to invoke these interests.

This raises the difficulty of acknowledging new areas within a discipline. Consider the differences between the study of artificial intelligence and that of teaching philosophy or critical thinking. AI was easily incorporated into university classes, APA meetings, and the paper presentation system because it was seen as an obvious extension of traditional issues in philosophical psychology. The same may be said for business or medical ethics. Teaching philosophy and critical thinking, however, have had a much more difficult time in gaining acceptance within the APA. Indeed, whole new organizations and professional journals have had to be formed to give an outlet for those who wish to deal with these areas as professional topics themselves. (How ironic, given that many who see teaching philosophy or critical thinking as marginalized subjects are themselves professional teachers of philosophy!) Feminism lies between AI and teaching philosophy and critical thinking. For many years feminism was marginalized as merely a social/political movement of dubious value and not as a serious academic study. The same can be said for the philosophical study of sexuality. All that is now in the past. All of these additions to the canon of philosophy are flourishing. They have gained more or less full-fledged niches in the APA as, à la Kuhn's *Structure of Scientific Revolution,* the old guard slowly ages out of the profession and new blood enters with the requisite need to establish status via professional presentations and publications.

Why should the same not be true for the philosophical study of popular culture? If the philosophy of popular culture is ever to achieve acknowledged status in the APA, it will have to follow a course similar to feminism, critical thinking, the teaching of philosophy, and the philosophical study of sexuality. There will have to be rising young philosophers who stake their future within the profession on achieving recognition as specialists in this area. It is not good enough that there are regional, national, and international popular culture association meetings. That is only a start. Currently these meetings have few sessions specifically devoted to philosophical issues and few philosophers who attend them. Until our attendance at popular culture association meetings and the number of sessions and papers devoted to philosophical issues increase, popular culture, like early feminism, will remain at the margins of our profession. Until the APA devotes sections to the philosophy of popular culture and universities invent undergraduate and graduate classes specifically devoted to the philosophical study of popular culture, this embryonic entity will remain in the process of gestation.

Afterwords

Academically, philosophy has a long way to go in our failure to interface with popular culture. Popular culture ignores us because we ignore it. The academic study of religion is way ahead of philosophy on these matters. In religion there already exists a journal, *Religion and Popular Culture*, and it is possible to obtain a master's in religious studies and popular culture. Surely we philosophers do not think that the academic study of religion is applicable to modern culture while the academic study of philosophy is not.

To be fair to ourselves, it is not as if no one in philosophy is currently paying attention to popular culture. Philosophy is a big tent and it is getting bigger every decade. Martin Benjamin has published a book, *Philosophy and This Actual World* (2003), which by its title would seem to be a textbook applying philosophy to popular culture. But the title in this case is somewhat misleading, as this text is really a topical introduction to philosophy that includes only a few cultural examples firmly embedded amidst the old chestnuts of traditional philosophy. A work such as this is merely a small step in the right direction. Recent works such as Irwin's *Steinfeld and Philosophy: A Book About Everything and Nothing* (2000) and Irwin, Conard, and Skoble's *The Simpsons and Philosophy: The D'oh! of Homer* (2001) have successfully bridged the gap between traditional philosophical analysis and popular culture in that they are (frequently humorous) attempts to use these well-known TV shows as vehicles for serious philosophical themes. Other texts such as Hanley's *The Metaphysics of Star Trek* (1997), in which Richard Hanley examines concepts like warping space, time travel, and the nature of human (and android) nature in the context of a group of long-lived TV series very familiar to many of our students, and Irwin's *The Matrix and Philosophy: Welcome to the Desert of the Real* (2002), in which a group of philosophers discuss some of the many philosophical issues raised by *Matrix*, or "Simulacra and Simulation," in which Jean Baudrillard discusses the cultural impact of imagination and gaming on culture, are more serious works that apply philosophical analysis to a range of issues raised by aspects of popular culture. Then there is *Matrix Reloaded*, "starring" Cornel West, whose line "Comprehension is not prerequisite for cooperation" is sure to become a cultural icon in between the status of Descartes's "Cogito, ergo sum" and Schwarzenegger's "I'llll bee bak!" (And West can sing too.) Texts about these and other current cultural artifacts could fill important philosophical needs, but if we are ever to break through into mainstream culture what we really need are philosophical popularizers, philosophers who fill the niche of Stephen Jay Gould or Carl Sagan. We need Professors Phil and Phyllis to continually get our messages out via mass media, especially TV. Any takers?

References

Aristotle. *Posterior Analytics*. Richard McKeon, Editor. New York: Random House, 1941.

Benjamin, Martin. *Philosophy and This Actual World*. New York: Rowman & Littlefield, 2003.

Baudrillard, Jean. "Simulacra and Simulation." In *Selected Writings*, Mark Poster, Editor. Stanford, CA: Stanford University Press, 1988.

Hanley, Richard. *The Metaphysics of Star Trek*. New York: Basic Books, 1997.

Irwin, William, Editor. *The Matrix and Philosophy: Welcome to the Desert of the Real*. Chicago: Open Court, 2002.

Irwin, William. *Steinfeld and Philosophy: A Book About Everything and Nothing*. Chicago: Open Court, 2000.

Irwin, William, Mark T. Conard, and Aeon J. Skoble, Editors. *The Simpsons and Philosophy: The D'oh! of Homer*. Chicago: Open Court, 2001.

Kant, Immanuel. *Critique of Pure Reason*. Norman Kemp Smith, Trans. New York: St Martin's Press, 1965.

Mill, John Stuart. *Utilitarianism*. Oskar Piest, Editor. Indianapolis: Library of Liberal Arts, 1957.

Plato. *Republic*, Robin Waterfield, Trans. New York: Oxford University Press, 1993.

9

Interdisciplinary Opportunities

Therapeutic Culture and the Study of Religion in the United States

GREGORY THOMPSON

Popular culture has always served as a barometer of religion in society. In fact the proliferation of popular culture in the United States can be directly attributed to the expansion of religions, especially evangelical movements, in the 19th and 20th centuries. The awareness and acknowledgment of the interconnection between religion and popular culture can only help to provide a broader and deeper understanding of religion's function, influence, and importance in society. As cultural institutions that share common heritages, the study of religion can only be enhanced by a healthy infusion of studies that seriously approach the intersections of religion and popular culture. Perhaps more so than any other department in an academic setting, religious studies critically examines, questions, and analyzes that aspect of human culture that is often the most private, personal, and subjective to individuals. From this examination, religious studies scholars attempt to understand, define, and examine religious experience and religious practices. Often, however, the examination quickly loses the subjective experience of the everyday practitioner and finds itself mired in the phenomenological exploration of the defining and refining religion as an academic discipline. This definition is then disseminated from professional religionists to other religionists in a process that builds up rather than tears down walls of separation between scholar and everyday participant. "Intellectuals and historians," historian Warren

Susman (1984) scolds, "would do well to begin to see ideas in things and to see that there is in fact some connection between the most ethereal of ideas and common, even basic, human behavior" (284).

There is, however, a development that is only just beginning to be explored and approached with academic seriousness. The problem is this, when one attempts to study religion with a strict, reasoned, and scientific approach, the emotional aspect of the religious experience is removed. This is why, for example, religion and art/theater are so intricately intertwined. Both expressions are intended to evoke emotional reaction. The importance of emotion and the examination of "therapeutic culture," provide an opportunity for academic scholars to address the importance of religion and religious institutions in creating shared emotional communities. Scott McLemee pointed to the growth of "emotion" scholarship in his 2003 essay "Getting Emotional." His exploration while detailed in its examination of emotion in some of the humanities and particularly in classical studies, is lacking in the connection that should be obvious between studies of religion and emotion. This realization has found some voice in scholarship over the past decade but so far has primarily been limited to the understanding of material culture and religion. As further understanding of therapeutic culture grows, the connection between religion, emotion, and popular culture will grow. These explorations should examine religion and expressions of therapeutic culture in both rhetorical and material forms of popular culture.

In his 1996 book, The *Spirituality of Comedy*, Conrad Hyers argued, "If one of the purposes of the humanities and social sciences is better to understand the human world, the resulting picture is often skewed by a presentation that largely ignores the playful and comic side" (1). In his excellent examination of the connection between comedy and spirituality, Conrad Hyers examines the important distinctions between comedy and tragedy as portrayed in Western dramatic literature and film. He extrapolates this examination to include an understanding of what can be called tragic or warrior virtues versus comedic virtues. While the warrior will stand firm, fight, and think in one-dimensional terms of honor, the comedian (fool) will turn and run, taking no shame in the pragmatic decision to preserve his or her life. Hyer's argument can easily be expanded to more broadly include popular culture.

Religious studies scholars dismiss popular culture as transient fad and fashion, unimportant to a long-term understanding of expressions of religious belief. When popular culture is examined in a religious studies context, it is usually when there is a clear representation of religious iconography present in the popular expression. Explorations such as Tona

Hangen's 2002 *Redeeming the Dial: Radio, Religion, and Popular Culture in America*, begin to examine the historical interconnection between religion and popular culture as it relates to cultural phenomena in American society. Hangen's text is an excellent if somewhat cursory overview of the development of religious broadcasting in the early 20th century. It is less an exploration of what the religion brought to the radio or why the religion played so well on the radio. Hagen more than accurately asserts, however, that in the 20th century, while some prognosticated that religious institutions would fade, the reality was that these same institutions, especially Protestant evangelical movements, simply redefined how their religion was disseminated and in some ways practiced. "Religion," she wrote, "even the kind that bills itself as 'traditional' or 'old-fashioned,' found a ready place in modern mass media, enhancing and strengthening certain forms of religious behavior and practices" (5).

John M. Giggie and Diane Winston also addressed the early belief that urbanization and industrialization led to the destruction of religious institutions, in the 2002 text *Faith in the Market*. This book, like Hagen's, addressed the predicted demolition of religious institutions only to find that these institutions, in order to survive, adapted themselves to American consumer and popular culture. Like Hagen, Giggie and Winston acknowledged the scholarly neglect of the interconnection between popular culture and religious studies as a subject largely ignored in academic circles. They realized that it is not enough, however, to simply examine the number of churches in an urban environment in order to gain knowledge of that city's religious beliefs.

> It would not be unusual to see the faithful, acting with the full blessing of their leaders, purchase clothing that telegraphed their beliefs, buy household objects embodying their devotion, advertise their brand of salvation in newspapers, or use the airwaves to publicize their unique revelations. The lesson learned would be plain: in urban areas, sacred life and commercial life are deeply intertwined [1].

The examination of commercial and popular culture expressions of religion found its voice initially in the 1993 Colleen McDannell book *Material Christianity*. While the realization of a connection between material goods and Christian expression may not have been new, it was McDannell's text that argued for the realization that the domestic, feminine, and adolescent expression of religious beliefs held as much importance as the traditionally male-dominated expressions found in the doctrine and dogma of religious institutions. It was McDannell's argument that in fact the "lived" expression of religion may be more valid than the spoken and

written expressions from church leaders and scholars. "These case studies demonstrate that 'genuine' religion has always been expressed and made
real with objects, architecture, art, and landscapes." Her examination of
the cultural artifacts of popular material culture led her to this assertion.

These explorations of the interconnection between popular and consumer or commercial culture and religion in the 20th century, form an
important base from which to study religious expression. Certainly by no
means must we limit our exploration of the material and spiritual to the
20th century. Indeed forms of popular culture and religion are found
throughout cultures, both Western and Eastern, and time periods both
contemporary and ancient. The most obvious immediately to come to
mind is the interconnection between religion and theater, both of which,
as organized institutions, find their common roots in western culture from
the 5th century B.C.E. Athenian festivals of Dionysus. The theater/religion
connection and the evocation of emotional reaction on the part of the religious congregant/theater audience, points to the necessary understanding
by religion scholars of therapeutic culture in society.

In several instances, throughout his 1984 book, *Culture as History: The
Transformation of American Society in the Twentieth Century*, Susman
hinted at ideas that he wanted others to expand. Among the simplest yet
most notable is his inclusion of photographs and captions that suggest further study but are not incorporated into the text. In a photo that shows two
images of what Susman titled "Our Church," he wrote in the caption, "Religious experience in America today is often defined in terms of traditional
institutions and traditional structure. In fact, there has been a wide range
of religious visions and associated practices" (286). The images are of an
African American storefront religious gathering and of a man standing on
a street corner with a sign expressing his religious opinion to passersby. This
is the extent to which Susman explored the question of various religious
visions and practices. Other references to religion found in his book were
related to discussions of Puritan value systems, a 20th-century version of
Jesus entitled *The Man Nobody Knows* (1925), and other minor references
to traditional religious institutions that helped shape the transitional characters about whom Susman wrote. The photos and caption leave open the
possibility for studying, using Susman's method of cultural exploration,
nontraditional religious experiences in depth and inquiring about the
importance of such experiences in further establishing what Susman
referred to as "the culture of personality" in America (275). Even more
obvious in Susman's "hint" for study is the idea that religious experience
and expression are interconnected through an emotional binding that
requires understanding the importance of the self in culture.

"One of the things," argued Susman, "that make the modern world 'modern' is the development of consciousness of self" (271). The exploration and the importance of self-realization was perhaps the most understated and important aspect of Susman's interpretation of American culture in the 20th century.

Susman, in the final section of his chapter on personality and the 20th century discussed what he referred to as "unproven assertions about the emergence of a culture of personality" (284). Susman recognized moments of clearly definable problems with the identification of the self in the 20th century. These problems, according to Susman, translated into time periods that were associated with leading psychological or psychiatric thinkers of the 20th century. "In the period from 1910 through the late 1920s, the problem was most often defined in terms of guilt and the need to eliminate guilt ... the age of Freud ... the period from 1929 to 1938 was dominated by Shame ... the age of Alfred Adler ... 1939 through the 1940s ... thought of itself as the age of anxiety.... Let me call this the age of Jung. From the end of the 1940s to almost the end of the 1950s the problem was fundamentally redefined as that of personal identity ... the age of Erik Erikson" (Susman, 1984, 284). While he presented these short categories of the ages and their psychoanalytical interpreter, Susman did not define the "therapeutic culture" (284). Susman's lack of definition underscored the difficult starting point for the scholar who hopes to understand the importance of the therapeutic culture in the American mind. The cures that the psychological and psychiatric professions provided for American anxiety told only a small part of the story of therapeutic culture in the United States. Furthermore, these scientific approaches to self-understanding rarely if ever included looks to religion and religious movements for understanding.

In 1966, Philip Rieff, in his book *The Triumph of the Therapeutic*, noted a shift in American culture that occurred over the first half of the 20th century. Rieff understood culture as a system of controls and releases that were diametrically related to one another. These controls and releases played out in the form of demands and permissions for social activity. Controls accounted for what one must or must not do and releases account for what one may do. According to Rieff, in the 20th century the system of releases had overtaken the controls and had turned the culture upside down. He suggested that in order to understand these fundamental shifts in culture one must look at the balance of controls in the society. If the controls had shifted to areas that were formally releases, then culture had indeed fundamentally shifted positions with regard to systems of moral demands (Rieff, 233). Rieff identified this morally inverted society as *therapeutic culture*.

Rieff argued that the use of psychoanalysis acted as a buffer to personal responsibility; it defended "the private man from the demands of both culture and instinct" (Susman, 1984, 278). It was not a technique of analysis that concerned Rieff, rather it was the person made by this Freudian revolution. Rieff referred to this new person as "Psychological Man." For Rieff, Freud and Freudianism became a secular religion to "Psychological Man." This focus on releases and Freudianism indicated to Rieff a switch from a principle of religious authority to adherence to the pleasure principle. According to Rieff, salvation was "religious man's" goal; "psychological man" was born to be pleased (25). In this ideological construct, religion lost its position of authority in favor of an authority system based in the use of psychology and therapy. Rieff, however, did not see religion or its rhetoric swept from the face of the earth. Instead he saw that appropriated components of various religions would fulfill what individuals felt was necessary for personal spiritual satisfaction. In reality his prediction has proven to be remarkably accurate: "Psychological man in his independence from all gods can feel free to use all god terms; I imagine he will be a hedger of his own bets, a user of any faith that lends itself to therapeutic use" (a prophetic statement in light of e.g., Cimino and Lattin, 1999). This was true at the end of the 20th century when the growth of the "salad bar effect" of choosing bits and pieces of various religious traditions to create what worked best for the spiritual seeker became prevalent (Cimino and Lattin, 1999). According to Rieff, "Psychological Man" used the ambiguity of psychoanalysis to create the neatest position possible to fulfill his or her needs.

This sense of individual search for perfectionism was prevalent throughout the history of the United States, but it was most clearly institutionalized in the 20th century. This idea in America was as old as John Winthrop and the Puritans, and the idea found even greater relevance in the writing and life of Benjamin Franklin. In the 18th and throughout the 19th century, at the beginning of the consumer age, individual perfectionism moved out of the traditional religious setting of the church and became institutionalized in the self-help and self-improvement movements in which the Horatio Alger myth of "rags to riches" took firm root in the American mind. Along with Alger, Temple University founder Russell Conwell was one the first great "self-help gurus" with his lecture "Acres of Diamonds." This was a frequently presented pep-talk and sermon about the positive potential within each man [sic] for prosperity and happiness in the United States. In each of these instances there was a connection with religion, not a separation from but a new interpretation of individual perfection based on changing perceptions of the consumerist world.

The continued use of therapeutic terms, terminology, and theory continued throughout the 20th century as various scholars examined American society though the lens of Freudianism. Often there was not specific reference to the use of Freudianism in these works, but the language, method, or approach clearly indicated an a priori understanding of Freud within the culture. This was evident in the work of T. J. Jackson Lears and Susman in the 1980s as it was of Rieff in the 1960s. In the 1950s, David Riesman's *The Lonely Crowd: A Study of the Changing American Character* provided a sociological study of therapeutic culture and its effect on American society (1950). Riesman's concern was that the emphasis on the self was taking over and that conformist behavior, driven by the therapeutic culture's concern with "normalcy" versus maladjustment, led to people who were no longer connected with those around them. His conclusion was that this led to a sense of alienation through conforming to the demands of a corporate society.

In her 1968 essay "The Concept of History," Hannah Arendt noted the effect of the therapeutic culture on American culture. As she characterized it, "the modern age, with its growing world alienation, has led to a situation where man, wherever he goes encounters only himself" (Quoted in June, 1980, 211).[1] This was particularly significant for Americans, because national identity has often been derived from the confrontation with frontiers that were natural in character. If the frontiers vanished, as Turner's 1893 essay insisted they did, then where were Americans to look for identity? More often than not, the form of identity realization that Arendt referred to was found through identification with celebrity or through advertising, especially as developed throughout the interwar period of the 1920s (Nash, 1970, 127).

Leading the growth of the therapeutic culture in America and the self-help industry of the 20th century, was not the church or exclusively the psychiatric community but rather the prophets of the "new culture of the self," men and women who were proficient at "getting into the minds" of individuals and convincing them that a better life awaited them through consumerism. Susman emphasized the importance of the advertising man Bruce Barton in helping to establish the new consumerist modes of thought in American culture in the 1920s. He also emphasized the importance of the fact that Barton was the son of a minister. The advertising men and salesmen of the early part of the 20th century completed the shift from

[1]*A good review of Christopher Lasch's work. It explores the question of why his work falls flat as a Jeremiad and why that work offers few if any solutions to the problems he highlights.*

culture of character to culture of personality, but they also helped bring religion into the new culture rather than leaving it behind. They did this because they were the sons and grandsons of preachers and devout parents who raised them in pious households.

Cultural critic James Twitchell observed:

> When you read the lives of the first and second generation of advertising impresarios, "the configuration [religion and retail] occurs with such startling regularity that it is hard to believe the combination was haphazard. Almost as if [Barton] has to shove aside the old father [the church] in order to get to the new text [commercialism], the youthful copywriter proceeds to apply what he has been taught about ecclesiastical hermeneutics to create a new parochial gospel of salvation" [1999, 64].

It was in the way Barton described Jesus in *The Man Nobody Knows* that gave insight into the importance of the image and personality that was evident in the new consumerist culture. "So Barton imagines a dapper Jesus at a cocktail party or a ballgame with the rest of us, a man among men who knows well what his people need and struggles to explain how to get it," 64–65). Barton's image of Jesus is one of "a canny businessman, a kind of Rotarian glad-hander" (Coleman, 2002, 141). Historian Roderick Nash reported, "*The Man Nobody Knows* 'redesigned' the image of Christ from a meek and lowly man into a sun tanned, hard muscled giant" (147).

The religious background was implicit. Nash wrote of Barton, "Believing religion indispensable to a full life, Barton long lamented that no professional clergyman saw fit to modernize ancient doctrine to fit current circumstances" (147). In creating an image of Jesus as businessman it was Barton's intent to merely create a metaphor that he believed had meaning in his contemporary society (148). "For Barton religion and politics and refrigerators were part of the same culture, a culture based on a kind of providential realism in which the powers of advertising could only spread the good word and reenchant the world" (Twitchell, 1999, 66). Barton no longer saw a necessity for the separation of the two realms of spirituality and the material world. It was Barton's contention that the way to understand spirituality in his contemporary culture was through the rhetoric of the material, consumer realm. The correlation between religion and advertising, according to Twitchell, was evident to Barton. "Sin, guilt, redemption: problem, anxiety, resolution — the process of transformation is clear" (67). Twitchell, Susman, Nash, historian Gary Cross, and others insisted that Barton was the culmination and the exemplary model of the 20th century Christian prophet.

The promotion of self-realization became not only the means for understanding the world but also the basis by which all morals were judged. In the therapeutic culture, traditional forms of restraint on behavior were supplanted by the development of psychoanalytic understandings. Historian Jackson Lears (1981) noted that this outlook was adopted by those for whom all "over-arching structures of meaning have collapsed and for whom there is nothing at stake beyond a manipulable sense of well-being" (54).[2]

Therapeutic culture was one in which the releases of previously repressed impulses became the dominant system of individual action or motivation. In this worldview, morality based in self-expression and self-realization became more important than traditional Victorian or Protestant beliefs of self-denial. Therapeutic culture provided a new set of values put forth by social scientists and therapists, supplanting religion, in this case Western European Protestant Christianity, as the primary foundation for moral restraint. It also provided the process through which one was in pursuit of self-identity and self-realization within society under these new values (Lears, 1981, 54).

"Indeed, the very term *therapeutic* suggests a life focused on the need for cure. But cure of what?" asked Robert Bellah. "In the final analysis, it is cure of the lack of fit between the present organization of the self and the available organization of work intimacy, and meaning" (Bellah, 1985, 67). The dominance of the business-oriented world on the consumer ethic in the 20th century became the defining principle of the American individual. "The bureaucratic organization of the business corporation has been the dominant force in this century" (45). In response, a need arose for the individual to understand and define herself within this new context.

"These diagnoses of individualism, with their rhetoric of crisis, terminality, loss and recovery, reflect and contribute to the therapeutic ethos governing late twentieth-century contemplations of the self," argued Gillian Brown (cited in Fox and Kloppenberg, 1998).

> The interests of the individual have become identified with psychological process and solutions, and expressed in terms such as *self-actualization* and *self-help*. Hence the psychic well-being of the individual has become a model for the rehabilitation of individualism. Modern health and leisure institutions—psychoanalysis, psychotherapy, counseling,

---

[2]*In two short pages Lears highlights the historical failings of both Rieff and Lasch's work. No Place of Grace is an exploration of how a reaction to modernity by elite Northeastern families actually helped spur the development of consumer and therapeutic culture.*

advice columns, talk shows, the diet and fitness industries and self-heal-
ing books and seminars—reiterate individualistic values in narratives of
self-restoration through individual effort [341].

The development of therapeutic culture owed its heritage to the roots
of the same northeastern United States thought from which the self-made
man grew. Simultaneous to the development of the success ethos of the
self-made man in the 19th century, was the countercultural movement created through rebellious members of the Unitarian Church such as Ralph
Waldo Emerson (1803–1882) and Henry David Thoreau (1817–1862). Ironically, by the later part of the 19th century the self-made man and the tran-
scendentalist, through the mindcure movement and its offshoots,
combined with the growth of advertising and consumer culture to create
a new hybrid ethos between business and spirituality seen in figures such
as department store magnate John Wanamaker.

Susman alluded to the irony that the very same line of thought that
was at the time the definition of the culture of character, later played a
significant role in the establishment of the culture of personality. "In an
important sense," suggested Susman, "the transition [from character to
personality] began in the very bosom of the old culture. For it was what
might be called the other side of Emerson — his vision of the transcendent
self — that formed the heart of that New Thought or Mind Cure movement
so important in the process from a culture of character to a culture of personality" (275).

In his discussion on the descriptive words in the culture of character, Susman made note of Emerson's importance to that understanding.
In the 19th century "The most popular quotation," Susman reported, "—
it appeared in dozens of works—was Emerson's definition of character:
'Moral order through the medium of individual nature'" (274). The intu-
itive ability of the individual, according to Emerson, was to be the found-
ing and primary source of moral guidance in the world. While many in
the culture of character may have lived by Emerson's words, it was the
commitment to individualism that led many to heed those words.

The rhetoric of the therapeutic culture provided many in the 20th century with an opportunity for shared cultural experiences. How those experiences have been expressed in popular culture remains a wide-open area
of academic study. Interdisciplinary explorations of this subject including, literature, theater, dance, art, religion, philosophy, and history and
open discussions about the communities created though popular cultural
expressions (both inclusive and exclusive) continues to be a necessary area
of academic exploration.

Bibliography

Baudrillard, Jean. *America*, C. Turner, Translator. London: Verso, 1988.

Beaudoin, Tom. *Virtual Faith: The Irreverent Spiritual Quest of Generation X.* San Francisco: Jossey-Bass, 1998.

Bellah, Robert. *Habits of the Heart: Individualism and Commitment in American Life.* New York: HarperCollins, 1986.

Cimino, Richard, and Don Latin. *Shopping for Faith: American Religion in the New Millenium.* San Francisco: Jossey–Bass. 1998.

Cloud, Dana. *Control and Consolation in American Culture and Politics: Rhetoric of Therapy.* Thousand Oaks, CA: Sage, 1998.

Coleman, John A. "Selling God in America: American Commerical Culture as a Climate of Hospitality to Religion." In, Richard Madsen, et al., Editors, *Meaning and Modernity: Religion, Polity and Self.* Berkeley: University of California Press, 2002.

Cox, Harvey. *The Feast of Fools: A Theological Essay on Festivity and Fantasy.* New York: HarperCollins, 1969.

Cox, Harvey. *Fire from Heaven: The Rise of Pentecostal Spirituality and the Reshaping of Religion in the Twenty-First Century.* Reading, MA: Addison-Wesley, 1995.

Corrigan, John. *Business of the Heart: Religion and Emotion in the Nineteenth Century.* Berkeley: University of California Press, 2002.

Emerson, Ralph Waldo. *Emerson's Pose and Poetry.* Joel Porte and Saundra Morris, Editors. New York: W.W. Norton, 2001.

Fishwick, Marshall W. *Great Awakenings: Popular Religion and Popular Culture.* New York: Haworth Press, 1995.

Fox, Richard Wightman, and James T. Kloppenberg, Editors. *A Companion to American Thought.* Malden, MA: Blackwell, Editor, 1998.

Frith, S. "Popular Culture." In M. Payne, Editor, *A Dictionary of Cultural and Critical Theory.* Cambridge: MA: Blackwell, 1996.

Giggie, John M., and Diane Winston, Editors. *Faith in the Market: Religion and the Rise of Urban Commercial Culture.* New Brunswick, NJ: Rutgers University Press, 2002.

Hangen, Tona J. *Redeeming the Dial: Radio, Religion and Popular Culture in America.* Chapel Hill: University of North Carolina Press, 2002.

Hyers, Conrad. *The Spirituality of Comedy Comic Heroism in a Tragic World.* New Brunswick, NJ: Transaction, 1996.

James, William. *The Varieties of Religious Experience.* New York: American Penguin Library, 1982.

Jameson, Frederick. *Postmodernism or the Cultural Logic of Late Capitalism.* Durham, NC: Duke University Press, 1995.

Jung, Sharron. "Beyond Narcissism," *Religion Life,* 49 (1980): 211.

Kaplan, Amy. *The Social Construction of American Realism.* Chicago: University of Chicago Press, 1988.

Krapohl, Robert H., and Charles H. Lippy. *The Evangelicals: A Historical, Thematic, and Biographical Guide.* Westport, CT: Greenwood Press, 1999.

Lasch, Christopher. *The Culture of Narcissism: American Life in an Age of Diminishing Expectations*. New York: W.W. Norton, 1978.

Lears, T. J. Jackson. *Fables of Abundance: A Cultural History of Advertising in America*. New York: Basic Books, 1994.

Lears T. J. Jackson. *No Place of Grace: Antimodernism and the Transformation of American Culture 1880–1920*. Chicago: University of Chicago Press, 1981.

Lundén, Rolf. *Business and Religion in the American 1920s*. Contributions in American Studies, no. 91. New York: Westport, CT: Greenwood Press, 1988.

Lutz, Tom. *American Nervousness, 1903: An Anecdotal History*. Ithaca, NY: Cornell University Press, 1991.

McDannell, Colleen. *Maternal Christianity: Religion and Popular Culture in America*. New Haven, CT: Yale University Press, 1995.

McLemee, Scott. "Getting Emotional." *The Chronicle of Higher Education*. 21. (2003).

Meyer, Donald. *The Positive Thinkers: Religion as Pop Psychology from Mary Baker Eddy to Oral Roberts*, 2nd ed. New York: Pantheon Books, 1980.

Nash, Roderick. *The Nervous Generation: American Thought, 1917–1930*. Chicago: Ivan R. Dee, 1990.

Noble, David W. *The Progressive Mind, 1890–1917*. Minneapolis: Burgess, 1981.

Nolan, James L. *The Therapeutic State*. New York: New York University Press, 1998.

Rieff, Philip. *The Triumph of the Therapeutic: Uses of Faith After Freud*. London: Chatto and Windus, 1966.

Riesman, David, et al. *The Lonely Crowd: A Study of the Changing American Character*. New Haven, CT: Yale University Press, 1961.

Rischin, Moses, Editor. *The American Gospel of Success: Individualism and Beyond*. Chicago: Quadrangle Books, 1965.

Rubenstein, Richard L. *The Cunning of History: The Holocaust and the American Future*. New York: Harper & Row, 1975.

Susman, Warren L. *Culture as History: The Transformation of American Society in the Twentieth Century*. New York: Pantheon Books, 1984.

Tocqueville, Alexis de. *Democracy in America*, Book 1. Henry Reeve, Trans. New York: Bantam, 2000.

Turner, Frederick Jackson. *The Frontier in American History*. New York: Holt, Rinehart and Winston, 1962 (1893).

Twitchell, James B. *Lead Us Into Temptation*. New York: Columbia University Press, 2000.

10

Pop Goes the Geographer

Synergies Between Geography and Popular Culture

THOMAS L. BELL AND MARGARET M. GRIPSHOVER

Geography is one of the few disciplines that straddles the natural and social worlds. Geography as a subject area has a long and venerated tradition that can be traced to the ancient Greeks. But, at the same time, it is a relatively new university discipline, having been accorded separate departmental status only in the 1870s in Germany and even more recently in the United States. It was relatively slow to integrate themes of popular culture as an area of scholarly inquiry. This is curious because elements of popular culture are so visible on the landscape and, one would think, would provide the fodder for many geographic studies and interesting maps, especially within the subfield of cultural geography. To understand the slow adoption of popular culture topics into geography one needs to understand a little about the history of the discipline. What follows is a general overview of that history targeted to the concern about the potential linkages between geography and popular culture.[1]

A Definition and Brief History of Geography

It has been said, somewhat facetiously, that there are as many definitions of geography as there are practicing geographers. The definition

[1]The interested reader is referred (if more background on geography's historical development is desired) to such reference volumes as Holt-Jensen 1999; Martin and James 1993; Gould 1985; and Haggett 1995.

that we like is the following: Geography is the study of human/environment interaction across space and time. Geographers examine spatial distributions—the pattern and place-to-place variation of phenomena over the Earth's surface. Geography is not confined to a particular body of subject matter, but rather is more defined by its viewpoint on the world. If history is chronological and concerned with variability through time, then geography is chorological, concerned with variability over space.

Geography is more than an encyclopedic compendium of earth description. Geographers need to know *where* things are as surely as the English professor must know grammar and syntax. But, the more important and penetrating question is: *why* are these things where they are? This "why?" question touches on issues of generative process, morphology, and diffusion of phenomena over space and time.

The types of geographic insights that would be of greatest interest to persons interested in popular culture would probably be those developed within the social scientific tradition. As we come to realize that even nature itself is a social construction, however, the humanistic and even the natural science perspective will become more important to the popular culture specialist seeking geographic insights.

Popular Culture versus Folk Culture from a Geographic Perspective: Sauer Grapes?

The historic emphasis of folk over popular culture in geography is not surprising give the history of development in cultural geography and the overwhelming influence of Carl O. Sauer, a geographer at the University of California, Berkeley. Sauer virtually defined the field of cultural geography in America for several decades, well into the 1950s. The Berkeley school of cultural geography is still associated with Sauer, his faculty colleagues, and his students. Sauer himself was deeply steeped in the naturalist tradition of geographers, having been trained during the early decades of the 20th century. He was also greatly influenced by his anthropological colleague at Berkeley, Alfred Kroeber.[2]

Sauer's concerns were complex. He was interested in the morphology of landscapes (1925) as well as the generative processes that produced them. He traced the evolution of what he labeled *cultural landscapes*, for

---

[2]*Kroeber said that anthropology is the most humanistic of the sciences and the most scientific of the humanities. Carl Sauer would probably have substituted* geography *for* anthropology.

indeed, there were few places on the earth's surface where humans had not modified the natural landscape thus creating cultural landscapes. Sauer was especially interested in the early cultural landscapes of California and Mexico; those produced by the indigenous peoples of the areas he examined (Sauer, 1956). One of Sauer's students, Fred Kniffen, carried the Berkeley tradition to the South. He became a mainstay of the combined department of anthropology and geography at the Louisiana State University for several decades, further refining the methods of interpreting folk cultures from their material artifacts, especially the types of houses that they constructed (Kniffen, 1965).

Derwent Whittlesey of Harvard University was the other cultural geographer of note during this early period. He and Sauer were geographically separated, but they were quite alike in their shared interest in folk cultures. Whittlesey called his method of analysis "sequent occupance" (Whittlesey 1929). He suggested that the present cultural landscape of any region could be viewed as a palimpsest in which the layers previous cultures could still be "read" by the cultural geographer attuned to the nuances of the historical evolution of the region.

Geography was a discipline on the rise at the beginning of the 20th century when the theory of environmental determinism held sway. The theory was based on the rather simplistic notion that the physical environment (e.g., climate, landforms) caused humans to behave in predictable ways. This was not a new idea; in fact, environmental determinism dates back to the time of the ancient Greeks (Gould, 1985, pp. 8–21).

While environmental conditions are, indeed, important constraints on what any society can accomplish, they are not determinate in a one-way causative sense. The natural environment influences human behavior, but humans can, in turn, modify their environment. When other sciences realized the fallacies underlying the simplistic theory of environmental determinism, geography bore the brunt of the criticism and many of the Ivy League schools dropped geography from their curricula altogether. It was then up to the large public institutions in the Midwest and California to pick up the gauntlet of geographic scholarship. Had eastern private institutions been more influential in the theoretical development of geography after the 1920s, it is conceivable that cultural geographers in the United States might have turned to popular culture topics sooner than they did, because the dominance of the Berkeley school might have been tempered. It really wasn't until the late 1960s that the first inklings of interest in popular culture began to emerge in geography. And it wasn't until the 1980s, that the first specialist publication incorporating popular culture themes appeared — Popular Press's *Journal of Cultural Geography*.

Few geography departments in the public institutions of the heartland at the midpoint of the 20th century showed much interest in examining any aspect of elite culture either. This disinterest is perhaps a throwback to the populist roots of the land grant movement represented by many of the leading departments of geography at the time. Instead, cultural geographers during this period displayed a great interest in folk culture under the influence of Sauer and his many students, who emulated his interests and diffused into geography departments throughout the heartland. Add to this cultural geography's natural affinity with anthropology, and it is easy to see why cultural geography's interest in popular cultural was so slow to emerge.

Hula Hoops to the Rescue?

Perhaps the first major cultural geographer to embrace popular culture and thus change the culture of cultural geography as it was practiced in the mid 20th century, was Wilbur Zelinsky. Zelinsky was himself a product of the Berkeley school and a disciple of Carl Sauer. The anecdotal (and perhaps apocryphal) story of his Pauline conversion to popular culture goes like this:

As a newly minted Ph.D. from Berkeley, Zelinsky, who is now emeritus professor at Pennsylvania State University, had to move his family east from Berkeley for his first university teaching position. He fully intended to continue his study of "primitive" cultures in the well-established Berkeley tradition. But truckloads of hula hoops interfered with his plans. His progress across country was interminably slow because the family station wagon had to keep stopping behind large delivery trucks dropping off shipments of Wham-O's popular fad invention of the 1950s—the hula hoop. Zelinsky was impressed with the fervor that people showed for this cultural artifact (Jordan-Bychkov and Domosh, 1999, p. 309). He might have thought: Why not study the cultural items that impact contemporary culture rather than something more esoteric like the evolution of harpoon handles in Polynesia?[3]

Fortunately for cultural geography and the field of popular culture in general, Zelinsky has been making major contributions to our understanding of the geography of American popular culture ever since. His organization of the Society for the North American Culture Survey

[3]This is the example used in a cartoon parody of the Berkeley school that appeared in Gould's brilliant but quirky look at the history of geography (Gould, 1985, p. 33).

(SNACS) eventually led to the production of *This Remarkable Continent: An Atlas of United States and Canadian Society and Cultures* (1982), the first atlas of popular culture. That volume still bristles with interesting mapped patterns of popular cultural phenomena.

The Emergence of Geographic Research of Popular Culture

Aspects of popular culture started to appear in many courses in cultural geography in the late 1960s and 1970s. This was, of course, a reflection of the increasing attention that cultural geographers were devoting to popular culture topics in their research. In an interesting early article, Larry Ford (1971), a cultural and urban geographer at San Diego State University, demonstrated how the origins and diffusion of rock-and-roll music could be used as a way to illustrate spatial diffusion mechanisms in general. His concerns were mainly pedagogic, as befitted the nature of the journal in which his article appeared (i.e., the *Journal of Geography*, a publication of the National Council for Geographic Education). It was clear that Ford thought his use of an important element of popular culture would resonate with students at a variety of educational levels.

The topics most likely to be covered in the section of a cultural geography course devoted to popular culture would be music and sport. These topics stand out because of the research and dominant influence of a few individuals—historian-turned-geographer George O. Carney for music geography, and the triumvirate of John Rooney, Richard Pillsbury, and John Bale for the geography of sport. Although many other geographers contributed to these areas of inquiry as well, Carney's love of country and bluegrass music as well as blues and jazz was infectious, and has led others to bestow upon him the sobriquet of "dean of music geography." His popular reader on music geography is now in its fourth edition (Carney, 2003).

In like manner, John Rooney, Carney's colleague at Oklahoma State University, might be considered the father of sport geography. His book *The Geography of Sport: From Cabin Creek to Anaheim* (1974) was the first attempt to put in book form some of his pioneering research on topics such as the influence of distance on the catchment areas of football player recruitment. This was followed in the United Kingdom by a volume written by John Bale in which he examined not only the "proper" British sports of football (i.e., soccer) and cricket, but also their diffusion throughout the Commonwealth as a form of postcolonial hegemony (Bale, 1983). Bale was the first geographer of sport to establish firmly the link between sport and the political economy within which it was produced (Bale, 1989–1994). Finally, the research of Richard Pillsbury on stock car racing should be mentioned. In a fascinating series of articles, Pillsbury traces the origins of NASCAR from the Southern dirt track circuit to the extravaganza that NASCAR events have become today (Pillsbury, 1974; Pillsbury, 1995a–1995b). Although Pillsbury has explored many other aspects of popular culture, including the geography of fast food franchising (Pillsbury, 1990), his editorship of the journal *Sport Place* has connected him with this aspect of popular culture more than any other.

Upon reflection, most of the early research on aspects of popular culture in cultural geography was mainly descriptive and somewhat naïve, as befits a new area of exploration. Little attention was paid to theoretical advances in popular culture. Recent geographic studies into popular culture are more theoretically informed and relate their findings to the societal meaning of cultural production and consumption. One has only to compare the groundbreaking early pioneering work of Pillsbury on NASCAR with the more sophisticated recent geographic analysis and cultural interpretation of the same subject area by Derek Alderman and his students (Alderman et al., 2003) to see how far studies in the geography of sport have evolved.

It is curious that during the early years of concern about the geography of popular culture (i.e., the 1960s and 1970s), so little attention was given to media such as television or the movies. Gould et al.'s (1984) interesting examination of television in the third world is an important exception to this generalization. Since the late 1980s though, geographers have delved into aspects of both television (Adams, 1992) and movies (Aitken and Zonn, 1993; Zonn 1990) with increasing relish.

Changing Postindustrial Geographies: From Production to Consumption

Within the last few decades, geographers have switched their attention from the geography of production to the geography of consumption. This shift reflects the change of the American economy to a postindustrial society (Bell, 1973). The bulk of research in the geography of consumption is related to popular culture. There has been a lot of recent geographic research, for example, on fast food franchising. In addition to Pillsbury's work mentioned above, there is a series of books by the well-known historical geographer John Jakle, who has examined fast food eateries (as well as motels and gasoline service stations) with an eye to explaining the origins and diffusion of these archetypes of vernacular architecture (Jakle and Sculle, 1994, 1996, 1999).

Geographers usually choose large targets for their popular culture focus. Both Carstensen (1986) and Curtis (1982) have, for example, examined the origins and diffusion of McDonald's in the United States and elsewhere. Graff seems to have made Wal-Mart his life's work (Graff and Ashton, 1994), perhaps because he teaches at the University of Arkansas, and Hopkins, a Canadian geographer (1990), opines about the cultural meaning of the West Edmonton Mall in Canadian society. This critical take on the world's largest mall may be contrasted with the Chamber of Commerce-like enthusiasm of Gerlach and Janke (2001) in their geographic study of the only slightly smaller Mall of America in the Twin Cities. More reasoned geographic discourse and a postmodern interpretation of the cultural meaning of the shopping mall in our society of spectacle and consumption has been provided by Goss (1993, 1999).

Translating Research in the Geography of Popular Culture into Teaching Materials

The subject matter of popular culture appears to be of most direct relevance within the subfield of cultural geography. There was, of course, a lag time between the heightened research interest in popular culture topics and the translation of the research results into the form of textbooks and other teaching materials. There are some recent textbooks in cultural geography that devote separate chapters to the topic of popular culture (e.g., Jordan-Bychkov and Domosh, 1999; Shelley and Clarke, 1994). There are other textbooks in either cultural or introductory human geography in which popular culture topics are folded in with considerations of folk culture in the same chapter, forming an almost seamless web (Rubenstien, 1999; deBlij, 1996). For the aficionado of popular culture, it is dismaying to see that in the popular Jordan-Bychkov and Domosh text, now in its ninth edition, the separate chapter on popular culture found in the previous edition, (1999) has been melded with material about folk culture in the most recent incarnation (2003).

We think the concatenation of these two disparate aspects of culture may be confusing to students. There are such clear and distinct differences between folk and popular culture that they probably ought to remain as two separate chapters in such texts. Many would consider popular culture anathema to folk culture, because the homogenizing forces of the mass media and cultural production continue to annihilate the remnants of folk societies. At least that is how many traditional cultural geographers might nostalgically describe the "intrusion" of popular culture into the contemporary world. And traditionalism is one of the reasons why popular culture topics were so slow in being considered worthy of study in cultural geography.

But even more disturbing that the folding together of folk and popular culture in geography textbook discussions, is the omission of popular culture topics altogether. Many textbooks that are labeled as *human geography* rather than *cultural geography* do not in any way address topics related to popular culture (e.g., Austin et al., 1987; Lowe and Pederson 1983; Stoddard et al., 1989). Other human geography textbooks contain only snippets of material that would be considered under the rubric of popular culture, usually the origin and diffusion of rock-and-roll music, which is a topic that is relatively well-documented and researched (e.g., de Blij 1996; Norton, 2002).

Contemporary Examinations of Popular Culture in Geography: The British Invasion

American geography has been influenced by the contribution of British cultural geographers, especially since the 1980s. This particular British invasion has nothing to do with the Beatles or the Rolling Stones. It has to do with what has been labeled the "new" cultural geography and the extraordinary influence that British geographers have had on the course of North American geography (T.L. Bell, 1990; Abler, 1987). At the forefront of the "new" cultural geography is British geographer Peter Jackson (1989). Jackson does not work in isolation. There are entire research centers in the United Kingdom at a number of universities devoted to the study of popular cultural phenomena (Cloke et al., 1991; Cook and Crang 1996; Crang 1996). Many of these centers are multidisciplinary, and they usually include geographers and sociologists working together in a synergistic fashion to extract the cultural meaning from everyday local practices. Geography is prominent in such efforts because throughout much of Europe and the British Isles the discipline has a much greater presence and visibility in the precollegiate curriculum than it does in the United States.

The British have been influenced by continental philosophies to a greater extent than American pragmatists and empiricists. The "new" cultural geography, largely of British origin, set itself in opposition to what it perceived as the stodgy, antiquarian, and a theoretical nature of traditional cultural geography (read: the Berkeley school). In turn, members of the Berkeley school have countered that they have been misunderstood, misinterpreted, and turned into a cartoonlike caricature by some enthusiasts for the "new" cultural geography (Price and Lewis, 1993).

So this internecine battle rages on. The "new" cultural geography is touted as emanating from the tradition of critical social theory that has swept the social sciences and humanities. The concern of the "new" cultural geographers is supposedly more attuned to the daily lives of persons in contemporary society. "New" cultural geographers are sensitive to the issues of class, race/ethnicity and gender. And most importantly, their empirical work is informed by theory — whether that theory emanates from a radical Marxist perspective, a realist interpretation, or a postmodern repudiation of totalizing discourse in favor of local knowledge. All of their work appears to be theory-driven.

How These Disparate Approaches to Popular Culture Have Played Out: The Example of Music Geography

Given the sometimes withering attacks on traditional cultural geography by those espousing the "new" cultural paradigm, it is small wonder that the more traditional geographers, especially those in the United States, took chauvinistic exception to the characterization of their research. In the subarea of music geography, George Carney is a careful and meticulous scholar who wouldn't mind being classified as "old school." He has, for many years, called together like-minded geographic scholars who were interested in aspects of music geography to present papers in special sessions he organized and chaired. These sessions on music geography have been presented at the annual meetings of the Association of American Geographers since the mid–1990s and they always draw a large audience, perhaps because of the liberal use of media (including sound recordings) by the presenters and the excellent and well-illustrated research of Carney himself.

Into this tight clique of music geography scholars entered two British geographers, Andrew Leyshon and George Revill, both decidedly of the "new" school of cultural geography. Both have written extensively about the cultural meaning of music, even its importance as a means of national identification (Leyshon et al., 1998). It appeared at first that there might be tension between these two disparate strains of research on the same general subject area. But, everyone involved was won over by the enthusiasm for, and knowledge about, music that has been shown by these two

British scholars. There is truly a détente and mutual admiration for scholarship in this subarea, irrespective of the theory underpinning the research.

In a magnanimous gesture, Carney turned over at least part of the organizational duties for these continuing music geography sessions to the British duo, and the last two sessions at the national meeting have been greatly enriched by the synergies of scholars approaching the same general subject matter from a variety of theoretical viewpoints. In this subarea at least, the multipronged theoretical approach often suggested as the way out of the welter of conflicting and contentious methodologies in contemporary social science is finally coming to pass.

Structuring a Course in the Geography of American Popular Culture

Given that material on popular culture has yet to become standard fare in all introductory culture and human geography textbooks, it is not surprising that there is no geography textbook that focuses exclusively on the geography of popular culture in the United States. In the course on the geography of American popular culture that we teach, we use a reader edited by George Carney with the intriguing title of *Stock Cars, Fast Food, Stock Cars, and Rock-n-Roll: Place and Space in American Pop Culture* (1995) as a basic reference. Carney has three popular readers on the market. In addition to the volume dealing with popular culture, he has another dealing with aspects of folk culture (Carney, 1998), and a third that specifically focuses on music geography, which is now in its fourth edition (Carney, 2003).

Carney's basic reader is supplemented with reading material found in books, journals, and even popular magazines. This portion of the reading list will probably by idiosyncratic and geared to the interests of the instructor. As had been pointed out countless times before, the subject matter examined in a popular culture course matters less than providing students with the tools of analysis needed to interpret the cultural meaning of the events happening all around them on a daily basis (Cawelti, 1973). If one can raise the students' levels of consciousness about contemporary issues and make them think critically about the world around them and appreciate the place-to-place differences that make life so meaningful and exciting, then we have done our job well.

Where Do We Go from Here?

There are many topical areas to which geographers interested in popular culture need to pay closer attention. There should be, for example, a greater effort to incorporate the advances made in behavioral geography into popular culture. Within this subfield the notion of mental maps is especially appealing and related to popular culture research in defining meaningful vernacular regions (Gould 1973; Gould and White 1974). The mental mapping literature has shown quite clearly that there is no one monolithic image of a place but rather that the image varies by gender, income, ethnicity, and a variety of other relevant factors.

Behaviorists have also made great contributions to our understanding of consumer motivations. Because popular culture is driven by consumerism, the insights that have been made in marketing geography should be applied to popular culture phenomena. Studies on how commercial land uses "invade" and eventually "succeed" residential land uses along arterial strip developments (Jakle and Mattson, 1981), or how the mix of retailing activities varies as a function of neighborhood ethnicity and income composition (Harries, 1971), offer great insight to popular culturists interested in patterns of consumption.

There is potential for much more interaction between urban geography and popular culture. Urban sprawl is a topic that should be of inherent concern to those interested in popular culture. Our residential lifestyle choices involve more than just the increased cost of providing inefficiently urban services to low-slung and far-flung suburban populations. There is a humanistic element of the placeless landscapes that seemingly endless sprawl creates—sprawl is an affront to the uniqueness and emotional attachment we have to place. Placeless landscapes diminish our quality of life and the human spirit (Relph, 1976; Kunstler, 1993). Sprawled landscapes have been blamed for increases in air pollution because of our increasing dependence on the automobile. There are now more automobiles than licensed drivers in the United States (NBC News, 2003). This automobile reliance has been linked to unacceptably high levels of obesity and unhealthy environments (Ewing et al., 2003). Not only do Americans eat many of their meals outside the home at fast food restaurants, but they cannot gain access to those restaurants safely by walking or riding their bicycles for needed exercise even if they wanted to.

Humanistic geography also has much to contribute to the field of popular culture. We need to know more about our emotional attachment to special places. Yi-Fu Tuan (1974) has done an excellent job of drawing attention to our attachment to ordinary landscapes. But, we also need more research on our shadowed ground (Foote, 1997), those landscapes that evoke painful memories in our collective conscience, whether it is Waco, Oklahoma City, or ground zero in New York City (Tuan, 1977, 1979).

A Parting Thought

It is gratifying that graduate students in geography have more opportunities to pursue topics related to popular culture today than has been the case in the past. Because of the excellence of the pioneering work of Tuan and others in exploring the humanistic meaning of popular culture phenomena of interest to geographers, more avenues of study have been opened.

This increased interest in the geography of popular culture phenomena has only taken place because current research is sophisticated, broadly conceptual, and applicable in a variety of geographic contexts and at a variety of geographic scales from the local to the global. In most graduate programs, popular culture topics are now an accepted area of geographic study. The cumulative nature of the knowledge gained by research currently being undertaken, irrespective of the methodological stance of the investigator, assures that the geographer of popular culture will continue to be taught in the classroom. It is only a matter of time until there is enough market demand for a textbook in the area to be published as well.

References

Abler, Ronald. "What Shall We Say? To Whom Shall We Speak?" *Annals of the Association of American Geographers*, 77 (1987): 511–524.

Adams, Paul C. "Television as Gathering Place." *Annals of the Association of American Geographers*, 82 (1992): 117–135.

Aitken, Stuart C., and Leo E. Zonn, Editors. *Place, Power, Situation and Spectacle: A Geography of Film*. Savage, MD: Rowman and Littlefield, 1993.

Alderman, Derek H. et al. "Carolina Thunder Revisited: Toward a Transcultural View of Winston Cup Racing." *The Professional Geographer*, 55. 2 (2003).

Austin, C. Murray et al. *Human Geographer*. St. Paul, MN: West, 1987.

Bale, John. *Sport and Place: A Geography of Sport in England, Scotland, and Wales*. Lincoln, NE: University of Nebraska Press, 1983.

Bale, John. *Sports Geography*. London: E. & F. N. Spon, 1989.

Bale, John. *Landscapes of Modern Sport*. New York: St. Martin's Press, 1994.

Bell, Daniel. *The Coming of Post-Industrial Society*. New York: Basic Books, 1973.

Bell, Thomas L. "Political Economy's Response to Positivism." *Geographical Review*, 80. (1990): 308–315.

Bergman, Edward F. *Human Geography: Cultures, Connections and Landscapes* Englewood Cliffs, NJ: Prentice-Hall, 1995.

Carney, George O., Editor. *Fast Food Stock Cars and Rock-n-Roll: Place and Space in American Pop Culture.* Lanham, MD: Rowman & Littlefield, 1995.

Carney, George O., Editor. *Baseball, Barns and Bluegrass.* Lanham, MD: Rowman and Littlefield, 1998.

Carney, George O., Editor. *The Sounds of People and Places: The Geography of American Music from Country to Classical and Blues to Bop.* 4th ed. Landham, MD: Rowman and Littlefield, 2003.

Carstensen, Laurence W. "The Burger Kingdom: Growth and Diffusion of McDonald's Restaurants in the United States, 1955–1978." *Geographical Perspectives,* 58. (1986): 1–8.

Cawelti, John, "Why Pop?" *The National Humanities Faculty Why Series.* San Francisco: Chandler & Sharp, 1973.

Cloke, Paul et al., *Approaching Human Geography: An Introduction to Contemporary Theoretical Debates.* New York: Guilford Press, 1991.

Cook, I. J., and P. Crang. "The World on a Plate: Culinary Culture, Displacement and Geographic Knowledge." *Journal of Material Culture,* 1 (1996): 131–153.

Crang, P. "Displacement, Consumption and Identity." *Environment and Planning A,* 28 (1996): 28, 47–67.

Curtis, James R. "McDonald's Abroad: Outposts of American Culture." *Journal of Geography,* 81 (1982): 14–20.

deBlij, Harm. *Human Geography: Culture, Society, and Space,* 5th ed. New York: John Wiley, 1996.

Foote, Kenneth E. *Shadowed Ground: American's Landscape of Violence and Tragedy.* Austin: University of Texas Press, 1997.

Ford, Larry R. "Geographic Factors in the Origin, Evolution and Diffusion of Rock and Roll Music." *Journal of Geography,* 70 (1971): 455–464.

Gerlach, Jerry, and James Janke. "The Mall of America as a Tourist Attraction." *Focus,* 46. 3 (2001): 32–36.

Goss, Jon, "The Magic of the Mall: An Analysis of Form, Function and Meaning in the Contemporary Retail Built Environment," *Annals of the Association of American Geographers,* 83 (1993): 18–47.

Goss, Jon. "Once-Upon-a-Time in the Commodity World: An Unofficial Guide to the Mall of America." *Annals of the Association of American Geographers,* 89 (1999): 45–75.

Gould, Peter R. "On Mental Maps." In R. M. Downs and D. Stea, Editors, *Image and Environment.* London: Edward Arnold, 1973, pp. 182–220.

Gould, Peter R. *The Geographer at Work.* London: Routledge and Kegan Paul, 1985.

Gould, Peter R. J. Johnson, and Graham Chapman. *The Structure of Television.* London: Pion 1984.

Gould, Peter R., and Rodney White. *Mental Maps.* Harmondsworth, UK: Penguin Books, 1974.

Graff, Thomas O., and Dub Aston. "Spatial Diffusion of Wal-Mart: Contagious and Reverse Hiearchical Elements." *The Professional Geographer,* 46 (1994): 19–29.

Haggett, Peter. *The Geographer's Art.* Oxford, UK: Blackwell, 1995.

Harries, Keith D. "Ethnic Variations in Los Angeles Business Patterns." *Annals of the Association of American Geographers,* 61 (1971): 736–743.

Holt-Jensen, Arild. *Geography — History and Concepts, 3rd ed.* Thousand Oaks, CA: Corwin Press, 1999.

Hopkins, Jeffrey. "West Edmonton Mall: Landscape of Myths and Elsewhereness." *Canadian Geographer,* 34 (1990): pp. 2–17.

Jackson, Peter. *Maps of Meaning: An Introduction to Cultural Geography* London: Unwin Hyman, 1989.

Jakle, John A., and Richard L. Mattson. "The Evolution of a Commerical Strip." *Journal of Cultural Geography*, 1. (1981): 12–25.

Jakle, John A., and Keith A. Sculle. *The Gas Station in America*. Baltimore: Johns Hopkins Univeristy Press, 1994.

Jakle, John A., and Keith A. Sculle. *The Motel in America*. Baltimore: Johns Hopkins University Press, 1996.

Jakle, John A., and Keith A. Sculle. *Fast Food: Roadside Restaurants in the Automobile Age*. Baltimore: Johns Hopkins University Press, 1999.

Jordan-Bychkov, Terry G., and Mona Domosh. *The Human Mosaic: A Thematic Introduction to Cultural Geography*, 8th ed. New York: Longman, 1999.

Jordan-Bychkov, Terry G., and Mona Domosh. *The Human Mosaic: A Thematic Introduction to Cultural Geography*, 9th ed. New York: W.H. Freeman, 2003.

Kniffen, Fred B. "Folk Housing: Key to Diffusion." *Annals of the Association of American Geographers*, 55 (1965): 549–577.

Knox, Paul L. and Sallie A. Marston. *Human Geography: Places and Regions in Global Context*, 3rd. Upper Saddle River, NJ: Prentice-Hall, 2003.

Kunstler, James H. *The Geography of Nowhere: The Rise and Decline of America's Man-Made Landscape*. New York: Simon and Schuster, 1993.

Lewis, George. "Uncertain Truths: The Promotion of Popular Culture." *Journal of Popular Culture*, 20. 3 (1986): pp. 31–44.

Leyshon, Andrew. et al., Editors. *The Place of Music*. New York: Guilford Press, 1998.

Lowe, John, and Eldor Pederson. *Human Geography: An Integrated Approach*. New York: John Wiley, 1983.

Marin, Geoffrey J., and Preston E. James. *All Possible World: A History of Geographical Ideas*, 3rd ed. New York: John Wiley, 1993.

NBC Evening News, August 30, 2003.

Norton, William. *Human Geography*, 4th ed. Don Mills, Ontario: Oxford University Press, 2001.

Pillsbury, Richard. *From Boarding House to Bistro: The American Restaurant Then and Now*. Boston: Unwin Hyman, 1990.

Pillsbury, Richard. "Carolina Thunder: A Geography of Southern Stock Car Racing." *Journal of Geography*, 73. 1 (1974): pp. 39–47.

Pillsbury, Richard. "A Mythology at the Brink: Stock Car Racing in the American South." IN G. O. Carney, Editor, *Fast Food, Stock Cars, & Rock-n-Roll*. Lanham, MD: Rowman & Littlefield Publishers, 1995a, pp. 239–248.

Pillsbury, Richard. "Stock Car Racing." In Karl Raitz, Editor, *The Theater of Sport*. Baltimore: Johns Hopkins University Press, 1995b, pp. 270–295.

Price, Marie, and Martin Lewis. "The Reinvention of Cultural Geography." *Annals of the Association of American Geographers*, 83. 1 (1993): 1–17.

Relph, Edward. *Place and Placelessness*. London: Pion, 1976.

Rooney, John F., Jr. *A Geography of American Sport: From Cabin Creek to Anaheim*. Reading, MA: Addison-Wesley, 1974.

Rubenstein, James M. *The Cultural Landscape: An Introduction to Human Geography*, 6th ed. Upper Saddle River, NJ: Prentice-Hall, 1999.

Sauer, Carl O. "The Morphology of Landscape." *University of California Publications in Geography*, 2 (1925): 19–53.

Sauer, Carl O. "The Agency of Man on Earth." In W. L. Thomas, Editor, *Man's Role in Changing the Face of the Earth*, Vol. 1. Chicago: University of Chicago Press, 1956.

Shelley, Fred M., and Audrey E. Clarke. *Human and Cultural Geography: A Global Perspective.* Dubuque, IA: W. C. Brown, 1994.

Stoddard, Robert H., et al., *Human Geography: People, Places, and Cultures.* Englewood Cliffs, NJ: Prentice-Hall, 1989.

Tuan, Yi-Fu. *Topophilia: A Study of Environmental Perception, Attitudes, and Values.* Englewood Cliffs, NJ: Prentice-Hall, 1974.

Tuan, Yi-Fu. *Space and Place: The Perspective of Experience.* London: Edward Arnold, 1977,

Tuan, Yi-Fu. *Landscapes of Fear.* Oxford: Blackwell, 1979.

Whittlesey, Derwent. "Sequent Occupance." *Annals of the Association of American Geographers,* 19 (1929): 162–167.

Zelinsky, Wilbur, Editor. *This Remarkable Continent: An Atlas of United States and Canadian Society and Cultures.* College Station, TX: Texas A&M University Press, 1982.

Zonn, Leo, Editor. *Place Images in Media: Portrayal, Experience, and Meaning.* Savage, MD; Rowman and Littlefield, 1990.

11

Popular Culture and Women's Studies

JANE CAPUTI WITH MICHELLE SHARKEY

The collisions and collusions of popular culture and feminist theories and practices take vivid and entertaining form in the magazine *Bitch/Feminist Response to Pop Culture* (founded in 1998). *Bitch* is not only a useful text in any women's studies classroom; it is itself a popular version of much feminist scholarship. The website (*http://www.bitchmagazine.com*) first details the magazine's mission, outlining the range of advances made by—and the backlashes directed against—feminism. *Bitch* then exhorts writers and readers to direct their critical attention to the contributions of popular culture and to enter directly, and creatively, into the fray:

> Television demonstrates that most people still think what a woman is wearing is more important that what she's thinking. Magazines that tell us, both implicitly and explicitly, that female sexual urges are deviant, while reminding us that maintaining our sex appeal is the only way to wring commitment out of a man, without which our lives will be sad and incomplete in spite of dazzling careers and intense friendships. Billboards urge us to fork over our hard-earned cash for the glittery, overpriced wares of companies that depend on our unhappiness and dissatisfaction for their profits. Hollywood continues to churn out movies where women's only lines are "Help me," "C'mere, big guy," and "Oh, honey, I missed you so much while you were off saving humanity by tracking down that vicious serial killer/diverting that asteroid/killing those scary space aliens."
>
> *Bitch* was founded on the impulse to give a voice to the vast numbers of us who know in our hearts that these images are false, and want something to replace them…. Where are the girl-friendly places in the mass media? Where are the things we can see and read and hear that don't insult our intelligence? How can we get more of them?
>
> We can make them.

Bitch's mission statement neatly encapsulates the project of feminist thought in relation to popular culture: to critique, to search out the "girl-friendly" terrain that already exists, and to grow that territory by creating new stories, characters, and images. These directives also inform the dialogic and deeply overlapping relationship between women's studies and popular culture.

Women's studies can be understood as an interdisciplinary field of scholarship that asks us to look at the world as if women were not mere bit players on the stage of life, knowledge, and history. It centers women's perspectives, "challenging an androcentric/phallocentric notion of knowledge which can be defined as men's experiences and priorities being seen as central and representative of all" (Robinson, 1997, 2) and addresses not only the ways that culture shapes women but also the ways that women shape culture.

In this way, women's studies is much like popular culture studies in that both fields take what has been marginalized and foreground it. Popular culture questions the normative designation of the cultural products of elites as "culture" itself, allowing it to be seen as central and representative of everybody's experience of culture. It asks us to look at popular and everyday arts, entertainments, rituals, sports, fashions, celebrities, and our common values and beliefs as topics worthy of academic study, meaningful and aesthetically interesting in their own ways. Popular culture refuses class hierarchies for the designation and study of culture and proposes new areas for research and new methods for interpretation. So too women's studies challenges the ways that knowledge and dominant models of research have been riddled with sexist assumptions. It takes into account new theoretical and empirical sources — the experiences, theories, and lives of women. And it simultaneously interrogates traditional knowledge for the ways that it reflects and supports the sexually political status quo.

Our purpose here is to demonstrate not only that the two fields share some basic ground and assumptions, but also to explore the ways that popular culture is integral to the full comprehensiveness and understanding of women's studies. To do this, first we consider the emphasis of each field on everyday culture. Shared concerns include: popular representations and their propensities, variously, to stereotype negatively or to provide sites of identification and resistance; popular beliefs (about women, men, and proper gender roles); activities especially associated with women (romance novel reading, shopping, fashion); female celebrities; cult characters; women as creators of popular fiction, music, and film; and forms of popular culture (zines, slash fiction, music festivals like Lilith Fair) that foster female communities. Especially since the 1970s, feminists have used and shaped popular culture forms in diverse ways to directly address audiences and to generate the images and stories that they — as feminists, lesbians, women of color, and members of various subcultures— want, and that the mainstream has not given them.

Currently, feminists can look at popular phenomena from the successes of Oprah and Roseanne though the popularity of Madonna and Buffy (the potent character who vanquishes vampires, but who is played by an actress who hawks makeup) as reflecting, in complex, varied, and often diluted ways, the permeation of feminist ideals into everyday culture. The meanings generated by popular presences and phenomena are inevitably porous, complex, and frequently paradoxical. Feminist scholars, like many in the tradition of cultural studies as articulated by Stuart Hall (1993), recognize this complexity; the meaning of a text resides not only in the text itself, but also in a particular audience's values, beliefs, social position, and experiences. Feminists thus necessarily engage in lively struggles over these meanings, for themselves and for the culture as a whole. They propose widely varying interpretations of the Barbie doll (Lord, 1994; DuCille, 1996), consider the challenges and contributions of female artists to male-dominated subcultures such as hip-hop (Rose, 2001). They debate how and if the burgeoning popularity of cosmetic surgery signifies women taking control of their bodies or an acquiescence to yet another form of mutilation and manipulation (Covino, 2004) and argue vehemently about pornography in relation to the sexual liberation of women (Dworkin, 1981; Kipnis, 1991), mainstream pornography as well as that produced by women, often identifying as feminists and/or lesbians (Chalker, 2000).

Second, we approach the conjunctions of popular culture and women's studies by drawing upon basic feminist theory and stressing the need to understand the gendered nature of what is commonly understood as knowledge and culture. Women's studies examines any topic or research question through what Susan Moller Okin calls "the "prism of gender" (Nussbaum, 1998). Hence, a feminist perspective on popular culture immediately notices right-wing contempt for pop culture is itself steeped in an ingrained cultural misogyny, for popular culture, in the sexist oppositional and hierarchical gender system, is itself gendered as "feminine" (Huyssen, 1986). Marked with such stigmatized traits as sentimentality, conventionality, simplicity, and a tendency to overwhelm and even pollute, popular culture is viewed as inferior to the implicitly "masculine" high culture, marked with such valorized (and masculine-identified) traits as individuality, genius, autonomy, experimentalism, purity, and intellection.

Of course, from a feminist standpoint, this "feminine" nature of popular culture signifies not only class and gender bias, but also points to the ways that popular culture (in *some* though not all of its aspects) can serve as a site of oppositional and resistant knowledge, worldviews and wisdoms denied and trivialized because they historically have been associated with oppressed and marginalized peoples, paradigmatically women (Caputi, 2004).

We will next elaborate on these conjunctions in a greater depth, but ask readers to recognize that we are not attempting to be comprehensive but only offering select examples that illustrate some key concerns in the overlapping relationship of popular culture and women's studies.

The Personal is Political

An axiom of popular culture, transmitted on the Southwest Popular Culture Association Web site, is: "If it isn't popular it isn't culture." An analogous axiom structuring women's studies (and derived from the early feminist movement) is: "The personal is political." This recognition leads feminist thinkers to probe beneath the surface of the allegedly purely personal and trivial to locate deeper cultural influences and patterns. One aspect of that "personal," of course, is directly popular. Popular culture is "so much a part of the day-to-day lives of all Americans, that the values and beliefs on the surface and hidden beneath these products inevitably have an important impact on us all" (Geist and Nachbar, 1983, 2). Both women's studies and pop culture scholars share this interest in getting beneath the surfaces of the everyday.

One way to determine the extent of the intrinsic interest of popular culture to women's studies is to examine the content of core undergraduate courses in the field. Nearly every "Introduction to Women's Studies" class includes components that are directly related to popular culture: advertising, gender roles, beauty standards, pornography, sports, body image, family values, and the effect on consciousness and behavior of popular images of sexualized violence. An advanced undergraduate course, designed by Marjorie Jolles (2003) at the University of Iowa, "Feminist Cultural Studies," advances a theoretical argument for this focus on the everyday:

> [T]he practices of everyday life that contribute to the production of identity. Feminist cultural studies explores every day practices, institutions and contexts as they pertain to, produce, and regulate gender identities

and norms. In this course, we will study critical feminist work on domesticity, film, fashion, pornography, consumerism, and various other aspects of engagement with popular culture, along with important work on the cultural constitution of gendered [and raced, sexed, and classed] bodies and personal identity.

Jolles's course reflects a predominant interest of feminist scholarship in cultural identity — its construction, pleasures, complexities, and pitfalls. Psychoanalytic, object-relations, and social theory frequently are brought to bear on the ways that popular cultural beliefs, texts, and discourses participate in the ongoing construction of our socially influenced and inflected, subjectivities, however "natural" they seem (Fiske, 1992).

Communications scholar Gaye Tuchman (Tuchman, Daniels, and Benet, 1978, 9) used the term *symbolic annihilation* to describe the systemic treatment of female images in the mass media. Such annihilation is expressed through two ways: *absence*— women are simply disappeared from roles that convey social power, significance, and validity; or *negative stereotyping*— women are projected in images that are condemnatory, belittling, or victimized. Over time, as Stuart Hall (Grossberg, 1986, 54) observed, these reiterated negative images take on "lines of tendency," fixing perception into standard oppressive grooves, essentially colonizing or occupying consciousness, destroying group self-esteem, and encouraging stereotypic perceptions from group outsiders. Patricia Hill Collins (1998), in *Black Feminist Thought*, traced the evolution of the most central, and condemnatory, black female stereotypes, since slavery times. She also insightfully connected the development of pornography in the United States to the specific practices of display and derogation associated with the slave market.

Feminist film scholarship, most notably in a famous 1977 essay by Laura Mulvey (2003), "Visual Pleasure and Narrative Cinema," radically challenged the ways that gendered assumptions structure modes of viewing and experiences of pleasure. Using psychoanalysis and semiotics, Mulvey called attention to the ways that men have been positioned powerfully as privileged bearers of "the gaze," while women, as the objects of that gaze, are alternately fetishized or victimized. Mulvey's attention to the significance of the image to gender relations and social constructions of masculinity and femininity continues to provoke debate within film studies, popular culture, queer, and feminist studies.

Most theorists do recognize an ineluctable intermeshing of the feminist project with "visual culture"— a classification that includes fine art but also magazines, advertisements, television, pornography, and other popular forms. In her introduction to *The Feminism and Visual Culture Reader,* Amelia Jones (2003, 1) argued for the inseparability of feminist studies from those of visual studies:

> Academic versions of feminism theorize the ways in which all forms of culture condition, and are conditioned by, gender or "sexual difference...." Visual culture is a rubric and a model of critical thinking about the world of images saturating contemporary life ... feminism has long acknowledged that visuality [the conditions of how we see and make meaning of what we see] is one of the key modes by which gender is culturally inscribed in Western culture. Feminism and visual culture, then, deeply inform one another.

Images, bell hooks (1992, 2) put it bluntly, are "central" to any system of domination — racial, sexual/gendered, heterosexist. Questions feminist scholars have raised include: how have images of gender identities, both masculine and feminine, been expressed in popular culture; how are these identities differently inflected by racializations or by class associations; how are these images internalized and how are they resisted? When hooks addressed the ways that images of black female bodies have been characterized, variously, as expendable, excessively sexual, ugly and undesirable, animalistic, and otherwise inhuman, she also called upon participants in popular culture to develop critical consciousness. A primary component of that was for subjugated audiences to adopt an "oppositional gaze" (hooks, 1992, 115), one resistant to hegemonic meanings, and one that allowed audiences to articulate and affirm subjectivities and meanings that do not replicate the dominant order of sexual and racial injustices.

The Struggle Over Meaning

Both feminist and popular culture scholarship is deeply influenced by Stuart Hall's (1993) articulation of the ways that popular culture is used by individuals and groups in forming identity and, concomitantly, the ways that particular communities often read against the grain in order to select out aspects of a movie that provide fodder for resistance, while simultaneously critiquing the "dominant" and oppressive parts of the text.

The editors of one anthology, *The Good, the Bad and the Gorgeous: Popular Culture's Romance with Lesbianism,* explore the ways that Lesbians negotiate popular culture:

> Since political change centrally involves a struggle over meaning, it is not
> possible simply to dismiss popular culture as merely servicing the dual
> systems of patriarchy and capitalism…. It is here, in television, maga-
> zines, films, books, and music, that we are offered the culture's domi-
> nant definition of ourselves. We cannot dismiss the popular by always
> positioning ourselves outside it. Lesbians have now begun to look at how
> we can intervene in the mainstream, subverting hegemonic meanings
> and imposing our own in their place [Hamer and Budge, 1994, 2].

A great deal of feminist audience research takes a similar approach,
exploring, and often justifying, women's pleasure in relation to such dis-
reputably and conventionally feminine genres as soap operas and romance
novels. Numerous influential studies have documented the ways that
female audiences use popular forms strategically in their everyday lives,
drawing their own, often resistant meanings from the texts, and sometimes using these as bonding elements in female-dominated subcultures
(Radway, 1984; Bobo, 1995).

Popular forms themselves become a focal point for feminist activism.
Nayland Blake (1995) explored the ways that took place in the 1970s:

> Women's music became one of the most successful lesbian cultural
> expressions, generating not only a new roster of lesbian stars, but also
> providing through concerts and festivals new possibilities for women to
> meet each other and forge communities. Both punk and the women's
> music movement were attempts to confront social problems via cultural
> strategies [22].

Feminist activists and artists, the Guerrilla Girls, have also used popular culture to generate consciousness and activism through performances,
poster art, and richly illustrated books, most recently *Bitches, Bimbos, and
Ballbreakers: The Guerrilla Girls' Illustrated Guide to Female Stereotypes*
(2003). With historical contextualizations and barbed wit, the authors dis-
sect a parade of sexist clichés, also offering readers an "anti-stereotype kit"
to activate real-world world resistance.

Feminist scholars/activists also caution against only attending to
derogatory or victimizing images occasions for consciousness raising.
Martha McCaughey and Neal King (2001), in *Reel Knockouts*, collected a
series of essays on violent women in the movies. Their aim was not to
"look at whether they properly represent women or feminist principles,"
but to present them as "texts with social contexts and possible uses in the
reconstruction of masculinity and femininity." As they put it, "We can use
these images, whether they're lies or not" (McCaughey and King, 2001,
3) — use them, that is, as sites to generate feminist consciousness and to

radicalize public conversations about gender roles. Feminist interpretations of fantastic female violence, McCaughey and King argued, can be used to question "assumptions about gender, violence, pleasure and fantasy." They can spur "film theorists to question models of female passivity and narrative closure [and] ... help cultural historians and social scientists to question assumptions about the development of political community among oppressed peoples" (2001, 3). In other words, feminist thinkers can creatively discuss images of violent and otherwise nonstereotypic women to achieve consciousness raising — in their scholarship, in the classroom, and in public conversation about these, frequently iconic, characters and stories (e.g., Foxy Brown, Xena, Buffy, Thelma and Louise).

Discredited Knowledge

These images of modern day "Amazons" call to mind another facet linking women's studies to popular culture — its relation to the mythic or folkloric. As numerous scholars (most notably Harold Schechter, 2001) have noted, ancient oral traditions, myths, and folklores serve as the basis for popular culture narratives and characters. Clearly, some of that folklore is misogynist and much of commercial mass culture blatantly supports the prerogatives of the dominant order — violent masculinity, white supremacy, female sexual servitude, and so on. But it is imperative that we recognize that in the mélange that constitutes popular culture, there are the threads of an alternative worldview to the "androcentric," a worldview, which we can think of as "gynocentric" (Caputi, 2004).

Folklore scholar Harold Bayley, writing in 1912, averred that ancient fairy tales issued "from the soil" (1996, Vol. 1, 190), that is, from women's oral tradition, from enduring, if now marginalized, wisdoms. The popular work *Women Who Run with the Wolves* (Estés, 1992) is a more recent work based on a similar premise: that folklore thinly veils a tradition of female wisdom. From this vantage point we can realize that, however much some forms of popular culture serve as support to the status quo, other aspects of popular (which at root means *people's*) culture function, albeit in coded form, as a repository for knowledges discredited by racism, upward mobility, male supremacy, misogyny, elitism, colonialism, and heterosexual order.

In his musings on the folk antecedents of popular culture, literary critic Leslie Fiedler (1982, 51) reminded us that: "for a long time, in fact, all song and story was regarded as contraband except that canonized by the hierarchy of the church, i.e., declared inspired by God." Nonetheless, the Church was unable to stop the flow of popular culture and the "oral/aural song and story of the folk flourished, as it were, behind the backs of the fully literate" (51). These folk song and stories, Fiedler (41) observed, tended "to express the repressed" and "in patriarchal ages" popular culture, in part, "pays tribute to the matriarchal." Tania Modleski (1986, x) rightly called Fiedler to task for not distinguishing between "'popular art' which 'arises from the people,' and 'mass art,' which is imposed from above," revealing his lack of political concern for issues of power and profit. It also reveals that those, like Fiedler, who associate all nonelite culture with freedom and resistance, conveniently forget that what looks like freedom for one socially privileged group (e.g., men's access to pornography that treats women as a class of sex objects) is premised upon the compromising of women's freedom.

Modleski (1986, xii) reminded us that much of *mass culture* works to "keep people in a state of what used to be called 'false consciousness.'" Feminist approaches to popular culture necessarily critically interrogate these forms. Yet, feminist and otherwise resistant perspectives allow us to surface as well those aspects of the genuinely folk or popular tributes to the "matriarchal" that persist in popular culture, even when they come in disguised and backhanded forms. In these, we can trace a record of wisdoms that have had to go underground to survive the brainwashings wrought by patriarchal domination, taking form in: the suppression and domestication of women; the persecution of gender and sexual variance; imperialist colonizations; and a continuous assault on the elements, creatures, and the green world. This resistant wisdom tradition pops up, for example, in the ongoing belief in psychic phenomena; in the "green consciousness" (environmental awareness and nature reverence) especially prevalent in children's culture; in the cult adulation of semigoddess figures like Princess Diana, and in the recurrent narrative presence of *powerful* women as wicked queens, witches, monsters, Amazons, mystery ladies, sex goddesses, and femme fatales. In these figures, we find also a suppressed gynocentric religious tradition.

Foundational to the patriarchal worldview is the official belief in a solely male divinity, one that legitimates male supremacy in the mundane world. In this system, female divinity is demonized and women play closely circumscribed roles of virgin or whore. In *Goddess: Myths of the Female Divine*, David Leeming and Jake Page (1994, 7) set out to restore awareness of an alternative history and theology. They conceptualized their task as writing the "biography of an archetype, a potential being who exists in all of us" (men as well as women). This goddess, though excluded from official religion, continues to take shape in contemporary popular culture, as the sex goddess and femme fatale.

Originally, then, the female divine — the "source of life and death and regeneration" (Leeming and Page, 1995, 7) — is honored, though, as the patriarchal era takes hold, femaleness, animality, sexuality, nature, death, and darkness are increasingly seen as something abject, chaotic, "dirty," needing to be feared and controlled if not eradicated. For example, dutiful motherhood and (exploitable) fertility is honored while free sexuality is labeled *whoredom*. In the popular imagination, the unpacified, insubordinate, and uncontrollable goddess appears now as "whore," femme fatale, dragon lady, monster. Her domain is no longer established religion, but, ironically enough, the horror and fantasy genres of popular culture; she (and her priestesses) appear as the witches and fairies of children's culture, the Hollywood sex goddesses, and the 1-800 psychics. This approach to popular culture informs feminist analyses of female monsters and aliens (Rushing, 1989; Creed, 1996), and enables resistant and gynocentric readings of such figures as Aunt Jemima (Walker, 1998), the Barbie doll (Lord, 1994), various film stars (Paglia, 1994), and the figure of the dominatrix, bitch, vamp, and vampire (Keesey, 1997).

In sum, popular culture should be recognized as an especially rich source for women's studies teaching and scholarship, first, because it is the everyday culture that naturalizes gender hierarchies and unjust stereotypes. Second, because it is a principal site for women (in all of our variety) to "talk back," shaping popular culture in ways that reflect feminist worldviews and values. And third, because it is an evocative source for feminists to investigate women's suppressed knowledge traditions. The engagement of women's studies with popular culture is a necessary critical venture, an essential site for consciousness raising, and a fruitful site for strategic actions and interventions in the feminist task of social transformation.

References

Bayley, Harold. *The Lost Language of Symbolism*. 2 vols. London: Williams and Norgate, 1912; reprint, London: Bracken, 1996.

Blake, Nayland. "Curating in a Different Light." In, *In a Different Light: Visual Culture, Sexual Identity, Queer Practice*. Editors, Nayland Blake, Lawrence Rinder, and Amy Scholder, San Francisco: City Lights Books, 1995.

Bobo, Jacqueline. *Black Women as Cultural Readers*. New York: Columbia University Press, 1995.

Caputi, Jane. *Goddesses and Monsters: Women, Myth, Power and Popular Culture*. Madison: University of Wisconsin Press, 2004.

Chalker, Rebecca. *The Clitoral Truth*. New York: Seven Stories Press, 2000.

Collins, Patricia Hill. *Black Feminist Thought: Knowledge, Consciousness, and the Politics of Empowerment*. New York: Routledge, 1998.

Covino, Deborah Caslav. *Amending the Abject Body: Aesthetic Makeovers in Medicine and Culture*. Albany: State University of New York Press, 2004.

Creed, Barbara. Horror and the monstrous-feminine: An imaginary abjection. In Editor, Barry Keith Grant, *The Dread of Difference: Gender and the Horror Film*, Austin: University of Texas Press, 1996, pp. 35–36.

Dines, Gail, Robert Jensen, and Ann Russo, Editors. *Pornography: The Production and Consumption of Inequality*, New York: Routledge, 1998.

duCille, Ann. "Toy Theory: Black Barbie and the Deep Play of Difference." In *Skin Trade*. Cambridge, MA: Harvard University Press, 1996, pp. 8–59.

Dworkin, Andrea. *Pornography: Men Possessing Women*. New York: Perigee, 1981.

Fiedler, Leslie. *What was Literature? Class Culture and Mass Society*. New York: Touchstone, 1982.

Fiske, John. "British Cultural Studies and Television." In Robert C. Allen, (Editor), *Channels of Discourse, Reassembled: Television and Contemporary Criticism*, 2nd ed. Chapel Hill: University of North Carolina Press, 1992, pp. 284–326.

Geist, Christopher D., and Jack Nachbar. "Introduction: What is popular culture?" In Christopher D. Geist and Jack Nachbar, Editors, *The Popular Culture Reader*, Bowling Green: Bowling Green State University Popular Press, 1983, pp. 1–12.

Grossberg, Lawrence. "On Postmodernism and Articulation: An Interview with Stuart Hall." *Journal of Communication Inquiry*, 10. 2 (1986): 45–60.

Guerilla Girls. *Bitches, Bimbos, and Ballbreakers: The Guerrilla Girls' Illustrated Guide to Female Stereotypes*. New York: Penguin Books, 2003.

Hall, Stuart. "Encoding/Decoding." In Simon During, Editor. *The Cultural Studies Reader*, New York: Routledge, 1993, p.101.

Hamer, Diana, and Belinda Budge. "Introduction." In, Diana Hamer and Belinda Budge, Editors, *The Good, the Bad and the Gorgeous: Popular Culture's Romance with Lesbianism*. London: Pandora Press, 1994, pp. 1–14.

Hooks, Bell. *Black Looks: Race and Representation*. Boston: South End Press, 1992.

Jolles, Marjorie. Syllabus for "Feminist Cultural Studies," Women's Studies, University of Iowa, 2003.

Jones, Amelia. "Introduction: Conceiving the Intersetion of Feminism and Visual Culture." In Amelia Jones, Editor, *The Feminist and Visual Culture Reader*, New York: Routledge, 2003, pp. 1-8.

Keesey, Pam. *Vamps: An Illustrated History of the Femme Fatale*. San Francisco: Cleis Press, 1997.

Kipnis, Laura. *Bound and Gagged: Pornography and the Politics of Fantasy in America*. New York: Grove Press, 1996.

Leeming, David, and Jake Page. 1994. *Goddess: Myths of the Female Divine*. New York: Oxford University Press, 1994.

Lord, M. G. *Forever Barbie: The Unauthorized Biography of a Real Doll*. New York: Avon Books, 1994.

McCaughey, Martha, and Neal King, Editors. "What's a Mean Woman like You Doing in a Movie like This?" In *Reel Knockouts: Violent Women in the Movies*. Austin, TX: University of Texas Press.

Modleski, Tania. "Introduction." In Tania Modleski, Editor. *Studies in Entertainment: Critical Approaches to Mass Culture*. Bloomington: Indiana of University Press, 1986, ix–xix.

Mulvey, Laura. "Visual Pleasure and Narrative Cinema. In Amelia Jones, Editor. *The Feminism and Visual Culture Reader*. New York: Routledge, 2003, pp. 44–52.

Nussbaum, Martha. "Through the Prism of Gender — How New Scholarship About

Women's Lives is Changing Our Understanding of the Past, and the Present." *Times Literary Supplement*, 495 (1998): 3–4.

Paglia, Camille. *Vamps and Tramps: New Essays*. New York: Vintage Books, 1994.

Radway, Janice. *Reading the Romance: Women, Patriarchy, and Popular Literature*. Chapel Hill: University of North Carolina Press, 1984.

Robinson, Victoria. "Introducing Women's Studies." In Victoria Robinson and Diane Richardson, Editors. *Introducing Women's Studies: Feminist Theory and Practice*. New York: New York University Press, 1997, pp. 1–26.

Rose, Tricia. "Never Trust a Big Butt and a Smile." In *Black Feminist Cultural Criticism*, Jacqueline Bobo, Editor. Malden, MA: Blackwell, 2001.

Rushing, Janice Hocker. "Evolution of the New Frontier in Alien and Aliens: Patriarchal Co-Optation of the Feminine Archetype." *Quarterly Journal of Speech*, 71 (1989): 1–24.

Schechter, Harold. *The Bosom Serpent: Folklore and Popular Art*. New York: Peter Lang, 2001.

Tuchman, Gay, A. Daniels, & J. Benet, Editors. (1978). *Hearth and Home: Images of Women in the Mass Media*. New York: Oxford, University Press, 1978.

Walker, Alice. Giving the Party. In *Anything We Love Can Be Saved: A Writer's Activism*. New York: Random House, 1997, pp. 137–143.

12

Popular Culture in a Business Curriculum

ANN KNEAVEL

At first, a business school curriculum seems the least likely place to find popular culture topics. After all, business schools are all, well, "business," and not concerned with frivolities like teen horror movies, rap music, and boggle head doll collections. But a second look reveals perhaps the closest connection of all between pop culture and business majors.

By definition, what is "popular" in our culture is what generates the most attention and, therefore, often, the most income, making pop culture big business. The Disney Corporation, with its theme parks, hotels, cruise ships, TV networks, and movie studios, dominates both popular culture and the leisure industry market. Conversely, big business frequently becomes a phenomenon within pop culture — witness the Enron scandals.

The Martha Stewart story illustrates perfectly how intermeshed business and pop culture can be. Martha took her talent for setting standards for good taste and gracious living to such heights that she became the arbiter of culture. Within a few years, the corporation she headed — a vast conglomerate including a magazine, a TV show, and a product line with outlets in K-Mart stores nationwide — was listed on the New York Stock Exchange. "What would Martha do" became a catch phrase for style. Then something Martha did, in her personal financial dealings, made headlines *because* of the place she held in our culture. The resultant fascination prompted a made-for-TV movie that purported to portray both her business affairs and her personal life, thus bringing the cycle full circle; the tycoon who built a financial empire on pop culture becomes a pop culture subject.

Rather than present a theoretical essay on the ways in which popular culture topics *might* be used within a business curriculum, this details a case study of the ways pop culture *is* actually integrated into one college's academics.

The college being examined is a specialized institution; it offers only business degrees. Students earn associate, bachelor's, and master's degrees in accounting, computer science, finance, human resource management, and management, and marketing. Because it is a focused college, the curriculum is specifically tailored to most efficiently and effectively meet the needs of all its business majors. This means that the general education requirements, which for accreditation must comprise at least 40 percent of a student's transcript, are designed to cover the broadest range of material while keeping the connections to business as the foremost consideration. Unlike traditional colleges, this institution does not have a large selection of courses within, for instance, a sociology or literature department from which a student can choose. Because, then, the courses offered have been chosen solely with business majors in mind, the experiences of this institution can best exemplify an effective integration of popular culture into a business curriculum.

Popular culture plays a large role in the standard introductory level general education electives. The professor who teaches introduction to sociology, for instance, uses elements of pop culture to guarantee his material remains current and relevant. He sends students to K-Mart to survey customers on their shopping habits and to learn ways in which contemporary American lifestyles are influencing and being influenced by consumer culture. At least two class periods use lyrics to popular songs to explore current views of the family and social issues.

Psychology courses are another area of general electives which incorporate elements of pop culture extensively. The award-winning film *Ordinary People* is used as a case study for several psychological problems and ways of dealing with them. Films are also used frequently in the abnormal psychology class, because movies like *Analyze This, Anger Management,* and *A Beautiful Mind* have made psychological dysfunction a popular subject on the big screen. Another pop culture phenomenon scrutinized by students in the Abnormal Psych class is the confrontational talk shows like *Jerry Springer* and *Geraldo.*

Aspects of the popular are used even more in the psychology courses of special interest to business majors. In industrial psychology, for example, a field trip to a shopping mall provides an exercise in consumer psychology. The students were instructed to observe the displays, the merchandise, the crowds, the layout and decorations of the stores, and from their observations to draw conclusions about the culture as might occur to someone entirely alien — a Martian, perhaps. Films like *Roger & Me* give one view of the auto manufacturing industry.

A psychology course specifically tailored for business majors, "Gender and the Workplace," taps into the domain of pop culture to show how societal attitudes affect our lives in the workforce. One assignment is to view Saturday morning cartoons for the different roles assigned to males and females. Another part of the course looks at toy ads. Even in the 21st century, there are striking differences between what are traditionally marketed to boys and what are packaged to appeal to girls, and in the approaches to each gender. Yet another section concentrates on the way the workplace is portrayed on TV and in movies. The psychology department at this business college is well aware that popular perceptions shape our workplaces.

The introductory philosophy course, "Fundamentals of Philosophy," is structured entirely on the pairing of popular movies with categories of philosophy. This course deserves attention as the best example of the way popular culture can be extremely effective in bridging gaps and making real world connections for business majors. The chapter on ontology uses *Being John Malkovitch* or *Fight Club* to explore the mind/body duality; epistemology is discussed through *The Truman Show* or *Matrix*. (Here it seems appropriate to note that UC Berkeley has an entire philosophy course devoted to *Matrix*.) *Rapture* is shown for the chapter on philosophies of religion. *The Cradle Will Rock* or John Waters' *Pecker* (with caution) form the basis for discussion in the chapter on aesthetics, because both these films call into question the definition of art, who determines art, and whether art is co-opted by contemporary society. A movie like *Return to Paradise* is a perfect vehicle for ethics, because the entire film centers on an ethical dilemma and the views of so many schools of philosophy are represented by the different characters. One pairing, which is at once perhaps the closest fit and yet the most unexpected, is the coupling of the movie *Antz* with the social philosophies. The students learn how similar the social structure of Dreamworks' ant colony is to Plato's *Republic*, and see how that animated feature film interjects ideas from Hobbes, Locke, and Marx, among others. Part of the final evaluation in this philosophy course is to examine a complex film like *Existenz* from several different philosophical viewpoints.

The most widespread references to popular culture within specific business concentrations are, as might be expected, in the marketing courses, particularly in the marketing management course, which is required of all students, not just marketing majors. Each class meeting begins with a discussion of relevant current news items, providing insights into how the theory translates into everyday life. Focus of the course is on consumer marketing, so knowledge of what is most popular in the culture is vital. Every time the course is taught in the spring semester, the class after the Superbowl is devoted to the commercials (as is a sizeable chunk of time on the national news programs). Like the Superbowl, other major popular culture events are important for marketing management students. In fact, NASCAR is part of every marketing course, because the NASCAR culture encompasses every facet of the U.S. market. Case studies show how marketing professionals tap into pop culture to advance their products. Mattel gained market lead, for instance, because its research revealed strong trends in modern culture — the product tie-ins with TV shows and movies, the tendency in our culture for children to leave toys behind much earlier than a generation ago, and the paradoxical adult mania for collecting "toys" like Barbie dolls. Emphasis in the marketing courses in this business college is precisely on the need to be hyperaware of the popular culture.

Besides the important role of popular culture as part of many courses, there are some courses among the careful selection of general electives which are devoted to popular culture subjects. The business college recognizes the primary role of general education courses as providing the knowledge and skills necessary to participate meaningfully in society. In our society, that means the graduates should have acquired the vocabulary and contextual framework to discuss elements of our culture intelligently. One course designed to equip students for social exchanges is "Film and Literature," a 200-level elective which replaced a more traditional introduction to literature course.

The college catalogue describes the course as "a thematic approach to the study of literature represented in film" and continues, "Students will view films and read selections from literature treating such themes as love and hate, conformity and rebellion, heroism, family, freedom and responsibility, human vulnerability, and the relation of art to life." The stated objectives are to introduce students to the conventions of various genres, literary and film; to enable students to recognize and appreciate the devices for conveying meaning within those genres; to familiarize students with common themes of the human experience; and to teach students how to analyze works of literature and film. Teaching this course is a rewarding experience, and society benefits from having future business leaders gain a critical appreciation of this important subject in pop culture.

Even more specific to the business curriculum is the very popular seminar course, "Workplace in Film." The course pairs movies which deal with particular concerns of the workplace. For example, a movie like *The*

Associate or *Nine to Five* is compared to *Opportunity Knocks* or *Taking Care of Business*. Each of these movies uses the impersonation trope to move the plot. In each, the protagonist must pretend to be someone he or she is not to get ahead in the workplace. As the students examine the plot structures, a clear pattern emerges—the gender of the protagonist dictates two very different story lines. The female protagonist comes into the situation with all the qualifications and skills necessary to achieve, but she needs to change her look (for the females there is a heavy emphasis on wardrobe and makeup) to impersonate someone else. For the male protagonists in this model, however, it is precisely what they do *not* have which allows them to succeed. Often they are undressed, at least partially, so they are mistaken for someone of higher status. The antagonists actually possess the prerequisites for the job, but are ineffectual in the position. Thus in the male version, qualifications stand in the way of success; childlike simplicity and common sense are all a man needs to rise to the top of the corporate ladder. Like PSY 330, this portion of the special English course amply demonstrates the differing views of gender in the workplace. A similar topic addressed in "Film and the Workplace" is career-related female fantasies and male anxieties. Films like *Nine to Five* or *Baby Boom* envision utopian ideals and transform hostile working environments through totally unrealistic solutions. Equally extreme are movies which deal with male fears. In *Disclosure* and *The Temp*, for instance, men at work are brought down by seductive, conniving women, sending the clear message to beware of displacement by beautiful, intelligent female colleagues.

Corporate corruption, all too real in this post–Enron era, is covered in films like *Office Space* and *Boiler Room*, works which deal with seduction of a different sort — the way big business, always an evil influence in Hollywood's perceptions, draws earnest young people into its ethos.

The final topic of the course, labeled *The Dilbert Workplace*, after the popular comic strip, reveals most strongly why pop culture needs to be an important part of a business major's education. This unit includes films which treat the absurdities of the contemporary workplace — *Office Space*, *Clockwatchers*, and *Haiku Tunnel* to name a few. All the students have seen one or more of these movies; many own them; several can recite all the lines along with the characters on the screen, demonstrating how pervasive these presentations of office life truly can be. In these works and others like them, the goal is "to succeed in business without really trying." All of the stereotypes of the business world are found in these films, and the students clearly identify with the main characters.

There is no more effective management training than analyzing the situations presented and the solutions offered by these popular films, because they reach students on a level not possible through any other medium. This film course amply demonstrates the crucial function of pop culture in the business curriculum. Before our business majors go out into the workplace as accountants or computer programmers or financial managers, it is vital to national interests that they examine the attitudes of popular culture toward the workforce they are preparing to enter, and that they be given the opportunity to affirm or deny the perceptions.

13

Linkages Between Popular Culture and Economics

HELEN YOUNGELSON-NEAL

The linkages between economics and popular culture were significantly shaped by the technological advances of the 20th century. The speed and efficiency of transportation and communication led to the expansion of mass consumer markets, first on a national scale and more recently on a global scale. The commodification of entertainment and the development of mass markets have forged an important base for the modern popular culture enterprises.

The sounds, images, and narratives disseminated by popular culture industries inform, entertain, build collective identity, and influence culture practices. The economic characteristics of these markets shape what people read in books, what they see in movies and on television, and what they listen to on the radio and recordings. Mass produced entertainment has thus come to occupy a central place in modern lifestyles and uses of leisure.

Much of what is produced by media industries (books, radio, television, movies, and recordings) is widely criticized for disseminating ever increasing sensationalism and violence, mediocre content, repetitive programming, and formulas of entertainment geared toward the lowest common denominator. Whether you agree with the criticism or view such output as a reflection of individual taste, an analysis of the economic characteristics of these markets for cultural commodities can clarify the context and fill an important gap in understanding how popular culture is shaped. This analysis will explore the characteristics of popular culture markets by drawing on perspectives from Robert Frank and Philip Cook (1986). They used the term *Winner-Take-All Markets* as the title of their book to help clarify the forces that shape what we view on television and in the movies, what books we read, and what music we listen to.

Attributes of Winner-Take-All Markets

Frank and Cook define winner-take-all-markets as markets in which the payoffs are determined by relative rather than absolute performances (23–26). Rather than concentrating on an entire industry, the focus is on a few big winners. Thus, in popular culture markets, monetary rewards are concentrated in the hands of a few top performers, hit television programs, and movie blockbusters. Success is not defined by the quality of creative output, but by the popularity in responses from intended audiences. The greater share of earnings in winner-take-all markets go as to the movies, TV programs, books, or recordings that achieve exceptional success, Through commodification, media industries either achieve quick success or no success at all. Popularity is the primary determinant, and popularity is frequently based on sensationalism, rather than the quality of the production. Thus, a characteristic of winner-take-all markets is the selection of performers and creative works on the basis of estimated audience appeal. This leads to a high degree of inequality in the earnings of both performers and the authors of creative works as well as of media firms.

Top stars and authors make exceedingly high incomes compared to the rest of their cohorts. For years Bill Cosby, was the most highly paid entertainer in the United States. His earnings frequently reached $50 million a year. Stars such as Tom Hanks, Tom Cruise, Julia Roberts, and Denzel Washington all receive $20 million or more for a movie. Ray Romano recently signed a $40 million contract for another season of *Everybody Loves Raymond*. The popular singer Mariah Carey, signed a $80 million contract with EMI's Virgin Records (Carr, 2003). J. K. Rowling, who is already reported to be richer than Queen Elizabeth II, earned about $22.5 million after the first day sales of her new Harry Potter book, *Harry Potter and the Order of the Phoenix* (Kirkpatrick, 2003). Senator Hillary Clinton received an $8 million advance on her autobiography, *Living History,* which in the first month sold 1 million copies. After the sale of 1.3 million copies, she will earn 15 percent of the retail price of each copy sold, which amounts to $4.20 per book (Wilson, 2003). This is in contrast with rewards in manufacturing in which earnings are tied to the number of units produced or productivity.

What are the attributes of the economy of popular culture that generates winner-take-all markets? On the supply side, creative works can be reproduced at very low cost, giving rise to production economies of scale. New technologies have dramatically reduced the costs of all forms of communication and information transmission (Acheson and Maule, 1999). The introduction of digital technology has significantly reduced costs of production and improved the quality in each of the traditional media industries (publishing, radio and television, film, and recording).

The use of the digital format in publishing has substantially reduced costs of preparing material for publication. The functions of editing, formatting, and typesetting are performed on computers, requiring less expertise. These functions have increasingly been shifted from the publisher to the author. As a result, publishing has become more decentralized than before.

The introduction of the compact disc in sound recording has increased quality, portability, and flexibility. The digitalization of sound adds new editing and mixing possibilities. Digital audiotapes outperform their analogue predecessors in both reproduction and as a means for carrying original content that was missing in the older analogue.

Digitization introduced in the film industry has reduced the capital cost of equipment and the number of technicians needed to operate the equipment. The new digital imaging has revolutionized special effects departments of movie and television programming studios. Producers of animated television and feature films are increasingly dependent on computer-generated images. What was once a labor-intensive activity is now computer and software intensive. These cost reductions, together with the developments in videocameras and desktop video will make it easier for independent filmmakers to enter the industry now dominated by the large Hollywood studio.

New innovations have also changed the way films are distributed and exhibited. Multiplex cinemas in shopping malls and downtown office complexes have replaced the old palatial theaters and increased the number of screens. For the first time, a digitized version of *Jurassic Park Part III* is being exhibited in a movie theater by satellite. With the introduction of the VCR and the newer DVD player, living rooms have been transformed into household movie theaters.

The electronic and optical innovations in television broadcasting have broadened the channels along with information that can be transmitted on a communication network. The use of fiber optical cables increases by a very large factor the amount of information that can be carried over coaxial cable. The introduction of wireless communication in the form of microwave cellular technologies, coupled with the use of satellites as a base for redirecting the signals back to earth, have become a integral parts of delivery systems.

Digital television allows more channels in the same amount of bandwidth. Multichannel television began in U.S. homes in 1975 and spread very rapidly to other parts of the world. Multichannels spread across Europe in the 1980s and the rest of the world in the 1990s (*The Economist,* 2002, p. 8). This increase in channel capacity, together with the means of compressing the data transmitted, has dramatically expanded the communication capacity of all transmission media.

The introduction of the Internet and the World Wide-Web has provided an environment for experimentation and international participation in communications. With sufficient bandwidth brought to the home, cultural content becomes available on demand. When they wish to do so, individuals are now able to access video on demand, live and taped television programs, recorded music, and an array of printed material. Songs can be downloaded from the Internet and played on a home computer. Radio broadcasts can also be accessed on the computer. Video clips are standard fare on Internet sites. Newspapers and magazines make their content available on the computer. Books are being published on the Internet. Disney has *http://www.Disney.com* as a standard entertainment company site with movie and television news. It also has a children's magazine online, *Disney Blast,* and an online shop that sells 2000 Disney products.

These accelerated advances have led to the reshaping of traditional media industries. Cultural industries have undergone a process of internalization, realignment, and progressive concentration. Cultural industries are both vertically and horizontally integrated through ownership and complex contracting agreement. This integration process has resulted in a few, very large media conglomerates. Horizontal integration lowers costs by taking advantage of economies of scale in production, by distributing the same creative content in different places.

Vertical integration is reflected in the scope and depth of production and distribution by industry conglomerates. For example, starting with an original product or fictional character, conglomerates now handle the production, the movie studio, the music, the merchandising, the theme parks, the Internet site, and the e-commercialization of all derived products. All stages of content, process, and format are combined to create synergies that result in lower costs and reduced risks. Major media conglomerates own film studies, broadcasting networks, recording studios, book and magazine publishing companies, theme parks, and merchandizing stores. High profile mergers have included Disney's purchase of ABC, Viacom's purchase of CBS, Time-Warner's purchase of Turner Broadcasting and AOL, and Bertelsmann's purchase of Random House (New York Times, 2001, CS).

On the demand side, consumption of popular culture goods exhibits economic characteristics that give rise to winner-take-all markets. Most important of these are "nonrivalry" consumption and the "popularity" effect (Frank and Cook, 1996, 199–200). The principle of scarcity is an important basis for establishing the value of economic goods. For example, if one person consumes an ice cream cone, it is unavailable for another person to consume. Economists call this "rivalry" in consumption. This type of consumption is absent in cultural goods. Viewers watching a feature film or a television program do not preclude other viewers from consuming the same content, and thus exhibit "nonrivalry" in consumption. Books and magazines exhibit this nonrivalry in a limited sense because it is difficult to have a number of persons read one copy of the same book at the same time. However, the print medium has a quality of durability because it can be reread. Thus, for example, used books can compete with new books of the same content.

This nonrivalry consumption is only limited by the crowding effect. As more consumers of content are supplied, some crowding occurs, reducing an additional consumer. Television and radio programs are unaffected by the number of viewers up to the capacity of the network. In the same way, the numbers of viewers of a feature film are unaffected by the size of the audience up to the capacity of the theater. As a result, cultural industries exhibit large economies of scale because they have low incremental costs. The cost of additional copies of a television program, or extra prints of a feature film, or additional CDs of a sound recording, or additional books is negligible compared to the cost of the original production.

In addition to personal enjoyment of television programs, films, music and books, consumers also enjoy sharing entertainment property with friends and significant others. This is reflected in the popularity of book clubs and viewer clubs that arise around TV programming and movies. Such examples include Star Trek and Jackie Chan clubs. Rational consumers choose what popular culture they watch, listen to, and read based on a number of factors that they use as proxies for quality. These include, past experience, reviews, advertising, and popularity ratings. The most important of these is popularity, although popularity is not predictor of quality. Examples can be cited of movies, TV programs, and books that have had both critical and commercial success: such TV shows as *Mash* and *The Sopranos*; classic movies, such as *Gone with the Wind* and the *Wizard of Oz*; and books such as John Le Carré's espionage novels. However, quality does not guarantee popular success. There are many critically acclaimed books, movies, and TV programs that never gain financial success.

Implications of Winner-Take-All Markets

The characteristics of winner-take-all markets identified above shape the kinds of cultural goods offered and produced in all the popular culture industries. Large integrated media firms feel the need to make a quick financial success in order to win the competitive race with other firms for their share of market. This has led to a continuous and intensifying search for the hit blockbuster movie, TV program, or book that has mass audience appeal. This results in giving priority to early financial success over the consideration of creativity and quality content. This is further reinforced by *Variety* reports that nearly half of a film's overall revenue is made in the opening week. Given the high cost of initial production, the need to reach a large audience both at home and abroad becomes a primary concern of the broadcasters, movie producers, and book publishers.

This is reinforced by the risk and uncertainty characterized by cultural industries. Most films flop, most records lose money, and most TV series fail. Choosing winners is very risky. For every commercial success of movies such as *Star Wars* and *Titanic,* there are many more losses such as *Water Works* and *Treasure Plant.* For every surprise hit like *My Big Fat Greek Wedding* there is an unexpected dud such as *Wild, Wild West.* This is also true in TV broadcasting. For every hit such as *CSI: Crime Scene Investigation* and *Friends* there are flops such as *Dragnet* and *Big Brother.* Shows that were successful in a previous season may be met with audience's boredom in the next season, as was the case with *Who Wants to be a Millionaire?* The combination of risk and the need for a quick win makes it rational for cultural firms to choose content that has the potential of a hit based upon past experience. Thus, it is not surprising that when there is a choice between quality and probability of financial success, financial success is chosen even if it causes creative quality to slip. This occurs in all popular culture markets to some degree.

In book publishing, it is rational for a publisher faced with the choice between a book manuscript by a unknown author and one by a celebrity to select the manuscript by the established celebrity author even though it may not be as good as that of the unknown author. This invariably leads to lowered quality standards and often the publishing of formulaic offerings from authors such as Danielle Steel and Jackie Collins.

In the movie industry, similar dynamics occur. Producers are more concerned with financial success than experimenting with new creative works. Relying on sequels and remakes of previous movies such as *Star Trek* and *Terminator* represents a somewhat safe approach. After the launch of *Jaws*, the first modern blockbuster, movie audiences have been subject to the blockbuster and its sequel such as *Terminator 3, Star Wars 2, Matrix 2,* and *Beverly Hills Cops 3.* Each year an every increasing string of sequels and prequels is produced. Of the top 10 box office earnings in 2002, five were sequels, and one was a remake. The obsession with maximizing global box office earnings has given priority to the blockbuster that reaches every demographic group and has the widest possible audience. This results in action movie genre that crosses different cultures, contrasted to dramas and comedies.

These market forces are evident in broadcast TV as well. The introduction of digital cable has led to the fragmentation of the TV audience. In the 1950s a show such as *I Love Lucy* could capture over 70 percent of an evening's audience. By the 1970s only about a half of the viewing audience settled down to watch *All in the Family.* Today, however, even the most popular TV series, *Friends* can only capture 24 percent of the viewing audience (*The Economist,* 2002, 8). The remainder of the viewing audience is spread over a vast array of the other broadcast and cable channels. This shrinking market has led to pressure on network heads from advertisers to re-create "great event" TV or "water-cooler" TV (*The Economist,* 2002, 10). By this is meant that advertisers want to sponsor the blockbuster show that can generate a buzz and gets people talking around the office water cooler the next day. The problem is that even successful blockbusters may not subsequently last with audiences. For instance, ABC's *Who Wants to be a Millionaire?* was a success during its first season, only to falter in its second year.

Competition for audience size and the high costs of production have resulted in the production of more concept shows that are formulaic and ever more sensational. Seven out of the top 10 programs in 2002 were reality shows like *Joe Millionaire* or procedural dramas such as *CSI* and *Law and Order* dramas and their spin-offs. Two of the popular spin-offs from *Law and Order* are *Law and Order, SVU* and *Law and Order, Criminal Intent.* Spin-offs from *CSI* include *CSI :Miami* and *CSI: Crime Scene Investigation* . The venues for creative programs are to be found primarily on paid cable stations, such as HBO and Showtime. This is primarily due to their freedom from advertising pressures and the need to appeal to mass audiences.

In the present review of linkages between economics and popular culture, the analysis has been restricted to perspectives derivable from "the winner take all" philosophy. This indeed seems to be the dominant perspective in a variety of popular culture industries. Among the market forces, a dynamic interplay occurs among advertisers, producers, and the viewing audience. Advertisers can exercise censorship by deciding not to sponsor a particular program. Producers exercise an influence through their perceptions of the uncertainty of audience reaction and their direct control over scheduling and production. Through their exercise of preferences on reading, viewing, and listening, audiences have a major impact on what is offered by the popular culture industries. Thus, freedom and control operate in a variety of ways in the economic underpinnings of popular culture.

References

Acheson, Keith, and Christopher Maule. *Much Ado About Culture: North-American Trade Disputes*. Ann Arbor, MI: University of Michigan Press, 1999.

Carr, David. "Major Stars Not So Crucial as Concept Trumps Celebrity." *New York Times*, June 23, 2003.

Economist, The. "Power in Your Hand: A Survey of Television." April 13, 2002, pp. 8, 10.

Frank, Robert H., and Phili U. Cook. *Winner-Take-All Society*. Harmondsworth, UK: Penguin Books, 1996.

Kirkpatrick, David D. "New 'Harry Potter' Book Sells 5 Million on First Day." *New York Times*, June 23, 2003.

New York Times. "Sizing Up an Industry and Disney's Place in It." July 2, 2001, p. C5.

Wilson, Michael. "Senator Clinton Has a Cure for Foot-in-Mouth Disease." *New York Times*, July 20, 2003.

14

Popular Culture and Ethnic Studies

Curricular and Pedagogic Reflections

C. RICHARD KING AND DAVID J. LEONARD

Although often ignored by audiences, commentators, and even scholars, race centers popular culture. However, one need look no farther than the often used introductory texts on the study of popular culture to see the exclusion of ethnic studies (Strinati, 1995; Storey, 1996). While each text provides sufficient introduction to Marxist, postmodern, poststructuralist, and feminist theories as they relate to studying popular culture, neither offers any insight into the place or usefulness of theories of race. And conversations about specific popular fields, from movies and television to music and sports, too often foreground others issues at the expense of serious consideration of race and racism. For instance, the recent literature on video games, while limited, further reveals the peripheral place of race within the larger field of popular culture. The focus on gender or the fetishization of violence is done at the expense of examining its racial content. In light of such marginalization, a concern for popular culture must play an integral role within ethnic studies curricula, and, we would argue, race must occupy a more central place in classes and programs devoted to popular culture.

Today, (1) multinational media-culture conglomerates cynically manipulate notions like diversity and multiculturalism, constantly reiterate racial stereotypes, package programming for (supposedly) discrete racial communities, and create advertising campaigns for specific ethnic niches; (2) programs in the humanities and social sciences must become more practical and enlarge enrollments and majors while reducing their spending; and (3) universities intensify efforts to recruit and retain students of color. They often do so, however, without regard to racial stratification and its implications or to the erosion of cultural values and social policies like affirmative action that promote more democratic learning environments. These propositions, true as they are, raise difficult questions for faculty and departments. How have and should race and popular culture be taken up in ethnic studies classes and programs? How can faculty integrate such courses into the curriculum? How should one respond to students or administrators who suggest that such courses are at best frivolous distractions from the real world that obscure more urgent problems and undermine commitments to ethnic communities? How can departments design an area of study that simultaneously attracts students and critically engages difficult subjects? How can faculty and programs on campus without ethnic studies contribute and benefit?

The relationships between race and racism, popular culture, and pedagogy are neither idle nor abstract subjects for us. Rather, they are topics we regularly contemplate as we design courses, formulate lessons plans, talk with our students, listen to the latest release from Eminem or Jennifer Lopez, and watch *The Matrix*, an episode of *Friends*, or a Los Angeles Lakers basketball game. Like many of our peers, we engage the popular and its entanglements with race from multiple positions as fans, consumers, scholars, and teachers, taking pleasure at times, formulating critiques at others, but always thinking about what texts, performances, and trends mean. We constantly ask how the public, particularly our students, make sense of and use them, and how we might bring them into the classroom to talk about issues like racialization, stratification, resistance, and identity. With this in mind, here, we pause to situate ourselves and more fully ground our subsequent argument.

We teach in an ethnic studies department at a land-grant university in the Pacific Northwest. It brings together individuals working in African American studies, Asian-American studies, Latina/o studies, and Native-American studies and like many similar programs across the United States stresses comparative, critical, and increasingly global perspectives. Indeed, our department offers a bachelor's degree in one of five areas or concentrations, cultural studies, ethnic studies, multicultural literature and pedagogy, multiethnic studies, and prelaw. In common with our colleagues, we regularly teach service classes (such as introduction to comparative American cultures), core courses for our majors (including the cultural politics of race and ethnicity and seminars in culture and power), and courses in our areas of study (Native Americans and film and the Civil Rights movement, for instance). Thus, we speak as scholars and teachers familiar with both ongoing trends in specialized ethnic studies and within the study and teaching of the subject as a whole (Bulmer and Solmos, 1999; Butler, 2001; Butler and Walter, 1991; Gutierrez, 1994; Yang, 2000). Our discussion, in turn, should be read as speaking to both general and specific theoretical approaches, substantive trends, and pedagogic strategies in ethnic studies.

We both have a keen interest in — some would say an obsession with — popular culture, which figures prominently in our teaching and research. King, trained as an anthropologist amidst the rise of cultural studies and in the wake of the poststructural turn, has spent much of the past decade studying race and sports, particularly the Native-American mascot controversy and indigenous athletes (King 2002, 2003, 2004; King and Springwood 2001a, 2001b; King et al., 2002). Leonard, educated in ethnic studies, has also studied sports, recently turning his attention to race and video games (Leonard, 2002). And together, we are now analyzing race in popular account of *The Matrix*. Our teaching follows from our research, often incorporating its findings or foci; that is, popular culture animates our pedagogy. On the one hand, we integrate examples from films, pulp fiction, advertising, sport, music, and video games into our more general courses on race and ethnicity; on the other hand, we have designed entire courses on popular subjects, including a comparative study of the representations of difference and courses focused on specific racial groups (African Americans or Native Americans and film).

On Ethnic Studies

struggling
to educate
and inform
about
how Amerika
screwed
us
      — Gary Eng,
      "Asian-American Studies"

The above epigraph essentially captures both the historic trajectory and mission of ethnic studies in that the story of ethnic studies is one of struggle and efforts to undermine the white supremacist orientation of American educational institutions. Founded in 1969, the field of ethnic studies did not evolve out of educational mission papers, or campus bureaucracy; it materialized out of the blood, sweat, and tears of activists at both San Francisco State College (now San Francisco State University) and the University of California at Berkeley.

In fall 1968, students of color at San Francisco organized a strike in demand of a Third World College. Despite the efforts of state authorities to crush student activism, the efforts to secure a Third World College proved to be successful. The presence of up to 10,000 armed men for almost two months did not deter students, who were eventually successful in leading to the formation of ethnic studies at San Francisco State College, while inspiring those across the Bay.

In the Spring of 1969, students at UC Berkeley embraced this challenge as well, initiating a Third World strike, behind the formation of the Third World Liberation Front (TWLF), a coalition of students representing the African American, Chicano, Native-American, and Asian-American communities. Having failed to make inroads through institutional channels, with demands to form a Department of Black Studies, and support the national grape boycott, students from the Afro-American Studies Union (AASU), Mexican-American Student Confederation (MASC), Asian-American Political Alliance (AAPA), and the Native-American Students Union (NASU), publicly spoke of the need for direct action in January 1969. Shortly thereafter, on January 22, the TWLF initiated a strike, with picket lines at all the major entrances to Berkeley's campus. The initial demands of the TWLF included: (1) The establishment of a Third World College with four autonomous departments; (2) greater efforts to hire and retain faculty, administrators, and staff of color at all levels in all campus units; (3) increased efforts to secure programs for admission, financial aid and academic assistance for students of color; (4) autonomy in that people of color were to control all minority-related programs on campus; (5) increased number of work study positions available for students of color that facilitated work within minority communities and on high school campuses; and (6) no disciplinary action taken against student strikers.

Despite the support that student strikers received from the American Federation of Teachers, faculty and staff of color, numerous whites, and others throughout the campus, the strike turned violent very quickly. On January 28th, the Berkeley administration called in outside law enforcement, which included the California Highway Patrol and Alameda County Sheriffs, joining numerous campus police in efforts to "protect classroom activities from disruption." Unfortunately, the police went beyond protection, immediately arresting student picketers and otherwise disrupting the picket lines. Over the next couple of months, this trend held, with support growing (the faculty senate voted 540:2 in support of an interim ethnic studies program); at the same time, violence and repression increased as well. Tear gas, pepper spray, helicopters, and violence clashes with baton-wielding cops defined the later moments of the strike. Ethnic studies was, in fact, born out of these violent clashes. With increased instability on campus and negative publicity throughout the country, Chancellor Roger Heynes relented to student demands, announcing the establishment of the department of ethnic studies on March 4, 1969. The department would "immediately offer four-year programs leading to a B.A. degree in history, culture, and contemporary experience of ethnic minority groups, especially Black Americans, Mexican Americans, Asian Americans, and Native Americans" (Ling-Chi Wang, 1997)

The central mission of ethnic studies was clear from its inception: to challenge the white supremacist orientation of the university curriculum, while simultaneously offering community relevant education. While a radical agenda, which was feared by administrators across the country, the efforts of activists successfully led to the formation of ethnic studies departments throughout the country. Initially, universities formed black studies programs, which by 1971 were found at 500 schools; nearly 1300 schools offered at least one ethnic studies course. This honeymoon was short-lived, as administrators, politicians, and conservative intellectuals, who often saw ethnic studies as "balkanized bastions of self-imposed isolation for students of color, shoddy scholarship and unqualified professors," succeeded in shutting down infant programs and purging radicals (Bob Wing, 1999). The contemporary trajectory of ethnic studies can thus be found in its initial years as battled between its radical mission and its institutional presence, which at times is contradictory and other times incompatible.

Historical Trajectory: The Scope of Ethnic Studies

The scope and mission of ethnic studies, while constantly changing, has remained relatively true to its original core. Emerging out of 1960s movements, and reflective of its violent inception, the ethnic studies movement embraced ideas of self-determination, autonomy, and models of internal colonialism as the basis of its disciplinary emphasis. More specifically, activists of color saw ethnic studies as part of a larger struggle to revolutionize the white supremacist university structure from the bottom up through curricular changes, and infusing the university with people of color.

Equally important to the continued mission of ethnic studies is community relevance and bridging gaps between the ivory tower and communities. "They demanded an education relevant to struggles for racial justice at home and aboard and for programs that would serve as powerful bases for launching and supporting student and community organizing" (Wing, 1999). The mission of ethnic studies, from its inception, was thus about creating and utilizing interdisciplinary scholarship about people of color, for their community's sake. In its early days this took the form of community organizing projects cooperative garment factories, farm worker organizing and fights for low-income housing. Howard Johnson, an activist from San Fernando Valley State, captured the essence of an ethnic studies mission in terms of its relevance within the community. "We had to take our commitment from the ivy-tower world of academe to the grassroots, where it really counts" (Van Deburg, 1992, 72).

The mission of ethnic studies was not limited to bridging the gap through material political struggles, but combating deleterious stereotypes promulgated at the university and through popular culture. To combat the systemic affects of "subtle cultural enslavement," black student unions and other organizations oriented toward decolonization, monitored classes, initiated forums, and created alternatives. The ethnic studies movement, thus, equally centered on providing alternative images and narratives to those offered by dominant white society. Bob Wing, a member of the Third World Liberation Front and an instructor at Berkeley during the department's early period, remembered how ethnic studies offered alternatives to dominant images/stereotypes of people of color. "The theory, that slavery turned all blacks into Sambos was wildly popular in the history department," was dispelled through courses offered in ethnic studies (Bob Wing, 1999). While not central to its written and self-proclaimed mission, an examination of culture, especially in the form of widely popular culture stereotypes, has always been within the scope of ethnic studies

While the original mission of ethnic studies did not emphasize the exploration of popular culture, focusing its rhetoric on authentic political struggle, an examination of popular culture has always been at the core of an ethnic studies mission — an idea that is often articulated against a focus on popular culture within ethnic studies embraces the history and mission of ethnic studies. Arguing that ethnic studies is based on community work and political struggle, popular culture is constructed as a space without material consequences. Before talking about the problematic nature of this binary, in that examining popular culture addresses the material needs of community, it is important to examine the centrality of popular media within the mission of ethnic studies.

The mission of ethnic studies developed out of the ideologies and goals articulated within radical nationalist movements of the 1960s. The necessity of combating stereotypes, undermining white imagination of otherness, and challenging self-perceptions, all led to efforts to protest popular images of people of color. Clyde Warrior, a prominent member of the American Indian Movement, wrote, in "What I Would Like My Community to Look Like in Ten Years," that "the white men tends to rate the Indian as being lazy and worthless." Such images, that often emanate from popular sources, ranging from television to the movies, dramatically affect Indian populations in material ways. "The Indian," wrote Warrior, "seems to make it a point to act and be exactly as he's rated" (Smith and Warrior, 1996, 41). While Warrior emphasized the importance of economic development, educational opportunities, fulfillment of treaty rights, technological assistance, and increased autonomy, the revolution would not begin until "Indian people changed their view of themselves and took pride in who they were" (Smith and Warrior, 1996, 41). Without the necessary efforts to combat hegemonic images of Indianness, any sort of structural or "material change" was seen to be futile. The systematic bombardment of images that constructed the Indian as "a problem," as "backward," and the necessity of copying of whites, had its affects on Indian identity and community, as well as white perceptions of Native-American populations. In other words, a fight against white supremacist images was seen by activists, such as Warrior, as not only part of the revolution, but central to its success. As the necessary step, understanding, challenging, and undermining popular cultural images of people of color, which affected both white imagination and visions of self, has *always* been central to an ethnic studies agenda.

Its centrality is even clearer within the Asian-American movement. The longstanding images of Asian men as sneaky, dangerous, "retarded, sadistic and bucktoothed," and Asian women as passive, exotic, and sexual, reflected the historic fear of "the economic competition of Asian workers and the threat of 'racial mongrelization' through miscegenation" (Wei, 1993, 50). Moreover, the ubiquitous stereotypes of Asians as foreigners reflect the hegemonic ideas of the Orient and white supremacy, reducing all Asian to a homogenous other not worthy of assimilation or white privilege. The construction of Asians as the yellow peril continuously impacted community development, as evident in the Chinese Exclusion Act (1882), Japanese Internment, and other forms of racialized segregation. Recognizing the power of popular cultural images and necessity of combating stereotypes, activists engaged in the Asian American movement positioned a battle against these racialized notions as central to the overall mission and agenda of the movement. One of the earliest efforts came with the organization of Asian Americans for Fair Media (AAFM), which was eventually renamed the Asian American Journalist Association. In 1972, the International Ladies Garment Workers Union (ILGWU) offered an advertisement on many New York subways that built on the longstanding stereotypes of Asians as the yellow peril and dangerous foreigners. Asking the very provocative question, "Has your job been exported to Japan," the billboard blamed Japanese, and by extension all Asian (Americans), for the economic struggles of its membership. This billboard elicited a significant reaction, leading a coalition of people of color and whites to demonstrate at the ILGWU headquarters. This small action spawned the idea for the establishment of AAFM, "a permanent body ... set up to coordinate racism in the media" (Wei, 1993, 51). The AAFP embraced a wide range of strategies to combat stereotypes. First and foremost, it sought to educate Asians about the seriousness of this problem and the omnipresence of deleterious popular images. In New York City, members of AAFP organized a task force to gather a spectrum of examples of racialized images, eventually displaying them on community billboards throughout the city. Increasing awareness was not the only strategy, in that AAFP developed coalitions with other radical organizations of color challenging media bias, while simultaneously educating whites on the serious effects of popular culture on Asian-American identity, community, and survival. Specifically, AAFP disseminated a handbook containing various images and commentary on Asian-American stereotypes and popular culture. Through the many educational efforts, AAFP attempted to elucidate the popular cultural "racial images had 'an explosive psychological force that warps human relationships and wreaks havoc on one's personal dignity" (Wei, 1993, 51). Similar efforts took place throughout the country. In 1980, the Coalition of Asians to Nix Charlie Chan (C.A.N Charlie Chan) organized to protest the making of *Charlie Chan and the Curse of the Dragon Queen*. Embracing dominant white stereotypes of Asian men as passive and effeminate, "Charlie Chan represents the most derogatory stereotype of Chinese, and in general, Asian America. To perpetuate such an inglorious and outdated myth in the 1980s is unwise, odious and insulting" (Wei, 1993; 52). Other organizations attacked the presence of stereotypes on television and within children's books. In the mid–1970s, the Council on Interracial Books for Children organized the Asian American Book Project, examining 66 books published between 1945 and 1975, concluding that, with only a few exceptions, they were "racist, sexist and elitist" (Wei, 1993, 49). The importance and centrality of combating stereotypes continues today, with actions taking place in response to the casting of *Miss Saigon* and the production of racist T-shirts by Abercrombie and Fitch. As with the Native-American movement, the Asian American movement saw the importance of both elucidating the falsehoods of popular constructions of Asians and the necessity for offering alternative images. The importance of popular culture within Asian-American communities, and the effects of stereotypes of Asians on other communities, were not lost upon activists. Setting the foundation, and giving the inspiration for the formation of ethnic studies, the insistence by Asian-American activists on examining popular culture provided a road map for future scholars within the field.

While it is impossible and unnecessary to go through the long list of organizations and efforts within the black and Chicano power movements, it should be clear that efforts to combat racialized stereotypes, often articulated through popular media, were commonplace during the 1970s. Whether protesting the acceptance and articulation of racist ideas from Hollywood or on television, or pushing for alternative images, issues surrounding popular culture were always central to these nationalist movements. The organization of the National Black Media Coalition, Black Citizens for Fair Media, Blkartsouth, and the Black Theater Alliance, all dedicated to combating the cultural information disseminated through popular culture, reveals the importance of popular culture within ethnic studies. The interconnection of these grassroots nationalist movements and the ethnic studies movement, in terms of ideology, political orientation, shared individuals, and overall agenda, reveals the longstanding place occupied by the study of popular culture within ethnic studies.

While the mission of ethnic studies remains linked to its historic antecedents, its contemporary praxis remains very detached from its ideological foundation. The greater emphasis on exploring popular culture within present-day ethnic studies, in examining representation, is often posited in opposition to community work, and thus the original agenda of ethnic studies. The failure to understand both the material consequences— identity formation, cultural enslavement, understanding of race, racial performativity, whites' views of blacks— and the historic presence of studying popular culture, results in the formation of this dichotomy. The creation of an artificial and historically inaccurate binary between those who study culture and those who examine political struggles is problematic to say the least. In addition to the simplicity of such a binary, the failure to see cultural productions as political, and the ignorance about the history of ethnic studies, this oppositional binary disregards the intersectionality of material conditions. Let's take a single example of the prison industrial complex to understand the nature of the discourse. An inter-disciplinary approach, to the prison industrial complex based on a tradi-tion of ethnic studies, might examine the economics of the prison industry, the social effects of massive incarceration of people of color, the history of resistance movements, and the impact of the many racist images (of people of color being savages, criminals) articulated in contemporary films, television, and within video games. The scope of ethnic studies is evident here in the examination of social processes and their effects on people of color, through an interdisciplinary lens. From its inception, and especially at our current historic movement, the interconnectedness of culture, power, and white supremacy necessitates the examination and discussion of popular culture. The continued acceptance of a binary represents a short-sided understanding of the field, especially its historical trajectory.

Teaching Popular Culture in an Ethnic Studies Department

It is nearly impossible to avoid including elements of popular culture in ethnic studies courses, whether as subject or illustration. Indeed, eva-sions of the popular, as our foregoing discussion underscores, would run counter to the history and spirit of the field. With this in mind, we first outline some of the general principles shaping ethnic studies pedagogy; then, we delineate the curricular models employed by faculty and depart-ment to address the relationships between race and popular culture.

Although ethnic studies faculty do not equally share theoretical frame-works, political orientations, or substantive foci, they do address strik-ingly similar aspects of popular culture. Concerned with racism, race relations, or ethnic communities, they emphasize the overlapping issues of power, representation, ideology, and interpretation. Many who teach ethnic studies begin with stereotypes, or images of others that reduce mem-bers of racial or ethnic groups to an arbitrary, binary, essentialized, and often naturalized attribute or set of attributes. For example, many schol-ars begin their classroom discussions of popular culture by creating a list of stereotypes of contemporary minorities. This laundry list, which often covers the entire chalkboard, serves as the basis for discussions of popu-lar culture, as television, music, film, and other cultural products are understood to be the source of these prejudices. In the classroom, stereo-types offer important occasions to question how students and society more generally create, understand, and use objectifications, while ideally clear-ing a space to introduce more accurate, grounded, and critical knowledge.

Consequently, most do not stop with exposing damage images and correcting false consciousness, but push discussions to consider what representations reveal about ways of knowing and being in the world. Attention here shifts from what might be said about the content of a particular set of images, texts, or performances to what they communicate about a broader sociohistorical context. For some, this means getting at the means of production: Who is making popular accounts of race, for whom, under what circumstances? Then there are the modes of reception: Who is consuming such accounts and what are they doing with them? Questions about racialization, or the processes whereby race is made real, reception, and internalization frequently frame such engagements with popular, encouragingly difficult discussions about how individuals and institutions fashion, negotiate, and claim a culturally meaningful and readable (racial) identity. Almost invariably, power underlies approaches to popular culture in ethnic studies, whether rooted in Marxism, poststructuralism, critical race theory, or postcolonialism. In part, this requires faculty and students to account for troubling inequities and their reproduction in performances, narratives, and spaces devoted to pleasure and play: how and why popular texts convince audiences to embrace their constructions of race, what some term hegemony and others false consciousness; how the realm of the popular feeds on the works of racialized community to create novel, fashionable, and meaningful expressions for mass consumption (think of rock and roll for instance); how popular forms produce social groups, regulating their relations, while delimiting their sense of self and other; how and why communities resist and refashion accepted understandings of race circulating in popular texts.

The significance of popular culture in ethnic studies pedagogy is only matched by its fertility as a teaching tool. Five distinct ways of including popular culture in the ethnic studies classroom merit attention. First, ethnic studies faculty frequently endeavor to integrate the popular into their general courses. They consciously mainstream discussion of popular works or artists into broader or introductory courses, as the subject of discussion or as a way to illustrate a concept. For instance, in a first year course on ethnic studies, one might focus a class period on Native-American mascots to theorize racial conflict and play hip-hop music to elaborate on readings concerned with identity formation and cultural resistance. Or, in an introduction to a Native-American studies course, one might ask students to bring in media images to work through historic and contemporary stereotypes; and then, nearer the end of the semester, screen *Smoke Signals* to illustrate the emergence of indigenous media and the importance of cultural sovereignty in the American-Indian experience.

Second, many ethnic studies departments offer specific courses on race and popular culture that establish boundaries by genre or by group. Many ethnic studies programs limit discussions of popular culture to classes on a specific ethnic group. It is common to find offerings like Asian Americans (or African Americans and so on) in popular culture. At the same time, others confine discussions of popular culture and race by medium; for instance, multicultural literature or race in cyberspace. In many cases, programs combine both of these limiting strategies in the construction of their curricula, resulting in courses like Native Americans and film and Asian-American memoirs.

Third, an alternative curricular model, favored by some faculty and departments in ethnic studies, might be best described as comparative; that is, courses that focus on multiple popular forms and a range of ethnic groups, attending to production, representation, and reception. King has taught a course that traces conceptions of racial difference in popular culture over the past two hundred years. It contrasts cinematic, commercial, and exhibitionary depictions of African American, Asian Americans, Latina/os, Native Americans, and Pacific Islanders. For example, University of California, San Diego, which has proven to be a leading voice of innovative ethnic studies scholarship, offers a class entitled, "Ethnic Images in Film," which explores "the social implication of ethnic images" and "the role of film in shaping and reflecting societal power relations." Ethnic studies at Bowling Green State University contains a similar class entitled, "Race, Representation and Culture."

Fourth, popular culture also serves as a wonderful space to push beyond race and consider the multiple, intersecting ways in which power, privilege, and difference shape forms of identification, affiliation, experience, and interaction in contemporary society. Often referred to as the matrix of oppression, such a course seeks to address the interpenetration of race, class, and gender (as well as sexuality and ability in many instances) in popular culture. The introduction of Michael Omi and Howard Winant's ideas of racial formation to discussions of popular culture is but a single of example of how to use ethnic studies scholarship to understand cultural productions. They argue that racial categories are "created, inhabited, transformed and destroyed" through a series of sociohistorical projects that provide common sense ideas of race (Omi and Winant, 1994, 55). In forcing our students to understand the process of constructing racialized meaning, which ultimately results in formalization as a distinct racial category, discussions of popular culture prove to be very useful. Commonsense ideas about race, about what is meant by black or white, emanate from cultural products. Taking a step further, this approach allows one to connect the dots between popular culture, racial formation, and public policy; from the image of the black or Latino criminal in *Sports Illustrated*, on MTV, and in too many movies, to the categorization or essentialization of blacks/Latinos as criminals, to public policy (more police and prisons), a study of race and popular culture goes hand and hand with discussions of white supremacy and public policy.

Fifth, ethnic studies faculty, more recently, following broader trends in the field, have begun to think about the relationships between race and popular culture in a transnational, global context. This model conceptualizes popular culture and race in transit, crossing borders, flowing within and between nations, states, and cultures. A course devoted to the movements of people in an era of globalization has proven productive for King. Contrasting tourists with migrants (often who work in industries devoted serving the former), he has successfully prompted students to think about how constructions of exoticism and authenticity and unequal power relations (whether these be economic, social, or sexual) structure these worlds of pleasure, and in turn, have troubling implications for discussions of identity, choice, and desire. An alternate approach to globalization pushes students to examine the spread of American media around the globe. Focusing on McDonald's, Disney, and the soap opera (among others), it encourages reflection on both production and consumption in terms of cultural imperialism, as well as the significance of these transnational popular forms for local cultural worlds. Other possibilities familiar to the authors include classes on world music, the centrality to popular forms to the formulation of imagined communities within contemporary diasporas, and the emergence of transnational markets and medias within the Americas.

Toward a Concentration on Race and Popular Culture

The many successful courses on race and popular culture, both within and beyond ethnic studies departments, combined with recent interdisciplinary efforts to rethink the curriculum, have produced a context for the creation of concentrations or major tracks devoted to the subject. Indeed, designing such a program of study should appeal to administrators, students, and faculty. Pedagogically, such a concentration promises to arm students with the media and cultural literacy essential to informed and active participation as critical citizens. Practically, a major track in ethnic studies and popular culture undoubtedly would increase enrollments in offerings, while arguably growing majors, precisely because it speaks to students where they are at, about subjects that matter to them often in profound and passionate ways. Intellectually, it allows faculty to connect their research and teach, make connections with peers beyond their home departments, and bond with students within the classroom.

Undoubtedly, the precise content and form of a concentration in race and popular culture will vary from one university to the next; however, we think it useful here to point to the kind of courses central to ongoing efforts at our home institution to create such a major track.

Required Core in Ethnic Studies (12 hours)

Introduction to Ethnic Studies
Cultural Politics of Race and Ethnicity
Research Methods
Seminar in Culture and Power

Concentration on Race and Popular Culture (24 hours)

Introduction to Race and Popular Culture
History of American Popular Culture

Choose One Course for Each of the Following Areas

African American Studies

African Americans and Cinema
Hip Hop America
History of Jazz

Asian/Pacific American Studies

Asian Americans and Film
Exotic/Erotic Visions of the Pacific
Blackness in Asian American Popular Culture

Latina/o Studies

Popular Cultural Citizenship: Latina/o Popular Culture
Latina/os and Film
Toward an History of Latina/o Music in American Cultures

Native-American Studies

Indigenous Media: Politics and Aesthetics
Native Americans and Film
Playing Indian

Comparative Approaches

Capitalizing on Race: Advertising, Marketing, and Multiculturalism
Digital Diversity
Race, Gender and Sport in American Society
Representing Cultural Difference
Stereotypes in the Media

Global Perspective

Debating Cultural Imperialism
Global Television
Orientalisms
Traveling Cultures
War, Media and Society: Vietnam to the Persian Gulf
World Music

SENIOR CAPSTONE (3 HOURS) CHOOSE ONE

Independent Study/Senior Thesis
Internship/Externship

The proposed concentration has a core of classes in ethnic studies, designed to introduce students to the substantive interests, political commitments, competing theories, and ongoing dialogues central to the field. It also offers the essential skills for the critical study of race and popular culture. On this foundation, students take courses devoted to specific ethnic groups as well as one course from a cluster designated as (respectively) comparative, global, critical, and theoretical. To integrate and apply learning, students complete a senior capstone during their final year, either a senior thesis rooted in independent study or an internship.

The absence of an ethnic studies department need not preclude the creation of a concentration devoted to race and popular culture. Faculty from a range of departments, including English, sociology, anthropology, communications, history, rhetoric, and women's studies, who have an interest in popular culture, race, or their articulations can work together to establish an interdisciplinary program of study. Such an initiative would require first the assessment of existing curricular offerings to determine which satisfy the ideals and aspirations of the working group, and then, the creation of novel courses, for instance, an introductory course on race and popular culture or a course that examines the themes of the concentration globally.

Conclusions

To close, we return to where we began: Race is central to popular culture; hence, popular culture has been central to ethnic studies; and race (as taken up in ethnic studies) should be central to the study of popular culture. We trust that many readers appreciate that ethnic studies is not merely replicating the work of other disciplines, nor borrowing established methodologies and theories. Indeed, our discussion has sought to direct attention to the vitality of ethnic studies and the uniqueness of its contribution to the study and teaching of popular culture.

Scholars and teachers in ethnic studies, do not merely examine stereotypes and racist images of people of color or their place in popular culture. This defines a number of other fields, including the field of popular culture. There tends to be a greater focus on plot, with people of color reduced to a cog in the larger issue of economics (profit), spectatorship, or at best societal prejudice. For example, Leonard presented his work at a popular culture conference, where one of its participants challenged his argument that video games represent a modern form of minstrelsy with claims that game content reflects an effort to design marketable plots.

In part this derives from distinct understandings of race and racism in ethnic studies and other disciplines. Whereas a majority of scholars in more traditional disciplines treat racism as a historical trope and embrace prejudice models (stereotypes; racism as ignorance), ethnic studies works from the premise of white supremacy existing as the guiding principle of American life. Popular culture merely reflects these dominant ideas, and the efforts to maintain white economic, political, and social dominance. These desperate foundations lead to a completely different understanding of the nature of popular culture in our society, while affording novel curricular and pedagogical innovations.

As a consequence, ethnic studies is poised to make unique and vital contributions to the examination of popular culture. Embracing a social constructionist position that recognizes the material reality of race, many ethnic studies scholars use racial formation as the basis of their work. Whether talking about immigration laws, Jim Crow, lynchings, or popular culture, ethnic studies examines how these projects contribute to our understanding of race, ultimately leading to the establishment of racial categories to explain and maintain inequality. Those engaging in popular cultural research through rhetoric, sociology, or history tend to treat race as real, or as a valid basis of research. In other words, ethnic studies treats race as a dynamic process, whereas other disciplines tend to see race as a fixed category of inquiry.

Finally in "studying the ethnic," the work outside of ethnic studies often lacks the necessary consciously political edge. It is crucial to contextualize our examination of popular culture within the material conditions that give rise to poverty, inequality, the prison industrial complex and state violence. Given these realities and the deleterious affects on people of color, it is futile, and contemptible, to treat cultural productions as pure texts. To detach popular culture and the dissemination of stereotypes from the conditions of white supremacy reflects the acceptance of studying ethnicity, rather than ethnic studies.

References

Bulmer, Martin, and John Solmos, Editors. *Ethnic and Racial Studies Today*. New York: Routledge, 1999.

Butler, Johnnella E., Editor. *Color-Line to Borderlands: The Matrix of American Ethnic Studies*. Seattle: University of Washington Press, 2001.

Butler, Johnnella E., and John C. Walter, Editors. *Transforming the Curriculum: Ethnic Studies and Women's Studies*. Albany: State University of New York Press, 1981.

Gutierrez, Ramon A. "Ethnic Studies: Its Evolution in American Colleges and Universities." In David Theo Goldberg, Editor, *Multiculturalism: A Critical Reader*. Cambridge, MA: Blackwell.

King, C. Richard. "Defensive Dialogues: Native American Mascots, Anti–Indianism, and Educational Institutions." *Studies in Media & Information Literacy Education*, 2.1 (2002). *http://www.utpress.utoronto.ca/journal/ejournals/simile*

King, C. Richard. "Arguing Over Images: Native American Mascots and Race. In R.A. Lind Editor, *Race/Gender/Media: Considering Diversity Across Audiences, Content, and Producers*. Boston: AB-Longman, 2003.

King, C. Richard. *Telling Achievements: Native American Athletes in Sport and Society*. Lincoln: University of Nebraska, 2004.

King, C. Richard, & Charles F. Springwood. (2001a). *Beyond the Cheers: Race as Spectacle in College Sports*. Albany: State University of New York Press, 2001a.

King, C. Richard, & Charles F. Springwood, Editors. *Team Spirits: Essays on the History and Significance of Native American Mascots*. Lincoln: University of Nebraska, 2001b.

King, C. Richard, Ellen J. Staurowsky, Lawrence Baca, Laurel Davis, & Cornel Pewewardy. "Of Polls and Race Prejudice: *Sports Illustrated's* Errant 'Indian Wars.'" *Journal of Sport and Social Issues*, 26 (2002): 382–403.

Leonard, David. "Live in Your World, Play in Ours." *ColorLines*, Winter 2002/2003.

Omi, Michael, & Howard Winant. *Racial Formation in the United States: From the 1960s to the 1990s*, 2nd ed. New York: Routledge, 1994.

Smith, Paul Chaat, and Robert Allen Warrior. *Like a Hurricane: The Indian Movement from Alcatraz to Wounded Knee*. New York: New Press, 1996.

Storey, John. *An Introduction to Cultural Theory and Popular Culture*, 2nd ed. Athens: University of Georgia Press, 1996.

Strinati, Dominic. *An Introduction of Theories of Popular Culture*. New York: Routledge, 1995.

Van Deburg, William L. *New Day in Babylon: The Black Power Movement and American Culture, 1965–1975.* Chicago: University of Chicago Press, 1992.

Wang, Ling-Chi. "Chronology of Ethnic Studies at U.C. Berkeley." *Newsletter of the Department of Ethnic Studies at U.C. Berkeley,* (1997).

Wei, William. *The Asian American Movement.* Philadelphia: Temple University Press, 1993.

Wing, Bob. "'Educate to Liberate!': Multiculturalism and the Struggle for Ethnic Studies." *Colorlines,* http://www.arc.org/C_Lines/CLArchives/story2_2_01.html), 1999.

Yang, Philip Q. *Ethnic Studies: Issues and Approaches.* Albany: State University of New York Press, 2000.

15

The Value of Teaching Popular Culture in the Community College

A Stew of Abstract, Concrete, Serious, and Not-So-Serious Notions

LYNN G. BARTHOLOME

Kathy Rodriguez sat in her car and tapped the steering wheel anxiously. "What a day," she thought. "First the sitter bails out on me, then I spend my entire lunch hour typing a report, and now, a traffic jam." She had hoped to reach campus early enough to get an extra 15 minutes of study time in before her psychology exam. Although she had managed to prepare some, she didn't feel ready to take the test. And on top of everything else, she was just plain exhausted. "Just three more hours of class—then I can go home and go to bed—right after I put a load of clothes in the washer." What Kathy doesn't want to think about is the fact that she will have to replay the entire scenario tomorrow.

Kathy's overfilled life exemplifies that of a typical community college student. On any given day, there are thousands of students, just like Kathy, attending classes at their local "JC." Community colleges have educational environments and missions that are uniquely different from four-year colleges and universities, because these two-year bastions of higher education cater to the lifestyles of the learners. Some of the environmental differences are directly attributed to the diverse characteristics and motivation of the student population — the community college student is generally older and usually employed. Some learners are on campus to be retrained or change careers and may not have attended school for quite some time (*http://www.maricopa.edu*).

Here are some of the common characteristics of the typical community college learner:

- 80 percent to 90 percent are employed; 50 percent hold down full-time jobs.
- Over 70 percent of students attend part-time; the students are almost exclusively commuters.
- The average age of a community college student is 29; 46 percent of community college students are 25 years or older.
- 58 percent are female students; approximately one out of three students is a woman over 25.
- Students are often married, have family responsibilities, or still live at home.
- Minority students account for 30 percent of the student population (American Association of Community Colleges).

There are some distinct advantages to a community college education. First, the tuition at a community college is more affordable, often less than half that of a four-year state school. This can be a determining factor, especially for those making career changes, needing to support family incomes, or wanting to "refresh" certain skills or knowledge. Second, the remedial education courses offered at most community colleges keep options of degree programs and vocational training open to those learners who need improvement in reading, writing, and computation skills. Furthermore, people can continue to enroll in two-year college courses at any point in their lives; in fact, many return to the community college again and again to keep up with the technology that pervades work and leisure activities.

A final reason to attend a community college is to increase income and opportunities. Nick Isenberg, a Colorado Mountain College public information officer, recently completed a study which concluded that community college graduates who transfer to four-year schools often earn more across most majors, on average $2,052 more in starting pay, than their university classmates who received their entire education at a four-year institution. Isenberg related, "Many people used to think of community colleges as 'schools of last resort,' where you go when you can't get into a 'good' college. This research shows that for many people, especially those who go to college primarily to increase their income and opportunities, community colleges should be their first choice." The reason that community colleges succeed is because they are open to everyone. These institutions get excellent results by letting people in, not by keeping them out ("Transfer Students Earn More" *Community College Times,* 2003).

So, as you can see, on any given day, the community college professor enters a classroom populated with students of all ages, backgrounds, and levels of educational preparedness. How do we get everyone on the same page? How do we teach the lessons that need to be taught to such an assorted assemblage of characters? Perhaps the answer can be found by utilizing common culture — the culture of everyday things, or *popular culture.*

What exactly do we mean by popular culture? In its broadest sense, it is the culture "of the people." When we define the word *culture,* we must think of it in anthropological terms. Culture is the distinct practices, artifacts, institutions, customs, and values of a particular racial, religious, or social group. In his book, *Against Academia: The History of the Popular Culture Association/American Culture Association and Popular Culture Movement 1967–1988,* Ray Browne (1989), the father of popular culture explained:

> Popular Culture to us was the everyday, the vernacular, the heritage and ways of life that we inherited from our predecessors, used and passed on to our descendants. It was the cultural environment we lived in. Popular culture is mainly disseminated by the mass media [word of mouth, print, radio, pictures, movies, television] but not necessarily limited to such media of dissemination. Popular culture probably should not include some ten per cent of so-called elite culture but it should include all folk culture. It is by definition international and comparative in scope, with no time limit; it is not restricted to the present [24].

Because popular culture is concerned with the everyday, it reflects and influences people's ways of living; because popular culture can be linked to a specific time and place, it is transitory, subject to change, and often an initiator of change (Petracca and Sorapare, 2001, 4).

Why study popular culture? First and foremost, studying popular culture teaches us about ourselves. We observe what is essential to us; popular culture reveals commonly held beliefs about ideals such as justice, success, love, and beauty. We can also ascertain the social contradictions and conflicts between races, genders, and generations. Perhaps the greatest argument for studying popular culture focuses on the influence that it exerts on us. By analyzing popular culture, we can assess and ultimately resist this influence (Petracca and Sorapare, 6).

Integrating popular culture into the curriculum at the community college provides an opportunity to learn a radically unfamiliar skill (i.e., critical analysis) through deeply familiar material (the surface of popular culture). For example, after reading *Meditations* three times, Omar, a first year student in an introductory philosophy course, still could not understand Descartes' evil genius. At the same time, Omar could give a detailed description of the problem of knowledge revealed in the plot of the cult film, *Matrix*. It is such a small task, with huge pedagogical rewards, to discuss *Matrix* before delving into *Meditations*. It helps students like Omar to connect something quite abstract to something concrete in their lives. The teaching of popular culture gives community college instructors a much broader spectrum in which to place their students' learning potential.

The first two years of college introduce students to modes of inquiry, historical contexts, and standards of judgment — all of which can be introduced very efficiently when applied to cultural artifacts with which the beginning student is already acquainted. In an introductory literature course it can be beneficial to have students watch an episode of *Seinfeld* before attempting Shakespeare's *Much Ado About Nothing*. This enables the student to compare the show about nothing to the play about nothing. Associations can also be drawn between Jerry and Benedick, Elaine and Beatrice, Kramer and Dogberry, and even Newman and Don John. While Shakespeare's language may be a bit formidable for students, his posture and milieu are quite familiar.

Popular culture facilitates the transmission of ideas from "long ago and far away" into recognizable social and behavioral venues. While studying the characteristics of Greek tragedy and Greek tragic plays such as *Antigone*, I sometimes have my students "experience" the modern version of tragedy — a short segment from the *Jerry Springer Show*, recently voted the worst program in the history of television. We first discuss the importance of the Greek chorus, particularly how the chorus chants and reminds the audience of the cultural values the play is trying to inspire. We even talk about the importance of the leader in separating from the rest of the chorus and speaking to the audience. We then watch about five minutes of a taped episode of *Springer* in which audience members chant, "take it off" to female participants; additionally, the audience rebukes the guests sitting on the "high stage" by lambasting them with negative comments. Could Aristotle deny that the audience experiences a catharsis? Viewers can also stir up the emotions of pity and fear by purchasing bumper stickers with slogans such as "You think you've got problems," "We talk to the freaks ... so you don't have to," and "Where do you find these people?" on the Springer Web site. At the conclusion of each broadcast, Jerry sits on a stool and preaches his "moral" to the home audience. Thus, the students can perceive how the classics continue to influence even contemporary genres, such as the talk show.

Exploring popular culture provides commonsense building blocks to more traditional studies, especially for students in their first year of college. Analyzing a current hit song or film bridges logically into analyzing a poem or novel; studying a street or mall subculture creates a conduit for wider studies in sociology and anthropology. Learners who become savvy about mass media develop an equivalent understanding of information-based economy.

Often dismissed as simple and crude, popular culture can be rewarding if respected and examined more closely. When a professor includes popular culture in the curriculum, it authenticates the culture that students already value. There ceases to be a "we-they attitude." Learners don't have to choose between watching television and appreciating Greek tragedy because there is room for both. Taking away the common culture that students are aware of and accustomed to is counterproductive. Utilizing it constructively produces an environment where students are involved, motivated and willing to become engaged because they are already "experts." Think of it in this way: many "old books" deal with the same issues that we still wrestle with today. For example, in 1818 Mary Shelley raised questions about the dignity of life and the limits of human experimentation in her enduring classic, *Frankenstein* (which, by the way, was considered at the time to be a work of popular fiction). More recently we have dealt with this issue of "humanity" or the lack of it, in films such as Ridley Scott's *Blade Runner* and Steven Spielberg's *AI Artificial Intelligence*. Where it might take days or weeks for the student to become familiar and somewhat accommodating to Shelley's stylized discourse, after viewing these films just once, the student gets the message — what exactly defines "life" and from what perspective do we humans really understand it? And at the same time, while human beings are not inherently evil, they are capable of acting without regard for their fellow man; therefore, is humanity's future really guaranteed? While Shelley's novel is a difficult read for many college freshmen, viewing the replicants' fight to survive in *Blade Runner* or the android boy David's search for love and acceptance in *AI* immediately captures a student's imagination. This becomes a catalyst for serious discussion and exploration — thus a longstanding ideology becomes vital, accessible, and fresh.

With the most widely diverse population in higher education, community college students often have very little in common except for their immersion in popular culture. A humanities instructor trying to demonstrate the pursuit of the American dream might be hard-pressed to find a teaching method that will reach both the 16 and the 60 year old; popular culture eliminates this dilemma. Using contemporary examples, such as Ruben Stoddard's victory on *American Idol*, an enormously popular Fox Network reality based show viewed by a wide-ranging cross-section of Americans, illustrates that anyone — even a working-class boy from Alabama — can realize his dream with hard work and perseverance.

Popular culture almost inevitably raises questions about social class; community college students often belong to a class that has been encouraged not to think critically about this central issue. For example, on a typical evening of network TV, a viewer watches programs that make a conscious attempt at defining his or her economic and social lifestyle. But do they really? If you look at the homes of TV sitcom families such as those on *Everyone Loves Raymond* or *My Wife and Kids*, you see furnishings, décor, and ways of life well beyond the means of the average community college learner. This "sleight of hand" by network producers and corporate interests ultimately deludes the viewer into perceiving that everyone, including himself or herself, lives like this or should. Additionally, blue-collar employment is nearly invisible on network television. Even when it is, on programs like *The George Lopez Show* and the 1990s hit *Roseanne*, the higher standard of living noticeable in their home interiors does not correlate with their occupations. Rarely does the plot revolve around common "sticky situations" of the blue-collar worker, such as late mortgage payments or delinquent utility bills. Focusing on aspects of popular culture, therefore, affords the learner an opportunity to examine his or her actual role or status in society and the possibility or impossibility of effecting change.

Another reason to incorporate popular culture in the classroom is because of its interactive nature. Community college students engage with its manifestations, perform and observe its practices, and produce and consume its artifacts. It is the perfect laboratory for hands-on learning. An integral assignment in my popular culture course is the creation of a popular culture game. Students invent a board or video game based on some aspect of common culture. They fashion a playing board, game pieces, and other components based on a subject they have carefully researched. Complete game instructions are also provided, including the object of play. This exercise develops critical thinking skills, encourages proficiency in library and Internet research, and provides practice in writing. One memorable example was a board game based on the exploits of former senator Robert Packwood. Entitled *What About Bob? The Game of*

Sexual Harassment, the student inventor thoroughly researched the political career of the senator and examined sexual harassment laws that govern the workplace. The object of the game was to determine whether Senator Packwood was actually guilty of violating sexual harassment laws in his everyday dealings with female employees. The game board was both original and colorful; in the center was large picture of Senator Packwood with a ponderous look on his face. The game pieces were representations of his female employees. Through this exercise, the student honed his critical thinking and writing skills, learned valuable lessons about politics, the law, and the judicial system, and had fun in the process.

Which brings me to my final motivation for employing popular culture in the community college classroom. Even when you work with it intensely and rigorously, popular culture is, by its very nature, *fun.* If you were a two-year college student carrying 15 or more credit hours and working 25 to 45 hours a week at a minimum wage job, would it kill you to have a little fun? Popular culture perpetually promotes discussion, participation, imagination, and evaluation.

Put another way, popular culture is essentially multidisciplinary. One cannot conduct a popular culture course exclusively through lecture. Done well, the teaching and learning of popular culture occurs in the linguistic as well as the visual, auditory, and musical learning domains. These last three domains are where I find most of my community college students. They need to see the material and hear the material in order to understand the material. This is the true value of teaching popular culture in the community college — it allows me to go where my students are.

References

American Association of Community Colleges. Home page. *http://www.aacc.nche.edu.*
Browne, Ray B. *Against Academia: The History of the Popular Culture Association/American Culture Association and Popular Culture Movement 1967–1988.* Bowling Green, OH: Popular Press, 1989.
Community College Times "Transfer Students Earn More Than Traditional Classmates." June 10, 2003. *http://www.aacc.nche.edu/PrintTemplate.cfm?Section=Times_Articles....*
Maricopa Community College. Home page. *http://www.marcopa.edu.*
Petracca, Michael, and Madeleine Sorapure. *Common Culture: Reading and Writing About American Popular Culture.* Upper Saddle River, NJ: Prentice-Hall, 2001.
Springer, Jerry. Home page. *http://www.jerryspringer.com/store/.*

Acknowledgments: Thanks to my colleagues at Monroe Community College— Bob DeFelice, Beth Laidlaw, Jay Nelson, Phil Snyder, Tony Vinci, and Holly Wheeler— who provided many of the ideas and comments contained in this piece. You continue to be an inspiration for all of us.

16

Putting Methodology Where the Mouth Is

Integrating Popular Culture into the Traditional High School Curriculum

KATHERINE LYNDE

I was misguided and crazy—at least that's what my professors told me when I proudly announced my plans to become a high school English teacher. More to the point, they said, "You don't want to do that!" Fortunately, I remained steadfast to the dream. I had a vision of what *could be* for high school students, and it was drastically different from the one that my college freshmen English composition students lamentably described as their own public education experiences: literature they never truly appreciated and teachers who did not make enough effort to make sure it would happen. It is certainly possible for solid classic literature to be relevant to the present, and students relate to course material—even if they are reading *Beowulf*, the oldest surviving epic poem in the English language—if that material is connected to popular culture, something they believe they understand well. Can students analyze critically and fully comprehend classic texts without relevance? Of course. On the other hand, teachers should supplement lesson plans with whatever means guarantee deepest understanding for all students.

Don't get me wrong; the dream did not turn out to be a breeze. Teaching high school, and doing it thoroughly, is an overwhelming commitment. I choose to spend most of my time with human beings who are caught between the end of childhood and the beginning of adulthood. Everything in their existence is felt with more intensity than it will be at any other time in their lives: hormones, relationships, independence, extracurricular activities, experimentation, and decisions about their futures often take priority over education. Add to the mix that 17 to 18 year olds tend to be the centers of their own universes, and a teacher's effectiveness can suffer a precipitous decline. However, if the elements that seem earth-shatteringly important in their lives can be illustrated, advised, or solved within the confines of my classroom and in connection with British literature, they form a friendship with that literature. Yes, that's what I said: friendship, because hostility toward a difficult text dissipates exponentially with complete comprehension.

Writer Michael Crichton might readily agree. While Crichton is known for writing and producing mass media hits, such as the *Jurassic Park* film series and television's *ER*, he recognizes the value of the classics. When he discovered that a friend was using *Beowulf* as the springboard for a new college course entitled "The Great Bores," Crichton took him to task: How could anyone call *Beowulf* a bore? Crichton pointed out that *Beowulf* contains all of the aspects of today's best action adventure stories. Subsequently, he set out on a mission to prove his point. In 1976, Crichton's answer, *Eaters of the Dead*, hit bookstore shelves.[1] His novel attempts to place the epic in a historical context in combination with Arab Ibn Fadlan's later journey through Viking territory. In 2000, his point was even more vividly demonstrated with the release of the film *The 13th Warrior*, a screenplay based on his novel. *Beowulf* becomes everything Crichton proclaimed, and even the most reluctant teenage reader is forced to concur. Thus, a high school student can trace the evolution of *Beowulf* from prerecorded history to a modern film for which they would eagerly pay $7.50 to see at the theater (Figure 16.1).[2] Instead of the cornerstone of British literature as the kickoff to literary boredom, Beowulf becomes intriguing enough to carry an entire course. Michael Crichton understands marrying a classic work to popular culture.

Even if Crichton had never taken the dare and written the novel, options to integrate popular culture with *Beowulf* exist if a teacher so desires. Within the past five years, my county school system adopted new textbooks for high school English classes. Senior English classes currently use McDougal Littell's *The Language of Literature*, a book that luckily includes prompts relating its selections to current student experiences and popular culture, often found in a question-and-answer section entitled "Connect to Life" but not restricted to the Teacher's Annotated Edition.[3] The added beauty lives in the teacher's ability to tweak a prompt to best

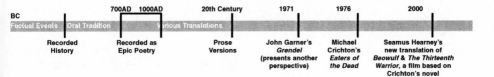

Figure 16.1

suit particular areas of inquiry or subject matter. Shortly after 9/11, I assigned a short response to my seniors and asked that each student choose the prompt that best sparked the imagination and easily provided enough support to ensure good composition. The responses were so well written and generated such great discussion that I have used them repeatedly. The prompts are as follows:

1. In *Beowulf's* Denmark, the Geatish hero must battle Grendel, a monster isolated from Danish society. After thinking about the Danes' possible culpability in Grendel's creation and reading the excerpts from John Gardner's *Grendel*, ponder that issue. In truth, every society has its monsters. Discuss how society has created one its own "monsters" based on your readings, observations, and experiences.[4]

2. Consider what the epic *Beowulf* reveals about Anglo-Saxon attitudes toward the following topics: courage, fate, the span of life, the deceased. Write a response comparing one of these attitudes and customs with those practiced today. This becomes especially appropriate in light of recent events.[5]

Both topics connect the Anglo-Saxon mindset to a student's experience and observations in modern times; however, the aim of each was extremely specific for Fall 2001: the first prompt required connections to areas of diversity, my school district's special-effort focus; the second prompt offered a forum for students to relate the literature to the terrorist attack in New York City. Fortunately, both topics are timeless, as are the thematic elements of *Beowulf*. A student can take the response as far as writing about foreign policy or make the response as personal as relating an actual experience in the high school or home. Coincidentally, when students are encouraged to associate literature with personal issues, not only does the teacher enjoy greater reading and grading pleasure due to the sheer variety of subject angles, but also the student has limited opportunities for plagiarism, a growing problem for educational institutions. Students *want* to write about themselves; it's part of the package that makes them who they are, and if students are careful to connect their experiences to the original text and to illustrate their claims with sufficient evidence, then both creating literary relevance and enhancing composition skills have been accomplished — *Voilà*!

On the other hand, literature, history, popular culture, and relevance become inextricably interwoven in another assignment used with *Beowulf* and my vocational-track general English students. These particular students frequently do not see the significance of studying what is traditionally recognized as good literature. Regularly infusing popular culture brings course literature to life and makes our time together more meaningful. They do read *Beowulf*, they do study the evolution of the text, and they do write short responses; however, they take the process one important motivational step further. General English students know local history; most of their families have lived in our college town for generations. They realize that Beowulf — the heroic, superhuman character — has become mythologized over the millennia, but actual historical events and a real-life human being most likely existed as the source. Accordingly, I assign students *The Myth and Legend Research Project* (Appendix 16.1). For the purposes of the assignment, students must research local folklore, choose the myth or legend that most interests them, find the source of the folklore, trace the storyline through what has become urban legend, and present their findings to their classmates while using a variety of media. Students gravitate to this project; young people who typically do not complete assignments outside of the classroom suddenly travel for on-site visits, make videos, conduct interviews, visit the town hall, type up reports, and spend quality time with each other. School is fun, even if only temporarily. This project would work equally well with upper level students. As a matter of fact, my college-track students desperately want to do the same project and demand to know why they are excluded. Doesn't every teacher daydream about students begging to do assignments?

Let's leave *Beowulf* and delve into what it takes for me and for my students to connect with other and to take popular culture seriously. First and foremost, teachers and students are in the learning process together. I learn from my students every day. We talk about life in and around talking about the required subject matter. We laugh — a lot. I open myself to them, and they, in turn, open themselves to me and to each other. Lectures, discussions, assignments, activities, methodology, and personality combine to create an atmosphere that fosters sharing; teaching English plays a notable role in the process because students, critical thinking, exploration, and communication combine as a natural part of the core discipline. Contrary to some educators' opinions, a teacher's closeness to students does not hamper deeper learning or ruin discipline in the classroom. Using educational time to build relationships actually creates mutual respect. Recognition of individuality is one key to both actualization and productivity; although my classroom environment is very interactive, disruptive, disrespectful behavior is never an issue. A sense of community becomes the overriding factor for both control and for learning.

Popular culture guru Marshall Fishwick defines popular culture as "what most people think most of the time about most subjects."[6] Of course, sharing common perceptions is useful in the classroom. Conversely, sharing unpopular beliefs and challenging popular perceptions is enlightening. Students need to be familiar with popular culture and its trappings in order to recognize and possibly validate what lies inside the average domain *and* affixes itself on the outer fringes of the sociological bell curve — and teenagers fall into both categories. Truthfully, most of them are still trying to define themselves, and often, popular culture becomes their dictionary. How else should they gauge their beliefs and behavior? For them, popular culture *is* normalcy. What happens if the dictionary by which they define themselves suddenly changes its terms?

For students enrolled in "11AP: Language and Composition," critical reading, rhetorical strategies, and grammatical structure are paramount. During the early stages of the course, students continuously omit necessary details required for truly great writing. I want to teach my students to show rather than to tell, and I want to teach it at the beginning of the school year. Consequently, one of their first assignments is entitled *The Personal Zine* (Appendix 16.2). The project is designed to replace the personal narrative essay so many teachers employ as a "get to know you and your skills" tactic. Instead of using words to describe themselves, students must define themselves *with* popular culture. Even though some students knit their eyebrows in perplexity on the day the zine is assigned, most of their classmates anxiously begin planning while I am still explaining the directions. Project requirements coincide with standard essay format; the design intentionally forces students to illustrate rather than state their assertions. Perhaps the most revealing part of the zine is the reflection paper that concludes the process. In retrospect, students describe the process of compiling their personal zines. Overwhelmingly, zine creators profess how much they learned about themselves and confess surprise at how easily they are defined by popular culture.

Ironically, cultural inscription process appreciation can be instilled with an evening's jaunt to Wal-Mart, one of America's newest popular culture icons. All this assignment requires is paper, pencil, and close observation. In the past, I have asked students to stand in the toy aisles of our local Wal-Mart Superstore and record the flow of young boys and girls. They must note where boys stop and show interest and which toys draw the girls' attention. Results rarely waver: boys will be boys, and girls will be girls. It becomes readily obvious that gender typing is well under way. Before leaving the store, students read and analyze toy packaging, especially of the items that appeared popular during the observation period. They begin to realize that cultural sorting and role determination begin early, even in the confines of a town or city's seemingly benign materialistic wonderland.

In case I have inadvertently implicated any negativity associated with high school students, I will dispel it now. The roller-coaster that is their lives makes teaching them pure joy. The tangible energy that exists in the high school classroom sustains my desire to teach, feeds my insatiable curiosity, and keeps me young at heart. In fact, I turned to my students in preparation for this article, asking my seniors to respond directly to questions regarding popular culture and its influence in their lives. Student definitions sounded oddly alike, which is not a bad result. In light of Fishwick's definition of popular culture, one student's answer resounds more succinctly: "It's all those things that everybody buys into."[7] Of course, in teenagerspeak, he means what *most* people buy into.

Apparently students are astute in their knowledge of what popular culture is; in sharp contrast, some are eager to deny its pervasive influence on their own lives — they are too cool for it; after all, these young people are in the throes of establishing independence. But, as my husband reminded me recently, there is no better audience for popular culture than high school students. They live in the moment. To them, back in the day was yesterday, and antiquity was a decade ago. They live, eat, and breathe popular culture. It is permanence vs. transience. They can be distraught, intrigued, laughing, immature, serious, and wise beyond their years in the course of 45 minutes. During the same period, students may discuss a trivial matter and imagine it as lasting an eternity. Popular culture is just as unpredictable, yet it can dictate attitude, belief, and behavior. Certainly, popular culture is more than just what the majority thinks — it is also about what lasts and what does not. What is the magical formula that dictates longevity?

While assessing students' personal zines in 2003, I discovered that many students included advertisements for or articles on the band The Vines. Because they had ignited my desire to know, I purchased their CD. Should I have bothered? I have not heard anything about The Vines since I spent my $14.95 at the record store. I guess they are not the next Beatles.

It makes me wonder if J. K. Rowling will have the staying power of Emily Dickinson. The fact that something affects people today does not mean that it will affect people in the next generation, the next century, or the next millennium. Understanding the machinations of popular culture offers students valuable assessment skills for their own culture.

In the October 27, 2003, *Time* magazine article, "Inside the New SAT," John Cloud discusses the restructuring of the test traditionally considered higher education's gatekeeper. In response to the banishment of the verbal analogy section, he quoted University of Iowa psychology professor David Lohman as saying: "Analogical thinking is at the very foundation of how we make use of old knowledge to understand new things."[8] His statement is the perfect summation of my pedagogy. Relating literature, both old and new, to what students feel that they already know — their own culture and lives— is as close as I will get to teaching popular culture for the foreseeable future, no matter how much I envision it as a separate course. Lohman goes on to say, "Students listen to a lecture and say, 'How did that relate to what I know?'" That's exactly my point. Effective teaching should relate material not only to its own historical context but also to a present context. It is how humans make sense.

Even though popular culture shifts constantly, pulling the majority out of its comfort zone is laborious and tiring. Hop on the bandwagon and help the cause. If you are a high school student, encourage teachers to incorporate popular culture into the curriculum and into the classroom. If you are a college student, imagine how much more you might have enjoyed the high school curriculum if it had seemed relevant, and seriously consider joining the teaching force. If you are a parent, become involved in planning and implementing effective teaching strategies for helping your teenager understand cultural forces. If you are a teacher and have not tried any of the methodology presented, try it; you may be amazed at your students' increased knowledge retention. If you are a teacher who creatively blends popular culture into your curriculum, rock on; spread the word to your colleagues. If you are a high school teacher who teaches popular culture, contact me; we need to talk. You can find me in room E-5, where I always am happy, sometimes go crazy, and rarely if ever feel misguided.

Appendix 1

THE MYTH AND LEGEND RESEARCH PROJECT

DIRECTIONS:

For this research project, you may work independently or form a group by choosing one to four of your classmates (no more than five members per group). Please choose carefully, because you will be spending extensive time working together; all group members will be expected to share in the research process and presentation. Shop through various Virginia myths or legends (preferably something from your local region). Select one that particularly captures your interest. Have fun finding its original history and tracing that history to what people say or believe about it today. This project will require more than visiting the location and taking pictures or filming a video for your presentation. Different areas of research might include the following:

➢ Interviews
➢ Available Photos
➢ Televised Videos
➢ Reference Books
➢ The Internet
➢ Site Visits
➢ Microfiche (old news stories)
➢ The Public Library
➢ Town Halls or Municipal Buildings

This is by no means a complete list of possibilities, but it does provide starting points for a thorough research project.

EXPECTATIONS:

• On the day of the presentation, your group will provide both factual (or thought to be factual) history and trace that history to today's story.
• All group members will be involved in the presentation. This is not a time for one or two group members to shine while others passively rest against the blackboard.
• Your group will use various methods to present your information (both audio and visual)
• Your group will submit all elements of the research project on the day of the presentation (with the exception of the course proposal).
• The presentation will be thorough AND entertaining.

RESEARCH PROJECT ELEMENTS:
- ➤ Formal Research Proposal
- ➤ Activity Log
- ➤ Participation Log
- ➤ Contribution Log
- ➤ The Presentation
- ➤ Works Cited Page

DUE DATES: _____

THE MYTH AND LEGEND RESEARCH PROJECT
MATERIALS REQUIRED FOR PRESENTATION DAY

- ➤ Activity Log
- ➤ Participation Log
- ➤ Contribution Log
- ➤ All Presentation Materials
- ➤ Reflection Paper

Activity Log:

The Activity Log is a list of dates and activities spent in preparation for your presentation. This may necessitate that you use approximate dates.

Available Library Dates: (Based on reserved library days for the class period)
- ➤ Several vocabulary workshops that count have been used for research purposes
- ➤ Friday, 10/10
- ➤ Monday, 10/13
- ➤ Thursday, 10/16
- ➤ Tuesday, 10/28
- ➤ Wednesday, 10/29
- ➤ Thursday, 10/30

Participation Log:

The Participation Log is an honest listing of activity dates and those group members who attended the planned activity. This listing is designed to fairly assign credit for participation in the project. Accordingly, group members who failed to "pull their weight" will not receive full credit.

Contribution Log:

This log must contain the elements of the presentation that were provided by different group members. For instance, individuals will have provided various items in the research process, typed logs and the paper, taken pictures, done the artwork, etc. Be honest in attributing work, because I assume your group members do not want someone getting full credit when no contribution was actually made to the presentation.

Presentation Materials:

The presentation cannot go as planned if all materials are not available at the time, so be sure to bring whatever items you promised to have on-hand for the presentation. This includes guest speakers.

The Reflection Paper:

You must have a typed essay that is a **minimum** of one, full page written in formal English. It can include any or all of the following areas of the presentation process:

➢ The selection of your topic
➢ What you liked best and least about the topic
➢ What you liked best and least about doing the project
➢ How well working together or individually worked for you
➢ Ease and/or difficulty experienced in conducting the research and completing the project
➢ What you learned from doing the project
➢ In retrospect, what you would change about doing the project
➢ Whether the project is worth pursuing for classes in the future

The Presentation:

All group members should be prepared to participate verbally in Friday's presentation. Group members not participating will be penalized accordingly.

Appendix 2

The Personal Zine
Creative Project: 1st Six Weeks
11AP Language and Composition

General Overview:

Yes, I want to get to know you — everything about you, and this should be an entertaining alternative to the "All About Me" paper. As the opening project of this school year, you will design a personal magazine. The objective is for you to put together both articles and advertisements that serve as a description of the elements, preferences, and characteristics that make up the package that is YOU. Anyone who should happen to pick up and thumb/read through your zine should know the editor of the publication (you). The reader should understand what the editor likes, believes, endorses, hates, and discredits. This project will require honest introspection on your part. It asks that you put yourself into visual and textual form without providing a narrative or an exposition. Only the cover you design, the articles you choose to include, and the advertisements that find themselves between them will serve to identify you.

Requirements:
- Magazine title (Not your name)
- Cover art and design
- Table of contents (see any magazine)
- A minimum of six articles
- A minimum of twelve advertisements
- A minimum of two pages of classifieds
- Project reflection

Assessment:

Your magazine will be assessed based on meeting the minimum requirements. This does not necessarily guarantee an A on the assignment. The care, ingenuity, and passion you put into the aesthetics and design will earn a superior grade. Important things to remembers are the elements that make you want to pickup and read any publication: color, graphics, and language.

Practical Applications:

1. The production of this magazine mirrors the composition of any good piece of writing.
   - The title and cover serve as an essay title — not merely the obvious (your name) but something extraordinary and eye-catching.
   - The table of contents serves as the introduction — why should any reader want to go further. What are your intentions for what follows?
   - The articles and advertisements serve as the body — these are the details and images that tell the reader exactly what the editor wants them to know.
   - The reflection serves as the conclusion — this is what the editor observed, gained from the compilation and makes sure the reader gets it too. This is what you've been thinking since writing the introduction and the body.

2. This project is also going to be a great way to kick off your plans for developing the class notebook (collecting, designing, and reflecting.)

**Due Date:

Notes

1. Crichton, Michael. "A Factual Note on *Eaters of the Dead.*" *The 13th Warrior: Previously Published as Eaters of the Dead.* New York: Ballentine, 1976. 270.

2. Figure 1 represents the visual timeline that I use while demonstrating how *Beowulf* has transformed historically.

3. *The Language of Literature: British Literature.* Evanston, IL: McDougal Littell, 2000.

4. The original prompt appears in *The Language of Literature: British Literature* as follows: "In today's society we have our own kinds of 'monsters' that threaten our safety or way of life. Who or what are today's monsters, and what threats do they pose?" 63.

5. The original prompt appears in *The Language of Literature: British Literature* as follows: "As students read the selection, have them consider what Beowulf reveals about Anglo-Saxon attitudes toward the following topics: courage, fate, the span of life, the deceased. When students have finished reading, have them write a short essay comparing some of these attitudes and customs with those practiced today." 33.

6. Fishwick, Marshall. Telephone Conversation. 29 Oct. 2003.

7. Mullin, Christopher. Short Answer. 3 Nov. 2003

8. Cloud, John. "Inside the New SAT." *Time* 27 Oct. 2003: 48–56.

17

Popular Culture in Sports, the Popular Culture of Sports

A Cross-Disciplinary Historical View

Douglas A. Noverr

Throughout history sports have been so much a part of cultures that they can serve as reflections of culture at any time. In earlier forms sports can provide insights into social values, interests, and attitudes about competition as well as the experience of athletic contests or endeavors. Sports are therefore especially helpful in courses in the humanities and social sciences—even in the so-called soft sciences from archaeology to zoology—especially in such seemingly unrelated college courses as architecture, the arts, literature, history, philosophy, sociology, and others as floating and evolving core elements of the culture of the time. At the same time, in many ways, sports are a constant in human attitudes and behavior.

Ancient and Medieval Sports

The initial connections and the interplay between sports and popular culture can be examined by reviewing the histories of three kinds of sports that each grew popular over different periods of time: the original Olympic games held in ancient Greece from 776 B.C. (the first Olympiad) to A.D. 394; the gladiator combats in Rome from 264 B.C. to A.D. 405; the Middle Ages tournament or tourney of knights from the 12th to the 16th century.[1] While these three different sports were carried out in significantly different contexts and had vastly different social meanings, the contests— whether ending in the glory of the head wreath of wild olive or the victor prizes awarded by the queen of beauty or the ignominy and brutality of bloody death on the floor of the amphitheater — established certain essential characteristics, features, or patterns that have remained a part of sports for over 2000 years.

- Pageantry preceded the contests with a dramatic entrance of the participants;
- Athlete preparation and training as well as specialization of skills;
- Connections of contests to social rituals, beliefs, or ideals;
- Special location or site of competition that is marked or laid out in a certain way;
- Rules or exclusions governing the qualifications of participants and observers;
- Use of specialized equipment by participants to demonstrate skill and to prevail in a contest;
- Distinctions among and between participants based on dress or equippage;
- Order of events or sequence of action with a duration for the contest or competition;
- Prizes or awards as well as accompanying glory or recognition in various forms;
- Accompanying activities, events, or rituals involving the observers before and after the contest.

The buildup to the Greek summer Olympic games, achieved through pageantry and anticipatory activities such as religious festivities and banquets, served to connect them to their purpose of honoring Zeus at the central site of this god's worship. One way of honoring Zeus was the demonstration and testing of the athletic skills of those who were fit and worthy of competing. The pageantry included an introductory procession and a trumpet call to signal that all was in readiness and that a special festival time had begun. Before this athletic meet the participants had to train diligently for 10 months, and be able to swear an oath that they had done so, and to put themselves under the scrutiny and supervision of those entrusted with the conduct of the games. Only free male Greeks of good reputation were allowed to compete. The pageantry also served the purpose of focusing on the athletes as individuals and as representatives of their city-states. As various types of sports were added to the competition of running events, athletes became even more differentiated physically as short or long distance runners (sprinters or marathoners), multiskill pentathaloners, boxers, wrestlers, or chariot racers.

The gladiator contests in ancient Rome also had elements of pageantry and physical exhibition. Unlike the Greek athletes (at least until later in the history of the Olympiad), the gladiators were professionals who learned their individual combat skills and use of weapons at special schools and were seasoned before they entered the arenas or amphitheaters. Gladiators were differentiated by their arms and armor. Some were heavily armed with sword, shield, and visored helmet; others fought virtually without armor or clothes, relying on a man catcher net and a trident. The combatants were paired off in twos, locked in what was intended to be mortal combat. For the thousands gathered to see these contests, the fascination was with the matchups of gladiators and respective weapons. Quickness, agility, and the skillful use of lighter weapons could possibly offset weight, massive strength or power, and protection. The goal was to create even matches that would result in prolonged struggles where the relative skills and weaknesses (or fatal flaws) of both combatants were displayed, and ultimately determined the victor. In the standard contest there could be up to 100 pairs of combatants, with a considerable variety of matchups in terms of gladiatorial types.

Unlike the Greek athletes who represented the pride and honor of their various city-states, the gladiators were either men without a future (unfree) or men who had dishonored themselves in some way and become social outcasts. Part of their popular appeal was the fact that they were desperate or defeated men who were considered dangerous and violent. Within the central ritual of the gladiatorial contests, they were given the arms they were otherwise denied and trained to be deadly with them. Their appearance in the Colosseum of Rome before 50,000 people, if they had made it to this apex of the sport, symbolized the struggle of their lives, with their life or death sanctioned by the gathered masses. Defeat ordinarily meant a death that was suffered by dispatch at the hand of the victor in the individual contest, unless the people indicated he should be spared. A few gladiators gained widespread popularity or notoriety as effective "killing machines" and specimens of highly developed mortal combat skills and use of specialized, exotic weapons. As professional fighters, they were considered equally adept at disabling and killing humans as well as wild beasts.

The tournament of knights in the Middle Ages had the richest pageantry of the early sports discussed here. Led by a champion, the knights rode with their entourages to near the site of the tournament field and camped. Judges considered their qualifications, experience, armor, quality of horses and equippage, and their weapons. After this inspection, which deemed them worthy and qualified for competition, they readied themselves and rode to the enclosed tournament field. Each group of knights was introduced by name, and trumpets sounded as they made their grand formal entrance. They passed by the local royalty and nobles with proper acknowledgment, with special attention to the ladies who sponsored the knights and provided the central connection with chivalry. A queen of beauty presided over the tournament and gave prizes to the victors. The contests included both individual matchups and groups vs. groups and were carried out to show the skills required by armed horsemen. A certain amount of danger was involved, since even with blunted weapons, knights were killed, seriously injured, or disabled in the ritualistic simulations of mounted battle. Because the tournaments were so popular and spread to the British Isles and western and southern Europe over four centuries, they were increasingly regulated by laws with changes made to make the sport safer.

The knights were viewed as proud and disciplined athletes who traveled to day competitions as teams led by a champion. On the tournament field they demonstrated the riding skills and deft handling of weapons while wearing full armor and simulating real battle, while at the same time following a code of honor and restrained aggression in the combats. These tournaments brought color, ritualistic pageantry, and excitement to the places that hosted them and spent the money required to build the tournament field. The ideal of knighthood and chivalry was kept alive, along with the military skills required in warfare. Eventually, however, the tournaments declined in popularity and disappeared as society became more commercial and warfare and weapons changed, making individual heavy armor an anachronism.

These early sports, each in its own way, established some of the essential elements or characteristics of games or competition. They were seasonal and established strong patterns of pageantry and ritual. Champions were accorded the status of celebrities and often given many gifts or privileges after their athletic victories by patrons or admirers. Stadiums or specialized facilities were built to accommodate spectators and to provide the stage for the spectacles or exhibitions.

Sports in Popular Culture, Sports and Popular Culture

These three sports, each of which extended its popularity over at least four centuries, also illustrate two basic concepts about the connections established between sport and popular culture. First, popular culture originates in or is created by sports, that is, the content, style, and qualities of the sport establish its appeal and its meanings to athletes and to spectators. The sport becomes popular with athletes and practiced because it offers certain physical and mental challenges, requires the mastery of certain equipment and the ability to use it to a certain end, and offers the test of competition with other athletes in a public arena in a contest with an outcome. The athlete accepts the demands and risks as well as seeks the possible rewards or honors. Spectators connect with the sport, and with the athletes, by way of identifying with certain competitors and by way of learning the specifics of the sports as well as admiring, rooting for, or finding fault with the execution of play.

Second, popular culture can attach itself to sports in the sense of surrounding it with attendant activities and rituals created by the spectators or by commercial enterprises. The experience of the actual sporting event or sports festival is preceded by an anticipation of it and followed by postevent discussion (the verbal re-creation of it or the memories of it) or even mimicking it in play or games (the acting out of it). Olympic victors, celebrated survivor gladiators, and champion knights became popular celebrities and legends because they had created a memorable or powerful experience of athletic triumph or exertion that carried over into everyday life. Chroniclers, poets, and historians provided the first recorded histories or celebrations of these early competitors, elevating some of them into mythic and heroic status as well as capturing the details of the sports.

Early Nineteenth-Century American Sports

Three sports in the period from 1840 to 1860 illustrate further how popular culture and sports develop close connections in the context of the urbanization and modernization of sports. Unlike the restrictive nature of the Greek Olympics, the Roman gladiatorial contests, and the knightly tournaments in term of those qualified or deemed worthy of competition (excluding the gladiators in this sense), the trend in the period from 1840 on in America was toward greater public participation under standardized rules and the formal regulation provided by sporting organizations. Bigtime sporting events became regular features of urban life but were no longer connected to religious festivals or dedicated to specific gods. Rather, these contests were created by promoters, sports enthusiasts or organizations, or rival groups (clubs, teams, or owners).

Two match races between thoroughbred horses in 1842 and 1845 at the Union Course on Long Island illustrate how horseracing became a focus of the popular culture of the times. In May 1842, Fashion, a New Jersey born mare, met Boston, a Virginia born horse that was about four years older than Fashion. Before an estimated 50,000 to 70,000 spectators, Fashion ran a world-class first four-mile heat and in the second heat defeated Boston, as jockey Joe Laird took Fashion from behind and won easily by sixty yards. William H. Gibbons, who owned Fashion, did not claim the $20,000 prize because he would not bet on his horse. The operator of the Union Course and a group of sponsors put up the stakes for this matchup of the greatest horses from North and South. The account in the widely distributed *Spirit of the Times* newspaper for May 24, 1842 noted the thousands in attendance:

> Among them the U.S. Senate and House of Representatives, the British Army and Navy, as well as our own, the Bench and the Bar, the Beauty and Fashion of New York were all represented.... The enclosed "privileged space" in front of the stands, reserved for the Members of the Jockey Club and strangers [who were charged $10 for admission without distinction!] was thronged with Turfmen, Breeders, and Amateurs [quoted in Kirsch, 194].

This account also noted how problems with crowd control for a time threatened the running of the race, as gate-crashers tried to gain access to the more privileged vantage points. However, a group led by James "Yankee" Sullivan, a professional boxer of New York City renown, cleared the course and restored order. The first heat was so exciting that the crowd tried to rush to the enclosed space where the horses were cooling down, and a portion of the track was covered with spectators. However, the desire to see the second four-mile heat prevailed, and the course was cleared.

In the 1845 match race for another $20,000, Fashion was challenged by an Alabama-born mare named Peytona. The crowd was estimated at 70,000 to 100,000, and the account in the New York *Herald* described the varied spectators.

> — All seemed eager to reach the ground. Long trains of carriages, filled with all sorts of people, reaching to Broadway, lined Whitehall Street. Here the magnificent barouche of a millionaire, full of gay, laughing, dark-eyed demoiselles, jammed in between a Bowery stage and a Broad-

way hack — here were loafers and dandies, on horseback and on foot — sporting gentleman in green coats and metal buttons — Southerners from Louisiana, Mississippi, and Alabama, with anxious faces, but hearts full of hope, "a pocket full of rocks," and a calm determination to await the results. The whole Union had in fact sent delegates to represent it in the grand contest which this day ushered in — all business seemed laid aside-one spirit animated the vast multitude [quoted in Kirsch, 200].

This account of the crowd noted the mixing of the social classes common to urban America in the Jacksonian period, as "rowdies" and gamblers rubbed elbows with gentlemen and self-styled sporting types. The gambling and drinking were heavy, and crowd control problems were again present, with a combination of distinguished gentleman and well-known tradesmen like Yankee Sullivan serving to clear the track. Peytona, the Southern mare who was about two years younger than Fashion, prevailed in both beats, winning by two lengths in the first and a length in the second.

This second intersectional match race illustrated how the popular excitement over thoroughbred horseracing had grown and how much high stakes gambling had attached itself to the sport. No longer was this a gentlemen's challenge wager, but drew the interests of the general population. All kinds and types had money interests in the race's outcome, including members of New York City ethnic gangs. The *Spirit of the Times* account also noted how important food and drink concessions were to the event:

Business in the tents-wigwams-the culinary camps and conventicles commenced at an early hour, and was carried on with a briskness that betimes looked like voracity, and fears were occasionally excited that the impetuosity of the hungry crowd might find a melancholy end in the prodigious tubs of lemonade and brandy punch that lay in elegant negligence around the tables, whose extended surfaces, supported masses of ham, sandwiches, lobsters, loaves, decanters, glasses, and all the paraphernalia of drinking that could be condensed in the spot [quoted in Kirsch 201].

Some elements of the ancient festival are evident (tents and food), but here, at the Union Race Course, this was a commercial business requiring planning, organization, and deployment for the purpose of profiting from the hunger and appetite of a large crowd willing to spend money on this special day of a "grand contest." Without the interest of the wealthy gentleman sporting class to buy, train, and race thoroughbred horses, these match races would not have been possible. But once the challenges were made and the stakes set, it was no longer a matter of which owner's horse was better on a particular day. The event became the stuff of popular excitement and interest as the horse's breeding, running style, training, speed, endurance, and jockey are all discussed and debated in infinite detail and from different sides.

Rowing or sculling was another sport that achieved great popularity during the 1850s in America. The first intercollegiate athletic contest was a rowing contest held between Harvard and Yale in a regatta on Lake Winnepesaukee, Vermont in August 1852. The Boston and Montreal Railroad Company paid all the expenses of one boat club from Harvard and three boat clubs from Yale. The high spirited undergraduate oarsmen brought excitement and a weekend of brisk trade to the local businesses. An article in the New York *Herald* for August 10, 1852, described the scene:

> On the day of the regatta, the boats came crowded to overflowing with passengers, and these, together with the people from the villages around, lined the wharfs and shore for some distance. The scene was extremely fine, as the boats lay all abreast, waiting for the sound of the bugle. The beautiful lake, with its hundred islands, stretching far off in front — the summits of the Red Hills in the backgrounds — the unruffled smoothness of the water, and the perfect silence of the throng around — all added to the beauty of the scene [quoted in Kirsch, 41].

In the prize regatta the Oneida Boat Club from Harvard outrowed the Yale teams and was presented with a "pair of fine black walnut oars ... as the prize." All oarsmen were treated to meals after the races and after the regatta. In the years following 1852, college challenge regattas, often held over two days on the weekend, were highly popular and attracted crowds of up to 20,000 to the picturesque sites where they were held. Prizes of oars or flags were given and taken back to adorn the boathouse clubs commonly found on Ivy League campuses. Although rowing was a collegiate amateur sport, rowing clubs were organized in most port cities of the northeastern United States and Canada with heavy betting and constant controversy over rules or decisions of regatta judges on fouls or illegal moves. It was harder to validate the lengths of courses over water or to compare times of rowers, unlike horseracing where times to the fraction of a second could be recorded and distance was exact. But the appeal of rowing was that it could be done on various kinds of courses (lakes, rivers, harbors) and that so many factors (including the weather, wind, currents, quality of boats, equipment problems, etc.) could affect the outcome.

This exciting sport was also available to anyone who could find sponsorship for a boat or be invited to join a rowing club, and who would submit to the rigorous training and the totally demanding exertion required.

No one was "born" a rower or sculler. It was a skill and a discipline, and under the right conditions a single rower or a crew could produce speed and precision that were truly amazing to spectators, with the boat and rower or crew united in the same way jockey and horse could become. Additionally, the sport was enlivened by the question of why amateurs were better than professionals, why Ivy League crews were superior to urban club crews.

The popular culture in the sport and of the sport find specific connection in this point of what is required by the sport (in terms of preparation and training, in terms of equipment, in terms of performance and effort, in terms of the conditions of competition) to be successful or distinguished. This knowledge, of course, varies in degree and content from athletes to spectators, with sportswriters or reporters providing a connecting link of "inside" information or direct experience.

Another connection is the realization of both competitors and spectators of what is required or comes together to create the special experience of a sporting experience, or what is needed to maintain the health of the sport as competition. In the 1852 regatta held between the crews from Harvard and Yale on Lake Winnipesaukee, it was described by the New York *Herald* reporter as the "perfect silence of the throng around" as they waited, with the rowing crews, for the bugle sound to start the race on the "unruffled smoothness of the water" (quoted in Kirsch, 41). In the New York *Clipper* account of the rowing race between the Metropolitan Club of New York City and the Union Club of St. John, New Brunswick, Canada on the Charles River in Boston, a contest rowed in heavy rain and a violent thunderstorm, the reporter noted:

> As the two boats reached the goal, they were received with rapturous applause. The crews of the opposing boats fraternized in the most cordial and friendly manner, and the losers [the McKay boat of the Metropolitan Club] convinced all present by their manly actions that they well knew how to bear their defeat. The victors received the honors showered upon them in a modest and becoming manner, making no boast, but on the contrary, endeavored to smooth the "rough edges" of their opponents' defeat [Kirsch, 47].

In commenting on the celebrated victory of Fashion over Boston in the 1842 match race at the Union Course, the reporter for the *Spirit of the Times* noted:

> Nor let us forget that to the gallant Boston we are indebted for maintaining the indomitable game and surprising speed of our Champion! Who else could have displayed it in such bold and beautiful relief. Arthur

Taylor brought him [Boston] to the post in the finest possible condition, and Gil. Patrick, his jockey, rarely distinguished him more than upon this occasion [quoted in Kirsch, 198].

In the development and evolution of "Base Ball" as the most popular sport in America by the end of the 19th century, initially as town ball, a folk or children's game, can be seen becoming a national sport played widely at the professional, semiprofessional, and amateur levels. It took some time for the New York City "diamond" version (with the batsman located at home plate) of the game to emerge as the dominant style and for the National Association of Base Ball Players, organized in 1858, to promote itself as the organization whose aim was "to improve, foster, and perpetuate the American game of Base Ball, and the cultivation of kindly feelings among the different members of the Base Ball Clubs" (quoted in Kirsch, 79). Under the rules and regulations the basics of the modern game were established and codified, except for the distance to the home plate from the pitcher's plate and box (the modern pitcher's rubber and mound), which was originally 45 feet (changed to 50 feet in 1889 and to 60 feet 6 inches in 1893); the system of calling strikes and balls (the umpire could only calls strikes if the batter tried to delay the game or gain an advantage by not offering at good pitches); and the underhand style of pitching until 1889. In 1859 the NABBP prohibited professionals. The goal of this New York City–based organization was to sanction clubs that abided by uniform rules, to establish teams with known rosters before contests, and to provide for umpiring that was firm and impartial.

The rise in the popularity of baseball was noted in an editorial from the March 10, 1860, *Spirit of the Times:*

Baseball has been a school-boy's game all over the land from immemorial time, but it was, until recently, considered undignified for men to play at it, except on rare holidays, and then they were wont to play on some out-lying common, where they would be unseen of their more staid associates. Within five or six years all this has changed; B.B. clubs outnumber the debating societies almost as much as they surpass them in enthusiasm. The infection seems to have seized all classes of people — intellectual youth, corpulent gentlemen, lawyers, butchers, dry goods clerks, doctors, every one, in short, if possessed of sound limbs and tolerable wind, must play one or two afternoons in each week, or be voted "slow" [quoted in Kirsch, 31].

The same editorial noted that shops all over the North were selling bats and balls as well as spiked shoes. This first baseball mania in the 1850s was followed by an even greater one in the late 1860s, as there were by then

300 member clubs in the National Association of Base Ball Players (Voigt, 1990, 3). The popular culture of early baseball became based on club identity, fraternity, and local pride. Gentlemanly behavior and sportsmanship were to provide the basis for the "cultivation of kindly feelings" that were one of the two stated objects of the Association. In match games the "trophy of victory" was the ball, and all gambling was prohibited, whether by players or spectators. The goal was to provide healthy recreation and the comradely experience of being part of a team or club that had community support. In the context of play, throwing, catching, fielding, running, and batting skills could be demonstrated. The game was learned by playing, with allowance for mistakes or inexperience. In comparing cricket and baseball, a writer for the New York *Herald* on October 16, 1859, stated: "It [baseball] is more lively and animated, gives more exercise, and is more rapidly concluded. Cricket seems very tame and dull after looking at a game of baseball" (quoted in Kirsch, 93). Early baseball matches were often followed by dinners where opposing teams shared fraternity and conviviality.

These noble ideals were, however, tested and strained by the enthusiasm and rowdiness of fans. In the three-game series between the Brooklyn Excelsiors and the Brooklyn Atlantics in 1860, the third and deciding game was ended when rowdies heckled the Excelsiors' team and caused the Excelsiors' captain to remove his team from the field and end the game in the sixth inning. An editorial writer for the New York *Clipper* attributed the hooting and heckling to heavy gambling and to the "spirit of faction" that prevailed in the ethnic conflicts between "the foreign element" and "native offspring" boiling over into politics, fire companies, gangs, and religion (quoted in Kirsch, 97–98). The popular culture of a growingly diverse urban city, with its increasingly ethnic and factional character, threatened to undermine the high social character baseball was attempting to cultivate. As the *Clipper* writer concluded:

> [T]he same evil spirit rules the actions and paralyzes the virtuous tendencies of all who succumb to its baneful influence, replacing kindly feelings with bitter hatred, and manly emulation and generous rivalry with revengeful retaliation; thereby turning every source of pleasure with which it comes in contact into a cause of feuds and quarrels that end in disgraceful and riotous conduct [quoted in Kirsch 98].

The history of professional baseball was marked by efforts on the part of club owners to control players and to make the sport profitable and respectable. However, baseball gained in popularity and attendance because the game was seen as spirited, fiercely competitive, and exciting.

Players were admired for their resistance to the controls put on their behavior and lifestyle. With overhand pitching and the calling of strikes, and with Sunday games and optional liquor sales, ballparks became places where a fast moving game could be experienced with a beer in hand and with "cranks" (fans) razzing the visiting team with catcalls and insults. Some teams adopted an aggressive style of play that featured baiting the umpire, intimidating other teams from the dugout and on the diamond, and rowdiness (Voigt, 5). It would take some time for professional baseball to gain respectability and for gentlemanly and Christian players to be admired for their restraint and class. Early professional baseball generally took on the character of the urban environment — aggressive, contentious, and competitive. Owners struggled with each other for the best talent as they tried to monopolize players and keep their salaries low.

The early popular culture of baseball had centered around an amateur game where spirited local or club rivalries were held in check by civic pride in the demonstration of fraternity and friendliness and in the players' commitment to this ideal. Fans appreciated the players' development and demonstration of skills as they learned the game and provided excitement with dramatic plays, unusual effort, and run-producing rallies within the limits of three outs per inning. However, the forces of commercial and business interests to make the game profitable for owners, and the desire by fans and supporters to have winning terms and star players, pushed baseball into the area of a larger popular culture of entertainment and commodification of players and the game itself. A national game displaced a local and regional game, although the local character of baseball would always remain a strong feature. Professionalism became the hallmark of the game, and skilled, paid professionals could be marketed and promoted to fans in ways that club amateurs could not. What had been an indefinite number of exhibitions or contests arranged by the clubs became a season schedule set and controlled by the league and the owners. All these changes affected the popular culture in the sport and of the sport in terms of the expectations and behavior of paying spectators and in terms of the ways champions would be determined. No longer were game balls awarded to the winners of match contests suitable. In the 1876 Constitution and Rules of the National League of Professional Base Ball Clubs "the emblem of championship shall be a pennant (of the national colors), to cost not less than one hundred dollars ($100)" and to "be inscribed with the motto, 'Champion Base Ball Club of the United States,'" with the name of the club and the year in which the title was won; and the champion club shall be entitled to fly the pennant until the close of the ensuing season" (quoted in Kirsch, 91). Here success and dominance were highly visible in a formalized emblem that flew at the home ballpark for the season following a championship. The memorabilia and keepsake business grew out of the championship emblem, and the display of victory pennants with dates has become part of the visual history of ballparks (and other sports arenas).

Conclusions

The origins and early development of sports reveal significant details, characteristics, and patterns containing information about the popular culture of the periods. It can be noted that a sports culture creates the interest needed for participants and that culture contains meanings or possible rewards to the athletes. That special sports culture, with its codes and style of play, is attractive to spectators in various ways and for various reasons. At key points during competition there can be a confluence or intersection of shared interests or needs that the sport satisfies, with a perceived unity or elevated moment. As sports develop and become popular, the push toward professionalization and commercialization is inevitable with sportsmanship, athletic camaraderie, and play elements harder to maintain. The popular culture that surrounds sports and attaches to them becomes an important part of the experience, with the expectations or needs of spectators sometimes driving changes in the sports over time. An examination of earlier European sports and the early history of American sports provides a means of understanding some enduring features as well as tracing why and how sports persist and change.

Notes

[1]For important works on the ancient Olympics *see* Heinz Schöbel, *The Ancient Olympic Games*, translated by Joan Becker (London, 1966); John Kieran and Arthur Daley, *The Story of the Olympic Games, 776 B.C. to 1972* (Philadelphia, 1973); David C. Young, *The Olympic Myth of Greek Amateur Athletes* (Chicago, 1985).

For the history of gladiators see Michael Grant, *Gladiators* (New York, 1967); Donald G. Kyle, *Spectacles of Death in Ancient Rome* (London, 1998); and Alan Baker, *The Gladiator: The Secret History of Rome's Warrior Slaves* (New York, 2000).

On the tournament *see* Francis Henry Cripps-Day, *The History of the Tournament in England and France* (London, 1918); Esther Josephine Crooks, *The Ring Tournament in the United States* (Richmond, 1936); and Juliet R.V. Barker, *The Tournament in England, 1100–1400* (Suffolk, England, 1986).

References

Kirsch, George B., Editor. *Sports in North America: A Documentary History*, Vol. 3. Gulf Breeze, FL: Academic International Press, 1992.

Voigt, David Q. "America's Game: A Brief History of Baseball." In *The Baseball Encyclopedia*, 8th Ed. New York: Macmillan, 1990, pp. 3–13.

18

Teaching Popular Culture in Relation to the Social Sciences

A Critical-Emancipatory View from Europe

MEL VAN ELTEREN

Over the past three or four decades there has been a growing interest in the study of popular culture in Europe within various disciplines and interdisciplines: folklore studies, cultural history, and history of mentalities — especially as practiced within the *Annales* tradition — as well as the "new social history" (originating in the 1960s), cultural anthropology, cultural sociology, and cultural studies. However, the study of mass popular culture in industrial and postindustrial or late-modern societies remains mostly confined to the domains of culture and media studies and is, to a lesser extent, also practiced within American, British, French, and German studies, along with some other area studies: urban anthropology, sociology, and social history.

To my knowledge, there are no special departments of *popular* culture with that name at European institutes of higher education, although departments of cultural studies — a number of which exist in Great Britain — focus mostly, albeit not exclusively, on popular culture. Some local circumstances have been conducive to the proliferation of cultural studies, such as those at polytechnic institutes or some of the new universities (mostly former polytechnics) as well as the Open University in Britain, and similar institutes of higher education in Scandinavia (especially Finland) since the 1970s (Bennett, 1998, 214–233; Davies, 1995, 45–53; Eskola and Vainikkala, 1992; van Elteren, 38–42).[1] Furthermore, most of the cul-

181

tural studies that developed in Europe outside of Britain are quite derivative, leaning heavily on British and American models, with notable exceptions such as Umberto Eco's approach to semiotics in Italy, and Roland Barthes's semiotics and Pierre Bourdieu's cultural sociology in France. The latter have also all three been of influence elsewhere in Europe, though often after having been filtered through Anglo-American interpretations and applications.

Probably the third most productive site (after Britain and France) of what can be seen as something like an indigenous cultural studies, is the former West Germany. This includes the development of the history workshop movement (inspired by its British example) and the interest in *Alltagsgeschichte* (everyday life history) since the 1970s; a number of feminist projects in Hamburg and Berlin and research projects on xenophobia and racism that developed around the *Kritische Psychologie Gruppe* (critical psychology group); and, in a more restricted sense, the work of the Ludwig-Uhland-Institut für empirische Kulturwissenschaft (empirical cultural science) in Tübingen on various forms of everyday social life, past and present, as well as its studies of the role of the mass media in the lives of their audiences in the 1980s. Youth studies also flourished in the former East Germany. Moreover, German scholars have produced a few significant general works on popular culture in their native language (e.g., Fluck, 1994; Maase, 1997). This all occurred despite a persistent hostility to the study of popular culture phenomena among many German intellectuals, due to a prevailing discourse about mass culture dominated by the critical theory of the Frankfurt School, particularly as this had been received by leaders of the 1968 student movement, which resisted such an opening up of leftist discourses on culture (Kreutzner, 1989).[2]

This resistance to popular culture studies has waned since the late 1980s, however, as German intellectual discourse also underwent the influence of neo–Gramscian Marxism and poststructuralism that led to more complex views of contradiction and conflict between processes of cultural production and consumption, and of popular culture as a site of contestation. German cultural studies— now including the study of the former East Germany after 1945 — has clearly linked up with cultural studies in the Anglo-American world (*German Matters*, 2000). But in a stricter sense it still remains a relatively small domain within German academia, which is in line with the predominant picture in Europe.

At most European universities, negative views on "mass culture" from both traditional and modernist high-culture perspectives left little room for the study of popular culture as a separate academic field. Institutional barriers against popular culture studies, although somewhat diminished, still persist in a predominantly inhospitable environment maintained by established disciplines and departments in the humanities and social sciences. The latter may themselves be at risk, reinforcing the tendency to close the ranks, and fostering even more resistance against the newcomer. Nonetheless, here and there faculties of letters and faculties of social sciences have incorporated popular culture courses into their educational programs, in order to cater to a growing demand for such content among students. (On the other hand, departments or individual teachers of sociology under threat have in some cases found a new niche within general educational programs in the liberal arts or social sciences under labels such as *social theory*, *social studies*, or *cultural studies*.) There is also the stiff competition with inter- or multidisciplinary fields such as business and management studies, social policy and public administration studies, leisure studies, European studies, and the like. These promise to offer students better job prospects, and are currently in favor among university managers (with their eyes on the bottom line of marketability and profitability), a tendency that is only exacerbated by the tight budgets of the great majority of European universities today.

In this essay I underline the merits of teaching popular culture in higher education and suggest ways in which it should preferably be taught in relation to the social sciences, but without severing existing ties with the humanities. These suggestions are derived partly from a critical diagnosis of problematic facets of the dominant strain of popular culture studies, which revolve around an uncritical cultural populism and a neglect of the structural dimensions and sociopolitical implications of popular culture, as well as aesthetic and moral-political appraisals. I will indicate how a further integration of popular culture studies with the social sciences may improve this situation. It is first necessary, however, to consider the diverse approaches of mass/popular culture that have been influential in Europe and America, and the development of (popular) cultural studies in both contexts.

Popular Culture's Societal Position in the Old and New World

Mass-mediated popular culture in Europe today has an all-pervasive influence in everyday life that comes close to the situation in the United States where this development is most advanced. Both cultures have also become much more intertwined — although with a predominance of U.S. input. In discussing the teaching of popular culture in Europe as compared to America, however, one needs to realize that in the United States popular culture is de facto still regarded as more legitimate than is common in Europe (Uricchio, 1996, 69). This remains the state of play at the moment, despite the fact that significant counterstrains in the United States severely contested this, including a longstanding, genteel Anglo-Saxon tradition and an odd coalition of anti–Stalinist leftists and liberals and conservative critics of mass culture in the 1940s and 1950s. A major reason for this difference with Europe is that American culture has for a long time been characterized by an aesthetics of performance at all of its different taste levels, including many of its most typical and original forms (Fisher, 1986). The new urban entertainment culture that emerged and soon began to flourish in the second half of the 19th century, was an early, large-scale manifestation of the culture of performance in the popular domain. This is a culture whose primary sources of attraction and gratification are the sensational spectacle, the outstanding performance, the extraordinary physical and acrobatic achievement, the intense emotional thrill, a special attraction, striking appearance, or simply the presence of a celebrity. This tendency also manifested itself in the silent film (immensely popular at the time), in which the level of performance, comprising physical skills, star presence, spectacular events, and special effects took priority over the narrative level that had been the traditional literary device for providing meaning (Fluck, 1996, 52–53). A good case can be made that this also holds true for many of today's Hollywood films, in which the narrative is often much less relevant than the performance features and the emphasis lies on other modes of communication (body language and action) rather than well-articulated phrases of actors. This tendency became manifest in forms of high culture as well, such as American literature, including self-conscious strategies of impression-management by certain authors and celebrity cults that sprung up around them.[3]

The German Americanist Winfried Fluck (1994), in his penetrating analysis of this culture of performance, stressed that:

> [T]aste levels and aesthetic forms were never separated as categorically as in Europe and…, as a consequence, it is characterized by a constant mixture and hybridization of aesthetic modes and forms of expression. This mixed, hybrid character with its connotations of "impurity" as well as lack of aesthetic control was, after all, one of the reasons why American culture was long considered inferior by many Europeans. But it was also one of the reasons why it was considered subversive and surprisingly "modern" by another group of Europeans [53–54].

One of the results of these differing traditions is that in America, a much greater diversity of social actors has access to the cultural stage. In other words, Americans generally tend to be *cultural* egalitarians, albeit with the clear exception of certain old and new elites who emphasize cultural distinction through all kinds of status markers. Europeans, on the other hand, are less inclined toward cultural egalitarianism, demonstrating a much stronger dislike of social and economic inequality — with the exception of the well-to-do, although even they tend to be more negative about socioeconomic inequality than their American counterparts (Hutton, 2003, 88–89; Lipset and Marks, 2000, 289). This sociocultural difference may also partly explain why some leading exponents of popular culture studies in the United States have resorted to an antielitist justification of popular culture studies by appealing to populist-democratic sentiments both in and outside academia (e.g., Browne, 1994; Fiske, 1991). Such a strategy appears much less effective and may even be counterproductive in the European context. Rather than privileging popular culture, I think that we should yoke the study of popular culture to elite culture as a programmatic starting point. Instead of justifying one culture at the expense of another, it is probably more productive to try to understand how high and popular culture interact, and how they change and complement each other over the course of time, in order to gain a deeper insight into the complicated cultural processes concerned (Freese and Porsche, 15; Fluck, 1994). For the same reason I also prefer the more inclusive term *cultural studies* to *popular culture studies*. This does not mean that one should opt for a combined study of both types of culture — whose domains are not always easy to delineate precisely anyway — in each and every case, but merely that the general relationships between the two must be kept in mind when planning individual research projects and curricula.

Of course, one should avoid essentializing the distinctive features of Europe and the United States as if they concern basic inherent differences that are set in stone. Each continent is a huge cultural-geographic entity which is internally diverse and changes over the course of time. While both the United States and "Europe" struggle with their multicultural composition, the latter also has problems delimiting itself geopolitically, as can be seen, for example, in the vicissitudes around new and potential member states of the European Union. The cultural-geographic borders of the United States have become a site of debate as well, manifested in the growing interest in border cultures and in current discussions among Americanists about a critical-internationalist or transculturalist approach toward their subject. Over the years, there have also been two-way cultural exchanges of various kinds, so rigid dichotomies between "Europe" and "America" should be abandoned (van Elteren, 1996a, 51–54). Importantly, Europe is experiencing the growing influence of the culture of performance, especially through the impact of U.S. culture as selectively borrowed and appropriated locally. Likewise, we find here a further blurring of boundaries between elite and popular culture, enhanced by thick globalization, which since the 1960s has produced a strong proliferation of cultural hybridizations, further eroding the strict dichotomy between high and popular culture.

Yet it can be argued (for the time being at least) that intellectual culture in Europe still differs from its counterpart in the United States in that European intellectuals are *relatively* better integrated into a "mandarin controlled" popular culture, carried by quality newspapers and magazines and public broadcasters, which solicits their opinions, according to sociologist Ben Agger (1992, 176).[4] These intellectuals do not simply endorse mass popular culture; on the contrary, when they do show interest in its manifestations, as some of them do, they usually tend to approach its various manifestations critically with a clear eye for negative as well as positive aspects. Only representatives of the dominant strain of cultural studies and kindred postmodernist thinkers are exceptions to this rule.

The transnationalization of America's culture of performance fits well with a more general shift of emphasis from narrative to performance as the primary source of meaning and gratification in contemporary Western culture. It is one of the driving forces behind an overall cultural development of de- and recontextualization, and dehierarchization and democratization on the aesthetic level. Needless to say, at the societal level it also involves the erosion of moral and social guardianship. The ongoing process of democratization in the aesthetic-cultural sphere must not be confused with economic and political democracy, however. While the latter forms evoke ideals of social equality and justice, cultural democratization basically refers to an increase in individual freedom and attendant freedom of self-expression — a tendency that may create problems of its own and is not necessarily good for democracy. As cultural sociologist Robert Wuthnow (1988) pointed out, it may turn into excessive expressive individualism and extreme "civil privatism," with only weak ties to any community life or common good whatsoever. Fluck contended: "In this sense of a continuous dehierarchization and an ever increasing freedom of self-expression we may speak of a global Americanization of culture." However, he hastened to add that "this process is one that affects American culture as much as other cultures (and even more so)" (Fluck, 1996, 74). Depending on the particular context, a culture of performance and self-expression may be either helpful or harmful for democracy — and sometimes both. In specific instances it may have detrimental effects in terms of equality, justice, and social cohesion. "The victory of mood over moral structure in contemporary society" (62), that accompanies the shift from narrative to performance, may also result in a narcissistic indulgence in aesthetic experiences with regard to both high and popular culture — which also offers significant rewards of "immediate experience"— and a weakened resilience against oppression and cultural imposition. In my view, a clear manifestation of this is the current emphasis on what has been called the "experience economy" by analysts of today's most advanced economies of the world (Pine and Gilmore, 1999).[5]

In the second half of the 20th century, U.S. popular culture as received among locals had become an integral part of the indigenous cultural repertoires in Europe. That means that by studying the local appropriations of U.S. popular culture, one learns more about national, regional, and other (sub)cultures in Europe. The same holds true for local crystalizations of transnational popular cultures carried by immigrants and refugees from countries outside the Western core (e.g., specific Arab, African, or Asian forms). In addition, special attention ought to be paid to populist-nationalistic rhetorics and rituals as strategically employed in political campaigns revolving around the politics of the popular. Indeed, populist movements in many parts of the world link up to globally mediated forms of popular culture and express themselves through local variants thereof.[6] Paradoxically, they may even do so when expressly distancing themselves from the homogenization tendencies of capitalist globalization. This has everything to do with the basic fact that transnational mass media (especially television) and communications technology (Internet) play a crucial role today in many people's everyday lives.

Developments of the Different Strains of Cultural Studies

The various versions of the critique of mass culture — from the left, right, and center that prevailed on both sides of the Atlantic from the 1940s and 1950s until the mid–1960s, shared a view of media manipulation of popular taste and ordinary people, and the passive consumption of commodified culture. This was challenged as a form of cultural elitism during the early phase of cultural studies in Britain, characterized by the recognition of a particular politics of popular culture. In British subcultural theory, the emphasis was put on identifying certain social groups with what Simon Frith has called "positive mass consumption," suggesting that, "The value of cultural goods could therefore be equated with the value of the groups consuming them — youth, the working class, women,

and so forth" (Frith, 1998, 571–572). It was a move away from the position of "if it's popular it must be bad" (taken by the Frankfurt School,
among others) to that of "if it's popular it must be bad, unless it's popular with the right people," according to this British sociologist of popular
music and cultural analyst (572). However, this meant that cultural value
was in the first instance gauged in terms of true and false consciousness.
Attempts at ideological interpretation, or "demystification" of a social reality mistaken by its inhabitants, prevailed over all other issues including
those regarding aesthetics, fun, pleasure, excitement, or grace. It also meant
that those consumers who were not approved because they did not fit in
the programmatic scheme of cultural-political resistance, were dismissed
as "dupes" in conventional Marxist terms.

Starting from a similar position of disdain for cultural elitism, but
from a populist-democratic rather than a Marxist perspective, popular
culture studies in America took quite a different course. Already at an
early stage, scholars in this vein looked for the redeeming qualities of commodity culture in the act of consumption. Within the positivist empirical tradition of mainstream American sociology, liberal practitioners in the
1950s—part of the then-prevailing consensus tradition in the social sciences and history—tried to find forms of mass consumption that were
not "passive" and types of mass consumers who were not "stupified." Thus,
they surveyed people's watching, reading, and listening habits, providing
data about "taste cultures" and "taste publics" to prove their case. (A
belated, full-grown result of this approach was the empirical study and a
kind of populist defense of popular culture by Herbert Gans, published in
1974, with a brief follow-up in 1985).

In the same period, C. Wright Mills, lone dissident within American
sociology, took an opposite, antimass culture stance not dissimilar to that
of both the Frankfurt School and the "New York intellectuals" (see below),
except for his more differentiated perspective on the cultural industries in
terms of the production of culture through the labor of cultural workers.
Mills's work has been depicted as an indigenous form of leftist American
cultural studies *avant la lettre* (Mattelart and Mattelart 1998, 40–42), which
is true to the extent that Mills looked at the cultural industries in terms
of the production of mass culture by "a stable of cultural workmen" hired
and managed by "the commercial distributor," and further steered by the
"marketing apparatus," in his unfinished book project of the late 1950s,
"The Cultural Apparatus" (1963). In this regard Mills had been influenced
by the cultural heritage of the Popular Front of the New Deal era, that creatively intermingled popular and "high culture" forms in literature, film,
musical theater, music (jazz, "cabaret blues," folk) during the 1930s and

1940s. But its leading intellectuals—including literary critics Kenneth Burke and Carey McWilliams, sociologist Oliver Cromwell Fox, "labor union intellectual"/fashion designer Elizabeth Hawes, jazz writer Sidney Finkelstein, and novelist, journalist, historian, and anticolonial activist C.L.R. James—held more nuanced views on popular culture, and wrote discriminatingly about the quality (aesthetically and otherwise) of its various manifestations at the time.

Between 1940 and the early 1950s, the Popular Front culture was severely criticized by a group of leftist anti–Stalinists (most of them then Trotskyist-inflected) associated with such journals as *New International, Partisan Review, Politics, Commentary,* and *Dissent* who took an uncomprising anti-"mass culture" stance, blaming the cultural industries for producing and distributing "stupifying" forms of culture among the populace[7] (and whose influence Mills had undergone as well).[8] These "New York intellectuals"—including James Farrell, Clement Greenberg, Harold Rosenberg, Dwight MacDonald, Robert Warshow, Irving Howe, Lionel Trilling—criticized the Popular Front from a modernist perspective for what they saw as an acceptance of both the "kitsch" of the culture industry and the "official" art of the state apparatus. Although the Popular Front, a radical "social-democratic" historical bloc gathered around antifascism, antilynching, and industrial unionism, had been defeated as a political movement by 1948, its aesthetics and cultural politics lived on as a subterranean culture during the McCarthy period and informed the works of a generation of artists and intellectuals, to be revived in the 1960s and 1970s, especially in music and film (Denning, 1996a, 1996b, 46, 49, 110–114; Aronowitz, 1993, 131–166*)*. Historian Michael Denning has argued that the intellectual and political origins of cultural studies in the United States lie in this heritage, in the "pioneering work" in the 1930s and 1940s of such figures as Kenneth Burke, cultural historian Constance Rourke, literary historian F.O. Matthiessen (a seminal figure in the development of postwar American studies), Oliver Cromwell Cox, and Carey McWilliams: "Though never a group of any sort..., they shared socialist or social-democratic politics, and interest in the popular arts, a desire to rethink notions of race and ethnicity, nation and people, and a concern for cultural theory" (Denning, 1992, 38). However, this legacy was hardly incorporated into the strain of cultural studies in the United States that emerged in the late 1970s from the reception of British cultural studies. It was not until the 1990s, that it was positively reassessed within some cultural studies circles (including a remarkable revival of Kenneth Burke's work on cultural theory).

During the 1960s, another countermovement against cultural elitism arose, growing initially out of a combination of folklore and American studies, that found a major publication outlet in the *Journal of Popular Culture*, established in 1967 by Ray B. Browne at Bowling Green State University in Ohio, and an institutional network embedded in the Popular Culture Association (PCA), founded in 1970 by Browne, Russel B. Nye, Carl Bode, Marshall W. Fishwick, John Cawelti, and others. Its members began to focus on the folklore and popular cultures of ordinary people, along with the output of the culture industries and mass media, as received by various audiences (mostly through textual analyses of popular novels and popular music lyrics). In some ways, their version of popular culture derived from Herder's "folk culture" concept — related to the discovery of folk culture in Europe in the late 18th and early 19th century by the Romantics — that led these scholars to an affirmative, if not celebratory view of mass popular culture. But next to a long-standing, populist antielitism strain in U.S. society, the American interest in popular culture derived also from a crisis within *high* culture circles stemming from developments within modern art during the 1950s and early 1960s (especially pop art), that questioned the validity of elite aesthetics by which art is judged. In addition, there has been a growing awareness among culture scholars and others that elite culture, like popular culture, is often distributed by mass techniques (films, records, audiotapes, books, more recently compact discs, videocassettes, DVDs, etc.). This realization prompted a further relativization of the distinction between high and popular culture among cultural critics and the public at large (J.R. Hall and Neitz, 1993, 7).

In his intellectual history of cultural studies, Ioan Davies indicated that Pierre Bourdieu and Roland Barthes in Paris, Umberto Eco in Milan, Marshall McLuhan in Toronto, and Ray and Pat Browne in Bowling Green, each practiced a form of cultural studies in their own way at about the same time as this field was developed by Richard Hoggart, Raymond Williams, Edward Thompson, and Stuart Hall in Britain (Davies, 1995, 38). But the field of cultural studies as it is internationally known today, largely (although not exclusively) originated in Britain. This is understandable given the fact that Stuart Hall adopted the term *cultural studies* from Hoggart and Williams and diffused it on a wide scale by developing a paradigm that came to constitute the core of the terrain widely considered to be cultural studies today.[9] Elsewhere I have sketched the origins and trajectory of popular culture studies as it developed out of Bowling Green (van Elteren, 2001). Here I consider both streams, which have so far remained at some distance from each other. Nevertheless, these two currents have influenced each other — as I see it, more traffic going from cultural studies to popular culture studies than vice versa.[10] PCA-style cultural studies remained mostly an American enterprise, and as yet had much less impact abroad (some in Mexico, Australia, New Zealand, Western Europe, Turkey, and Japan). British cultural studies made a stronger impact on the international scene, although it remained mostly confined to the Anglo-American world and other countries within its cultural orbit (Australia, New Zealand, Canada, Latin America, a few pockets in Africa, and Western Europe and Japan).

From the late 1970s onwards, cultural studies from Britain was exported abroad and selectively absorbed into American higher education. There it took another course, due to the very different social and cultural context. Importantly, the subject of social class never drew as much interest as in the United Kingdom. American cultural studies from the outset was much more focused on "race" or ethnicity as the basic social dividing line in everyday social perceptions and practices—even though class differences tend to overlap significantly with racial and ethnic divisions. This was not unexpected given the fact that most Americans see themselves as part of a broad middle class, a tendency evident in the hegemonic public discourse and in self-definitions. Besides, the dominant group routinely dismisses a residual category as "underclass."

In the background is a persistent and powerful (classical) liberal ideology within the national-popular culture that revolves around what has been called the "American Creed" (with liberty, egalitarianism, individualism, populism, and laissez faire as its major components), which is only contested in the margins by countermovements whose members hold other ideological views. Equality is first of all seen in terms of equality of opportunity and respect rather than of condition or results, and the existing social rank order is considered to be primarily the outcome of people's individual efforts, achievements and failures, and a certain amount of good or bad luck. The prevailing emphasis on equality of opportunity entails that the individual who is given the chance and takes it, also accepts the risks and expects no social intervention in the case of failure. It is especially in this regard that we can discern a crucial difference with the prevailing conception of equality in European countries, which not only pays tribute to equality of opportunity but also contains a strong component of equality of results. The hegemonic version of the American creed is foremost attuned to compensatory action; nevertheless various forms of affirmative action in the past decades amount to preferential treatment. However, these measures are under fire from various sides today, and considered to be a crucial deviation from basic American principles (Hutton, 2003, 56–57).[11]

More generally, a powerful tendency exists to perceive social phenomena primarily through a cultural lens, which explains why Americans tend to deal with sociopolitical issues in a culturalist way. Given the neglect of social class as a topic of public discourse at the macrolevel, it comes as no surprise then that societal issues connected with social inequality and questions of distributive justice are translated into questions surrounding cultural differences, identity politics, and cultural empowerment in local microprojects in the academic world. This occurs at the expense of involvement in social and political movements in the surrounding society and at the global level that try to tackle the causes of these problems. It has been argued that this privatization of the public sphere and the deliberate rejection of the notion of commonality — in terms of shared public interests and common goods among citizens— has in fact increased the social disempowerment of subordinate groups (Epstein, 1995; Gitlin, 1995, 100–102; Ostendorf, 1996).

Obviously, cultural studies changed significantly during the process of its transatlantic transplantation. Critics have pointed to the status quo affirming nature of cultural studies in America in that its practitioners tend to exaggerate the power and autonomy of the recipients of media and culture products and also confuse active cultural appropriation with political activity (Budd et al., 1990). Perhaps even more important is the fact that cultural studies in the United States was incorporated into a system of higher education that is quite different from that in Britain. Understandably, people in American academia tend to be less informed about the specific problems of culture and politics in Britain. As a result, theoretical notions that were initially formulated in the British context in relation to specific social issues, have been rather forcedly applied to situations in America. This also explains why the emphasis in U.S. cultural studies (and to a much lesser extent within popular culture studies proper) is on abstract theory — that allows for such use[12]— rather than theorically informed, empirical investigations of concrete cultural questions arising from the American sociopolitical context. Apparently, U.S. cultural studies proponents also overlook the fact that many of the relevant debates in England took place in nonacademic journals and magazines targeted at progressive intellectuals, while in the United States there are much weaker connections with political and cultural movements outside academia (O'Connor, 1989, 407). Academic isolation is also enhanced in America by the enormous size of the higher education sector and the crucial role played by private universities. This situation provides institutional conditions that allow critical debates to circulate in a semiautonomous arena at a far greater distance from the sphere of state and government. Indeed, there are few places outside the United States where similar circumstances exist (Bennett, 1998, 35). In sum, according to several observers, it appears that during the reception and academic institutionalization of cultural studies in the United States, the field underwent a much stronger depoliticization — in the sense of a diminished orientation on sociopolitical questions— in comparison to its place of origin, Britain.[13] Thus, U.S. cultural studies came to approximate the state of affairs of most of the homegrown variants of popular culture studies, which have shown little interest in the kinds of social engagement I mean here.

However, at least one leading representative of American cultural studies arrived at a very different conclusion in the early 1990s, which needs to be mentioned here. This took place in the context of heated public discussions about "tenured radicals," who had supposedly taken over university teaching and scholarship in the humanities, launching an attack on the basic values of "Western civilization." In response to various jeremiads about the decline of the public sphere in America and suggestions that leftist intellectuals had abandoned the public for the profession, Michael Denning insisted that what he called the "higher-education industry" is "a crucial public sphere, a key part of American mass culture," and that it is particularly within this sphere that critical public debates on major societal issues take place.[14] Here professors meet students, who should be seen as members of the "general public," in face-to-face encounters during the workday, next to encounters with the general public through the written word and modern communications technology. In Denning's view, cultural studies adopted from the British New Left entailed three related trends in American culture: "the emergence of the postmodern magazine; the reappearance of a leftist social-democratic conception of culture and cultural democracy; and an insurgent movement within the universities to reconceptualize the professional disciplines and the 'humanities' themselves." He saw the first component as perhaps the most important, referring to the emergence of a number of "postmodern cultural studies magazines and the imagined community of writers and readers surrounding them": *Social Text, Cultural Correspondence, Telos, Cultural Critique, Border/Lines, Cultural Studies, Boundary 2, Public Culture, Transition,* and a number of others. They constituted in his eyes an oppositional public sphere not unlike that carried by the legendary "little magazines" such as *Partisan Review, Modern Quarterly,* and *Politics* of the 1930s and 1940s (Denning, 1992, 22–23, 29–30, 32, 35–36). Yet, assuming that this estimation was correct, it still leaves the possibility that the movement toward changing the disciplinary structures and curricula has remained isolated from what is going on in the rest of American society — a movement with an aura of radicalism restricted to the universities themselves, and more interested in intellectual and cultural criticism than in social change, as critics on the left such as Barbara Epstein and Barbara Ehrenreich contended (Ehrenreich, 1991). One may also wonder how many among faculty or students in these disciplines have actually adopted the indicated conception of culture and cultural democracy over the past decade. Was this a movement that really counted (or counts) in academia and beyond?

Uncritical Cultural Populism and Its Affinity with "Market Populism"

In the 1980s, British cultural studies turned to a reappraisal of exactly what goes on in the "reception" or "consumption" of culture, and subsequently came closer to the more affirmative view of popular culture[15] held by the popular culture studies movement in the United States. The notion of consumption as the "passive" moment in the cultural circulation of commodities fell out of favor, replaced by an emphasis on active appropriations of commodities and differential interpretation of "texts" (in the broadest sense, including nonliterary cultural forms) on the part of consumers. Thus, the primary focus was on the output of cultural practice rather than its conduct, actual production, or the institutions and the social conditions of cultural production (Ferguson and Golding, 1997, xx–xxi). This led to what McGuigan has called an "*un*critical cultural populism" (italics added) in cultural studies: "Where cultural elitism had viewed popular taste as inferior, ill-educated and lacking in discrimination, latter-day cultural populism came to see exactly the opposite" (McGuigan, 1992, 138).[16] The attitude reflected in the "new revisionism" according to Frith (1991) was: "if it's popular it must be good!" (572). This in turn is likely to create an overromanticized view of the popular culture consumer, while simultaneously downplaying or even ignoring important institutional questions about cultural power. This tendency then misses Michel de Certeau's (1984) crucial distinction between the "strategies of the powerful" and the "tactics of the weak," or as David Morley put it: "the difference between having power over a text and power over the agenda within which that text is constructed and presented" (Morley, 1997, 125).

The idea of a "common culture" in the social-democratic tradition was a normative ideal that was given a radical and "productionist" bent by the New Left in early British cultural studies' investigations of working-class and youth cultures (Williams, 1968). The idea of some kind of "semiotic democracy" (Fiske, 1989, 1993) that came in vogue in the late

1980s also seemed to be such an "ought" concept, "identifying a desirable condition for which to strive rather than an achieved reality" (McGuigan, 1992, 141). The notion of "grounded aesthetics" coined by Paul Willis should be seen in the same light. It refers to "the creative element in a process whereby meanings are attributed to symbols and practices and where symbols and practices are selected, reselected, highlighted and recomposed to resonate further appropriate and particularized meanings" (Willis, 1990, 21). According to this perspective, there are as many aesthetics as there are grounds for them to operate in, and together they form "the yeast" of the common culture.

Importantly, in 1995 Richard Hoggart expressed his amazement and annoyance about the propensity on the part of cultural studies scholars to find subversion and resistance in every text, in every audience. What mattered most, he argued, was real-world political confrontation, not the ability of some subculture or group of fans to "resist" through expressive styles, thereby closing themselves off and even refusing to attempt to cope with the public life of their societies (Hoggart, 1995, 186). Two years later, Todd Gitlin coined the phrase "anti-political populism" to indicate this tendency within cultural studies, arguing that it merely reinforced the status quo and worsened the existing paralysis in U.S. politics:

> Seeking to find political energies in audiences who function qua audiences, rather than in citizens functioning as citizens, the dominant current in cultural studies stamps its seal of approval upon what is already a powerful tendency within industrial societies: the diffusion of popular culture as a surrogate for politics. It confirms the futility of trying to—indeed, needing to—organize for the public control over the mass media. Moreover, it is pressed willy-nilly toward a rapture of technological progress. It offers no resistance to the primacy of visual and nonlinear culture over the literary and linear.... In its disdain for elitism, cultural studies helps erode the legitimacy of the intellectual life that cultivates assessments of value that have the audacity to stand outside the market. In this way, cultural studies integrates itself nicely into a society that converts the need for distraction into one of its central industries, and calls "critics" those arbiters of taste whose business is to issue shopping advice to restless consumers [1997, 37].

The veracity of these observations is difficult to deny. They also correspond with a historical record that shows that time and again cultural industries have managed to defuse the critical potentials of counterstrains and protests against the hegemonic culture by co-opting them into their offerings of popular culture. This is well illustrated by the counterculture of the 1960s and British punk culture about a decade later, which were both transformed partly into a trend of radical chic and high fashion after some time, and became part of the mainstream culture in their watered-down and commodified versions (Frank, 1997). Another telling example occurred during the 1990s, when high-profile businessmen and political leaders of the neoconservative movement appropriated the issues, strategies, and even the vocabulary of the progressive movement of the 1960s, in a massive "market-populist" backlash against the social and cultural changes of that era.

Initially, the new interest in creative appropriation by consumers of popular culture was a daring approach that went against the grain of prevailing notions at the time; indeed, one positive aspect was that it took seriously consumers' active involvement in cultural reception. But soon it became the dominant stream with the detrimental effects indicated above. This cultural populism also has a close affinity with the idea of the sovereign consumer so prominent in neoclassical economics and free-market thinking within neoliberalism, despite the fact that it has been roundly criticized by institutional economists, economic sociologists, and psychologists on the basis of sound empirical evidence. The ideal conception of the consumer concerned has come under attack for good reason; here, however, I can only touch upon a few basic problems. Obviously, perfect knowledge of the full range of consumer choices remains elusive, and "demand" is not simply the aggregated sum of the rational choices made by consumers. Stimulated at least partly by suppliers through advertising and marketing, production has some determinacy overconsumption. Of course, consumers are also constrained to some extent by limitations of choice. The claim that we are all "sovereign consumers" is a distortion of the actual state of affairs; some consumers are more "sovereign" than others due to the privileged circumstances and advantages of cultural capital and competences resulting from family background and education: "Fundamentally, if you do not have the money or an appropriately cultivated range of competences, which in the 1990s includes a postmodernist picking and mixing of tastes, high and low, then, your potential choices in consumption are thereby limited" (McGuigan, 1997, 143).

It is no coincidence that the new revisionist tendency in cultural studies gained strength at about the same time as neoliberal concepts and practices—spearheaded by U.S. corporate businesses—became much more influential in the economies and politics of large parts of the world in the grip of capitalist globalization. Historian and cultural critic Thomas Frank has unraveled the direct connections between what he calls the "market populism" that became canonical in the United States during the 1990s, and the predominant ideas and practices of cultural studies at the time.

He also traced the influences of this market populism on intellectuals and think tanks affiliated with the "Third Way" of "New Labour" and an influential group of cultural studies proponents in Britain in these same years.[17] The central premise of this market populism is that markets express the popular will more articulately and meaningfully than elections do. The fundamental belief of market populists is simply that the market and the people are essentially one and the same. The market is supposed to be democratic, a perfect expression of the popular will through the operations of supply and demand, poll and focus group, superstore and Internet. This market fundamentalism even embraced the idea that the market was *more* democratic than any of the formal institutions of democracy (e.g., elections, legislatures, government) and that any and all tastes and preferences were articulated in the marketplace. Most importantly, the market by its very nature had no tolerance for snobs, hierarchies, elitism, pretense, which would all be driven away (Frank, 2000, 29).

At the same time that backlash conservatives rallied for "family values" and traditional culture, the corporate right propagated a market populism that associated the will of the people with the operations of the market, in broad agreement with cultural studies scholars "on the revolutionary power of popular culture and in the wonders of subjects who *talked back*, and gloried in symbolic assaults on propriety, on brokers, on bankers, on old-style suit-wearers of all descriptions" (287). This ideology of the American business community of the 1990s as expressed in the rhetorics of management theorists, CEOs (especially of "new economy" businesses), advertisers and PR people, account planners, investors, and bull market ideologues, shared many concerns with cultural studies. In fact, one could find the same frequently expressed desire to attack hierarchies, a similar tendency to see a form of elitism behind any critique of popular-mass culture, and a high regard for audience agency. In Frank's reconstruction, in market populism "too, the language and imagery of production was being effaced by that of consumption; class by classism; democracy by interactivity with the right of audiences to 'talk back' to the CEO (through stockholding), or the brand manager (through the focus group) trumping all other imaginable rights and claims" (290). In this new business climate, "listening executives joined forces with 'change agents' to see to it that we were all 'empowered,' where the old-fashioned leftist suspicion of mass culture was used endlessly as evidence of a distasteful leftist 'elitism' generally" (290). It is clear that the meaning of the term *empowerment* was given an odd spin here, actually referring to cultural incorporation and containment rather than genuine empowerment in terms of workers' participation and codetermination, or even self-management or workers' control, which all rely on countervailing power — some force that resists the imperative of capitalist power in the name of economic democracy. To the extent that cultural radicalism was at stake, this strain was targeted primarily at the Christian-traditional right rather than the neoconservative corporate right. Furthermore, in its praise for transgression and soothing talk about respect for "difference," the politics of the dominant strain of cultural studies appeared to be less cosmopolitan than its proponents tended to think from their self-ascribed position as "world citizens." A French literature scholar has even argued that in the almost exclusive focus on "the possibility of expressing oneself" as "the rightful beginning and absolute end of all social and political life," these politics closely resemble good old American libertarianism (Schwartz, quoted in Frank, 1997, 410, n 14).

Deconstructionism and Its "Principled Uncertainty"

The overemphasis on creative consumption of (popular) culture forms was also fueled by deconstructionism in literary studies and the associated textual turn in cultural studies at the time. In this context, the influence of French poststructuralism — exemplified by such thinkers as Michel Foucault (regardless of how he saw himself in relation to poststructuralism), Jacques Derrida, Jacques Lacan, Jean-François Lyotard, Ernesto Laclau, and Chantal Mouffe — filtered through certain departments of literary and cultural studies in America, has had a less-than-positive influence on popular culture studies in my view. It opened the door to an extreme social constructionism amounting to a form of neoidealism in the epistemological sense (i.e. from the perspective of the theory of knowledge). A philosophy of antiessentialism became dominant that considers the use of the term *real* as almost a provocation. According to historian Barbara Epstein, "the rejection of metanarratives, the insistence that everything must be understood as socially constructed, the rejection of any claims of truth or value, are exaggerated versions of one-sided, partial insights." Her critique suggests that this is a dead end to progressive thought, a view I share. Although the sort of Americanized poststructuralism I have in mind here is not driven by some conspiracy to destroy progressive movements, it nevertheless has negative effects on attempts toward a progressive analysis: "The implicit values of poststructuralism, its celebration of difference and its hostility to unity, make it particularly inappropriate as an intellectual framework for movements that need to make positive assertions about how society could be better organized and that need to incorporate difference within a collective unity for social change" (Epstein, 1985, 84–85). In other words, the resulting emphasis on identity politics makes it very hard to develop and sustain a broader progressive movement aiming for commonalities regarding an envisioned good society and a community life that disparate groups might share together.[18]

Because of poststructuralism's overriding influence, relativism has become absolute, and consists of a set of "relativistic certainties," to borrow David Morley's oxymoron (1997). The development of a relativist, self-reflexive stance (bordering on an orthodoxy in some circles) was partly the result of a proper concern with the politics of knowledge, and with taking into account the power relations between subject and object of knowledge as manifested, for example, in the case of "postmodern" or "self-reflective" ethnography (Clifford and Marcus, 1986). However, I agree with Morley and other critics who have come to the conclusion that the overall effect of deconstructionism in literary studies and cultural studies as influenced by this tendency, "has been a disabling one, as a result of which it becomes pretty hard for anyone to say anything about anyone (or anything) else, for fear of accusation of ontological imperialism" (1997, 122). The basic problem here is that poststructuralist theories are *hypermodern*, as sociologist Alan Wolfe (1992) has pointed out. Because they tend toward an extreme social constructionism and relativism, and are skeptical of supposed boundaries, these theories envision a world of almost perfect equality in which identities are more a question of choice rather than a result of a complex interaction between social determination and innate qualities: "If all differences are transient, then no firm basis for group life — short of some universal group that we share with all other species — is possible. Any effort by any group of people to protect and assign privilege to the particularities of their group will be understood as a futile and self-defeating strategy of protecting difference" (Wolfe, 310–311).[19] There is an elective affinity here with the free-choice thinking of neoliberalism, which could be an important reason why poststructuralism got a much stronger foothold in American academia (including the literary department at Yale University and some pockets at other Ivy League universities) than anywhere else in the world. It has even been argued that "the ... American passion for Derrida, Lyotard and other thinkers who speak well only of difference and implicitly reject any collectivity as a terrorizing totality is merely another manifestation of the lone rebel motif," a quintessential component of American culture (Tetzlaff, 1992, 62) — an interpretation that seems highly accurate. Similarly, Irving Howe has called it "a strange mixture of American populist sentiment and French critical theorizing" (Howe, 1991, 42).

According to this form of antifoundationalism, after the demise of the "grand narratives" there is no consensual basis for evaluating interpretative truth-claims anymore. Theoretical or methodological claims for interpretive adequateness—let alone for empirical validity and reliability, as in the mainstream social and behavioral sciences—are being identified as disguised power games: "The only consensus remaining seems to be that of a broadly defined antifoundationalism, which is strong in subverting arguments for general criteria on which claims for interpretive adequateness [or empirical validity] could be based, but weak in suggesting any criteria that would go beyond a mere performative voluntarism" (Fluck, 1998, 52). The latter is manifested in professional practices within the humanities (especially literary and cultural studies)—and kindred, as yet only very marginal, strains within the social sciences—that stress daring and strength and not necessarily substance of argument, in which the academic with the greatest persuasive power is likely to stand out most.[20] Thus, in judgments and praises of "innovative works," the decisive criteria concern performative qualities that are expressed through major keywords such as *powerful, on the cutting edge, dazzling* and so on (Fluck, 1990, 14).

Notwithstanding the declared political intentions of much of this kind of work within cultural studies, this is, in fact, also politically disabling. "It is hard to mobilize around a political platform of principled uncertainty, especially if one of those principles is that it is ultimately impossible to know what is going on" (Morley, 1997, 122). Importantly, poststructuralism has also rejected the concept of alienation—of estrangement from one's environment, from others, from oneself and from one's work and output—thus undermining a solid basis for social criticism. Epstein (1995) argued that:

> [T]he concept is incompatible with poststructuralism, because [it] ... implies that there are human needs that exist prior to the way in which they are constructed in particular societies, needs that are in some way innate and that are frustrated or met to one degree or another in particular social contexts. If there is no human nature outside social construction, no needs or capacities other than those constructed by a particular discourse, then there is no basis for social criticism and no reason for protest or rebellion [113–114].

Hence from this perspective, strictly speaking, there is also no ground for a critical analysis of specific forms of popular culture production and consumption in terms of cultural imposition, alienation and the like.[21] While broadly in agreement with this critique, I am also aware that the influence of deconstructionism has waned more recently, and that there are signs of a return to history and politics in literary and cultural studies which may make the previous remarks outdated at some time in the near future. Nevertheless, at the time of writing, there clearly is a need in (popular) cultural studies for a critical realism based upon cultural pluralism and a recognition of the theory-informed character of "social facts" in empirical research, without adopting any extreme epistemological or ethical relativism. A problem directly related to this concerns the rise of postmodern theories/worldviews and the textual turn in cultural studies, which has decoupled culture from structural dimensions, thus pushing "the social" back as an area of interest.

Neglect of "the Social"

A tendency to underexpose the social was already present within the indigenous tradition of popular cultures studies in the United States from the beginning, although in earlier years this was tempered by influences from folklore studies, ethnomusicology, anthropology, sociology, media studies, cultural geography, and social history that addressed relationships between culture and social structure. Within the textual-inflected cultural studies strain, a society (or a specific aspect of it) is simply "read" as a cultural "text" that is deconstructed in multifarious ways. In the extreme case, "the social" may even be completely nullified by proclaiming that the entire concept is historically restricted and obsolete in these postmodern times. Yet culture is still undeniably a *social* phenomenon that can very well be the object of empirical investigations from the perspective of anthropology, sociology, political science, or social history.

In a critical discussion of cultural studies, the British sociologist Bryan S. Turner has pointed out that practitioners of textual analyses within the dominant strain of cultural studies lack a clear awareness of the necessity to trace empirically the social effects of texts, signs or images. There is also little awareness of what he calls the "phenomenological concreteness" of people's experiences of cultural objects in specific times and places. The overriding tendency is "to subsume the social under the cultural" (Turner, 1994, 281). According to Turner's assessment (which echoes that of several other observers noted earlier), these tendencies have become more pronounced in the United States than in Britain and other countries of the British Commonwealth under the influence of cultural studies. With the growing emphasis on multiculturalism and the acknowledgment of cultural differences, multiculturalism's proponents contended that it was no longer possible nor desirable to hold on to a well-defined canon. Against this backdrop, cultural studies was enthusiastically received, and its practitioners managed to obtain and create institutional niches within some parts of the humanities and in certain media studies departments. Here the study of media, communication, and culture came to be dominated by a Foucauldean power/knowledge problematic — which initially was explored almost exclusively via texts, and subsequently also digitally by means of audiovisual and computer technologies.

These changes in (inter-)disciplinary approaches should also be seen in light of further commercialization of institutions of higher education. The humanities have difficulty surviving within an academic system that is often heavily dependent on external funding and financial support from the private sector. In the rush to attract funding, cultural studies can at least claim to be of some relevance for the media and cultural industries. At some campuses, cultural studies has become more or less a direct entry into employment in lucrative and trendy businesses such as television, film, and advertising production — hence a close rapprochement between corporate business and "cultural radicalism" at these strongly market-oriented universities (Frank, 2000, 294). With the further demise of governmental social policies and associated welfare arrangements, departments of sociology (and other social sciences) struggle to continue their education and research on the same footing as before. Sociology barely manages to survive as part of a general educational program in the liberal arts or social sciences under general labels such as *social theory* or *cultural studies*. As Turner rightly noted, such cooptation is very unsatisfactory for the discipline because the "reading" of all social relationships as cultural relations drives out the area of interest in what he called "the tensions between scarcity and solidarity," the terrain *par excellence* that the social sciences should focus upon (see also Turner and Rojek, 2001). The politicoeconomical dimensions of both the Marxist and the Weberian tradition of sociology run the risk of getting lost in a form of cultural studies that entails an "apolitical culturalism" because of the way in which multiculturalism tends to be approached here:

> Because postmodern cultural studies assumes moral relativism, it cannot produce, let alone accept, a unified moral criticism of modern societies. It is intellectually unlikely that cultural studies could develop an equivalent to Weber's notion of rationalization or Marx's concept of alienation. Postmodern cultural studies finds it difficult to promote a political vision of the modern world apart from an implicit injunction to enjoy diversity. This lack of politicomoral direction exists in a context of increasing alienation of intellectuals from McUniversity and

increasing rationalization of educational systems. Cultural studies, despite claims to a connection with critical theory, are not adequate as a contemporary response to politics and ethics [283].

Moreover, the multidisciplinary character of cultural studies is not without its problems either, particularly given the growing influence of neoliberal concepts and practices in higher education. Whereas true multidisciplinary presupposes powerful monodisciplines on the basis of which mutual cooperation and cross-fertilization will develop, these disciplines are offered but meager opportunities. In Turner's view, the prevailing form of multidisciplinary implied only weak interdisciplinary, because no assumptions were being made about the appropriate combinations of disciplinary perspectives. Perhaps even more worrying from the perspective of intellectual quality, is that multidisciplinary fits perfectly with the ongoing McDonaldization of universities: an emphasis on modular (= cafeterialike) educational programs on the one hand, and on the other, abolition of sections or sometimes whole departments based on the naïve assumption of a perfect world of limitless multidisciplinary in which each course (or discipline) can be combined with any other one, without further ado (283). This diagnosis brought Turner to the conclusion that the classical sociological tradition should be strengthened and critically thought through as to continuities and discontinuities of contemporary societal developments in comparison with the past. Predictably, he defended the disciplinary basis of sociology (and by implication that of other social sciences) on the basis of its penetrating character and — as he saw it — progressive accumulation of a solid stock of knowledge, while turning against cultural studies, the further expansion of which is likely to only exacerbate those tendencies.

Although Turner's criticism certainly has its merits, it first of all concerns the dominant strain in cultural studies that is one-sidedly textual-inflected and does indeed manifest the less-than-positive "postmodernist" tendencies that he referred to, including cafeteria-system educational programs that are free of obligations. A curriculum of cultural studies more attuned to the social sciences, as I propose below, is likely to suffer less from the deficiencies Turner brought up. It would also be wise, I think, to lay some monodisiciplinary basis for students who will learn the basic principles of a specific discipline (e.g., institutional and political economy, sociology, anthropology, history or literature — nation-based or comparative) when studying for their bachelor's, and then stream into a master's program of interdisciplinary cultural studies. Rather than a freewheeling modular system of courses, one should preferably opt for a master's core curriculum consisting of a strategic combination of basic subjects (including cultural sociology, cultural anthropology, cultural history, cultural philosophy, literature, cultural methodologies) with only a limited number of electives to be selected from a list of well-chosen optional courses (including, for example, sociology of art, cultural policy, social history, social philosophy, aesthetics, and ethics—next to thematic subjects). This will also make communication easier among students when attending courses, because they will all share the same basic stock of knowledge.

In practice, one finds forms of cultural studies at some places that lean toward the humanities, and in other places variants that are more oriented on the social sciences (Bennett, 1998, 57) as suggested here. This need not be a problem so long as introductory courses explore the wider spectrum of cultural studies in sufficient depth.

Reconnecting with the Social Sciences

Given the problems outlined above, I would strongly recommend that popular culture studies link up with the countermovement that has emerged in recent years within British cultural studies and their equivalents in the United States, Australia, Canada, and the European continent, which aims at a rapprochement with the social sciences, under the banner of "bringing sociology back in," and thus tries to do full justice to the sociohistorical context and structural dimensions of culture in its analyses (Ferguson and Golding, 1997; van Elteren, 2001, 111–116). My plea does not automatically imply the severing of popular culture studies' ties to literary studies, and more generally the humanities; on the contrary, a legitimate place remains for the latter. Neither should the two major orientations, or those of the humanities and the social sciences, be merged beyond recognition. Rather, each is a necessary complement to the other, because the substantive focus of each is, or ought to be, the context or ground taken as a given for the other. This is what cultural sociologist Richard Peterson argued about in the late 1970s with regard to popular culture studies, which in my view remains valid today (Peterson, 1977, 390).

The social sciences, in turn, are also likely to benefit from the further involvement with the study of popular culture, a domain which does not get the necessary attention, in particular within mainstream sociology and political science. In the classical sociology of the late 19th and early 20th century, "culture" (in the sense of shared values, belief systems, and lifestyles) was a major area of interest, especially in the works of Max Weber,

Emile Durkheim, Georg Simmel, and George Herbert Mead. In fact, all founders of sociology dealt with the cultural ambiguities involved in the emergence of modernity. In certain respects, this was also the case from the 1940s until the late 1960s within "modern sociology" dominated by structural-functionalism.[22] But with the decline of this sociological strain and the rise of forms of sociology primarily interested in social-structural dimensions, culture generally fell into neglect and was relegated to a separate discipline — cultural anthropology.[23] Rejecting Talcott Parsons's conception of culture as an overarching system of shared norms and values, theories emerged that emphasized social divisions and conflicts. Their proponents oriented themselves on Marx, Simmel, and Weber — whose intellectual legacy was now interpreted as a form of conflict sociology (rather than interpretative sociology), which offered a welcome complement to, if not improvement, of Marx's class theory. In a similar vein, around 1980, a form of historical sociology came in to vogue that saw social struggle and repression everywhere, in social processes such as state making and the mechanisms of imperialism, and in many forms of collective action (revolutions and social movements). Most of the work was radically anti-cultural. This tendency persisted until at least the late 1980s, if not longer (Calhoun, 1989, 1–2). In addition, the so-called rational choice theories that became popular in the late 1970s went even further in their rejection of culture as an area of interest. In assuming a society made up of rational, self-interested actors, the study of meaning systems was left aside in favor of game scenarios and mathematical equations that could best explain social actions aimed at profit maximization according to the protagonists of this approach (P. Smith, 1998, 1–3).

Meanwhile, to the extent that culture is studied within mainstream sociology today, popular culture still tends to be neglected, due partly to a strong influence of Bourdieu's sociology of culture that focuses primarily on sociostructural differences in cultural capital and associated differential participation in forms of elite culture rather than popular culture. Another problem is that mainstream American sociology continues to cling to a view of culture borrowed from classical social anthropology in which culture is conceived as a set of values, norms, beliefs, and attitudes of a population or specific subgroups— in terms of subcultures, counter-cultures, or civic cultures (Smelser, 1992). Diana Crane (1994) criticized this emphasis on "implicit culture" that is in the current, late-modern era certainly incomplete: "Culture today is expressed and negotiated almost entirely through culture as explicit social constructions or products, in other words, through recorded culture, culture that is recorded in either print, film, artifacts or, most recently, electronic media" (Crane, 1994, 2).

I would hasten to add, however, that one should not exaggerate the historical changes in this regard — the notion of implicit culture still has some relevance today, because beliefs, norms, and values remain basic components of human societies that can be traced through approaches as diverse as ethnographic field studies on the one hand, and cross-cultural surveys of values on the other.

However, the assumption of cultural integration and cultural consensus in the classical anthropological and mainstream sociological view of culture — if ever valid regarding preindustrial, tribal societies (because pure, nonhybrid cultures are a theoretical projection and probably never existed) — has certainly become problematic in large-scale contemporary societies that are increasingly becoming multicultural and characterized by all kinds of hybridization. The classic concept of culture as a consistent and coherent entity epitomized more an ideal or ideology rather than that is represented a reality, reflecting the modernist tendencies in the social sciences during the first half of the twentieth century. As Crane points out, mainstream sociology has yet to fully register that in this "postmodern era," the emphasis is on cultural manifestations that are inherently contradictory, inconsistent, and incoherent (4).

There have been some exceptions to the aforementioned one-sided approach of culture though, in specific areas such as the sociology of mass communication, leisure, sports, pop music, and within the microsociological strain of symbolic interactionism. More significantly, however, culture resumed its rightful place within the "new" (American) cultural sociology that emerged in the late 1980s and early 1990s and reclaimed the classical tradition filtered through insights derived from contemporary cultural anthropology and cultural history and British cultural studies. It also manifests a clear interest in popular culture. Compared to earlier cultural sociology, the new variant focuses much more on various manifestations of "recorded culture" as these have materialized in information, entertainment, science, technology, law, education, and arts. The aim, above all, is to avoid the normative consensus approach of Parsonian structural functionalism. Instead, one studies the role of culture in social struggles associated with all kinds of social inequality. Studies of subcultures and organizational cultures have replaced research of a supposedly overarching, united cultural system. Culture is now studied more closely from the perspective that it is heavily fragmented, contested, multifariously layered, inconsistent, internally contradictory, and unstable. There are also influences from French poststructuralism here, which have been processed in a distinctively "American way" within the institutions and academic culture of U.S. sociology, and have been mixed with domestic theoretical traditions, especially pragmatism in American philosophy. These poststructuralist influences may exercise similar negative effects on parts of the new cultural sociology as stipulated above with regard to cultural studies. Yet characteristic of the new cultural sociology is its greater emphasis on more precise conceptualizations and a preference for empirically grounded, middle-range research and the use of neopositivist methods that counter poststructuralism to some extent but also lead to a cutting away of philosophical speculations and societal critiques that one finds in the European tradition (Crane, 1994, 1–4, 17; B. Smith, 1988, 10–14; van Elteren, 70–79).

A specific variant of the newer sociology of culture approach is the flourishing production-of-culture perspective that focuses on the institutional conditions of cultural production. One can discern six lines of inquiry in this domain; these encompass the study of: (1) comparative market structures; (2) market structures over time; (3) reward structures; (4) gatekeeping and decision chains; (5) careers of creative workers; (6) structural conditions facilitating creativity. This perspective likewise offers a suitable framework for interesting comparisons across symbol-producing realms and distinctions between high and low, including patterns of cultural mobility and "differentiation/de-differentiation" of cultural distinctions (Peterson, 1994). However, in order to do justice to human agency and the institutional dynamics of cultural production, this perspective should not be interpreted in a mechanistic way. As Gaye Tuchman reminded us, "[o]ne can do theoretically informed and empirically rich studies of the production of culture without accepting a narrow, linear, sequential model" by marrying the production of culture to what she called "the production of consciousness" (Tuchman, 1983, 340). For that reason one should approach culture not simply as a thing that is produced but as a way of life, and consider the constitutive meanings and practices through which the creation and circulation of cultural goods occurs— a perspective that involves applying theories of culture to "industry" (Negus, 1997, 69). In other words, culture is not simply a product that is processed (like laundry soap) by organizational, technical, and economic factors; instead, culture should be understood more broadly as the means by which people create meaningful life-worlds. The latter are constructed through interpretations, experiences, and activities whereby material is created in connection with its consumption (Jensen, 1984, 104–114). Howard Becker's (1982) perspective concerning the worlds in which art, both in elitist and popular forms, is produced, is relevant here. Accordingly, the creation of works of art (painting, films, novels, music) involves collective practices that are coordinated by shared conventions and "consensual definitions" that emerge as various people form, are attracted to, and are actively recruited, to inhabit different "art worlds." For Becker, it is the cultural life and social values of the art worlds (overlapping production, distribution, and consumption) that are most instrumental in terms of generating the requisite conditions for creative collaboration (i.e., the production of culture) rather than a narrow production-of-culture perspective focused on formal organizational criteria and "product images" (Negus, 1997, 101).

Furthermore, critics such as Nicholas Garnham and Jim McGuigan have pointed out that the separation of culture studies from the political economy of culture has been a disabling feature of the field, a view I share (McGuigan, 1992, 40–41; Garnham, 1997). This means that the link with political economy, which looks at power in relation to the distribution of economic and social resources, and the means and relations of production, must be reintroduced and reinforced. More specifically, in regard to cultural studies, political economy focuses on structures of ownership, management, and control of culture production, and their implications for the outlines of the cultural landscape. Socioeconomic variations in access to, and availability of, cultural texts and practices are also examined. Yet as David Morley warned us, one should then not simply revert back to the "eternal verities" of political economy — as it prevails within orthodox Marxism (Morley, 1997, 121). Political economy as intended here needs to look in particular closely at the new communication and media technologies that have become an essential component of today's economy, which in some ways make it harder for peoples across the world to develop their own cultural lives (Bettig, 1996; McChesney, 2000). Not only do imperial strategies of transnational media conglomerates deserve the attention of cultural studies scholars, so do local and transnational countertendencies, including strategies of movements aimed against such globalizing forces (Davies, 1995, 154).

Toward an Integrative Approach of Popular Culture

These recommendations boil down to a plea for a truly integrative approach of popular culture. In his analytical overview of the cultural industries, the British sociologist Desmond Hesmondhalgh (2002) gave an excellent outline of such an overarching approach (except for the reception of culture, which is deliberately underexposed because it is well covered elsewhere). In the first chapter of his book, Hesmondhalgh introduced the major approaches to culture that are relevant for cultural studies: cultural economics, liberal-pluralist communication studies, various political economy perspectives, the production of culture perspective, radical mediasociology/media studies, and cultural studies, focusing on the meaning of "texts." In chapter 2 he presented criteria by which the cultural industries can be assessed in what he called the current "complex professional era of cultural production," outlined in terms of the organization of production in the cultural industries; the cultural labor market and system of rewards; ownership and structure of cultural-industry companies; and the form and degree of internationalization. The assessment criteria concern specific parameters with regard to the role of large corporations in the cultural industries and in society; conditions of creativity in cultural-industry organizations; international inequality; access to and participation in new technologies; diversity and multiplicity of cultural offerings, and opportunity of choice; quality of cultural supply; social justice and the servicing of interests. In the next chapter, the author focused on various ways in which the development of cultural industries can be explained: through three forms of reduction (technological, economic, and cultural) and a nonreductive, integrative approach that pays attention to politicoeconomical change, political and regulatory change (the rise of neoliberalism), changing business strategies, sociocultural and textual changes, as well as technological change (information technology and consumer electronics). The second half of the book goes into more detail with regard to changes in law and regulation since the early 1980s: deregulation, reregulation, cultural marketization, and attacks on and defenses of public service broadcasting in various countries (chapter 4); ownership and corporate structure; changing strategies of cultural industries, including conglomeration and vertical integration, next to the continuing presence of small companies; intercompany networks and strategic alliances; the increasing importance of marketing; changes in journalistic work, and the conditions of cultural work of technical personnel, creative management, and symbol creators (chapter 5); internationalization, globalization, and the issue of cultural imperialism (chapter 6); new media, digitalization (in the domains of music technologies, publishing, video and computer games, communication networks, the Internet and the World Wide Web, television) and convergence between the various media (chapter 7). The final chapter deals with choice, diversity, and multiplicity in the case of popular music, and the question of whether convergence is identical to homogenization; social justice and changes in cultural texts in terms of commercialization/commodification in relation to the cultural politics of entertainment and the provision of news; the question of declining quality (including the issues of shorter attention spans with regard to certain cultural texts, and the influence of cultural authority) and the rise of quality niche markets (e.g., in the film industry).

An introduction like this could be used as a general frame of reference in teaching popular culture in higher education. Complementary texts might then focus on subjects that get less attention in this book but are standard topics in introductions to and overviews of cultural studies (e.g., Barker, 2000). The latter include theoretical questions of culture, ideology, and power; cultural meaning and knowledge; various dimensions of cultural globalization (interplays between homogenization and heterogenization, creolization/hybridization, etc.); modernity and postmodernism; issues of subjectivity and identity, ethnicity, race and nation; gender, subjectivity and representation; television, texts and audience, and more generally the appropriation of culture by the recipients/consumers involved; cultural space, urban place, and cyberspace; youth, style, and resistance (youth subcultures); and cultural politics and cultural policy.

Fighting Western Centrism and Presentism

In order to obtain a critical awareness of other cultures, and by definition, one's own culture, students of popular culture should also be confronted with more comparative work than is customary, both diachronically (comparisons of a given culture or specific cultural phenomenon in time) and synchronically (comparisons of cultures or specific cultural phenomena across places at a given time). This implies that concerted attempts should be made to become more international or global in mental outlook by reading studies and taking part in discussions of popular cultures across the world, preferably without restriction to the territories of existing nation-states nor to the West. Fascinating in this regard are, for instance, the diverse ways in which the Islamic world in the Middle East has responded to Western mass popular culture, and the changes that the indigenous popular cultures underwent, partly through deliberate interventions by political elites involved in nation building (Stauth and Zubaida, 1987). Also relevant here are studies of a wide variety of border cultures and diasporic cultures (including Jewish, Arab, African, and Hindu diasporas and other immigrant cultures).

The overall aim is to foster cultural sensitivity among popular culture students, including cultivating a better understanding among Americans of the strong impact of U.S. culture on today's globalizing cultures in various domains. Next to the obvious fact of America's pivotal position in the area of popular culture, one must be aware that other cultural influences implicated in U.S.-style capitalist globalization may be even more important. These include corporate values and business culture, management and labor practices, strategies of private and semiprivate international relations forums and think tanks, cultural and political development policies for developing countries, as well as academic and professional cultures.[24] As I argued elsewhere, the notion of "U.S. cultural imperialism" retains its relevance today, although it should be seen in a different light from the conventional sense of the term, and in certain domains the idea of a broader "Anglo-American cultural imperialism" seems to be more accurate (van Elteren, 2003).

Europeans, too, will benefit from such conscious-raising underpinned by comparative approaches, becoming more aware of the cultural radiation of Europe more generally, or of individual nation-states such as Britain, France, Spain, and the Netherlands, and their continuing influence on the everyday cultures of their former colonies (Sreberny-Mohammadi, 1997, 50–51). The same applies to the vestiges of the former Soviet Union's cultural influences in its satellite states during the Cold War era and its aftermath.[25] In this regard, it is evident that Europe developed its own identity through a longstanding, all pervasive cultural discourse in which non–Europeans were assigned a secondary racial, cultural, and ontological status (Said, 1993). This also includes, of course, the hegemonic Euro-American culture of the United States.

Given the predominance of American scholarship[26] in popular culture studies, and more generally in many fields of the social sciences and humanities, that sets professional standards and offers models of theory and research,[27] European and other international popular culturalists should also make serious attempts to be less dependent on prevailing problem definitions in the United States as a starting point for comparisons.[28] For such constructions may hinder them in obtaining adequate insights into what is going on in other cultures and, paradoxically, even in the United States itself. A good example is the way in which a dominant conception of multiculturalism in America tends to downplay the issues of social inequality and injustice that are involved, focusing primarily on identity politics tied to cultural differences and differences in cultural power.[29] Above all, one must try to refrain from using a discourse of popular culture in which the various topics that draw most attention in the United States are considered to be more or less identical with "universal" issues of popular culture, and the American situation is taken as primary frame of reference (a similar problem is at issue in international American studies.) To counter such tendencies, international popular culture studies should not place itself in a position that privileges popular culture studies in the United States. Following a pattern like that employed by the U.S. film and music industries, the label *international* then functions as a stopgap, an euphemism that indicates the transformation of cultural products, streamlining them in such a way that they are more likely to draw the interest of a worldwide audience but which nevertheless retain a basic orientation on American culture. A prioritization of U.S. popular culture studies necessarily means giving up alternative approaches that might be beneficial for producing interesting contributions to a globalizing field of (popular) cultural studies. Because of their more distanced and broader perspective, such alternatives are also likely to produce rich insights into U.S. popular culture itself. In short, the value of worldviews that are not centered on the United States should be acknowledged. For the same reason, it is also wise to borrow from local intellectual traditions and areas of interest, as well as from non–American and non–English-language sources and literature, including those outside the European culture area, to help counter Eurocentrism.

In order to break through the prevailing frameworks of Western, or rather Euro-American centrism, one should also incorporate insights derived from the new cultural anthropology or ethnography that expressly tries to deal with such biases (James et al., 1997). This means another break with the dominant cultural studies stream. Remarkably, given all the interest in ethnicity, multiculturalism, and hybridization, cultural studies thus far has remained mostly a Western affair. Consequently, intercultural comparisons with the help of cultural anthropology may offer excellent opportunities to trace similarities and dissimilaries between cultures, and to sensitize students to the culture-bound character of many matters they tend to take more or less for granted. But they will, it is to be hoped, also learn more about the universal nature of basic components of human life that people the world over share.[30] Here it should also be noted that since the late 1980s, some anthropologists have developed macroanthropological approaches of cultural globalization that are very useful for contextualizing contemporary popular culture more adequately (e.g., Hannerz, 1992; Friedman, 1994). In contrast to classical anthropology (mostly of tribal societies allegedly bound to clearly delimitated local territories—a problematic assumption in itself, as research has shown), their perspective conceives cultures as social practices and collective meaning systems that belong primarily to social relationships and to networks of such relationships. Not necessarily and only indirectly do they belong to specific localities and are they delimitated by the geographic borders of nation-states (Hannerz, 1992, 39).

Related partly to the new anthropological line of inquiry, the teaching of popular culture would also benefit from drawing more on folklore studies. This field, often called ethnology nowadays, was drastically renewed via strong influences drawn from anthropology, sociology, and history, in which theories and concepts have been borrowed from the social sciences and cultural history in the *Annales* tradition,[31] and then applied to the study of folk-popular culture in its many dimensions and manifestations, including material culture, feasts and rituals, religious folk culture, oral culture, and popular singing culture. With modern ethnology, areas of interest include living folk cultures, as well as contemporary feasts and customs among ethnic minorities (Dekker et al., 2000). Further, interesting links to regional cultural history have also been made in this thriving field (Nissen; Bijsterveld).

Generally speaking, history should receive more attention in the study of popular culture than is the case at the moment, in order to avoid presentism.[32] Therefore, in my view, another link that needs to be strengthened is that with cultural history and history of mentalities (including historical anthropology) as well as those strands within historical sociology that incorporate meanings and cultural practices.[33] Popular culturalists also need to engage more with historical studies of popular cultural forms before the 20th century. Only then can popular culture students obtain a deeper understanding of the ways in which popular culture changed in the course of time, and its shifting relations with folk, working-class, ethnic, and elite cultures in different parts of the world. These historical investigations should also include the ways in which popular culture forms are related to their social contexts. This means a closer tie with social history than tends to be the case in cultural studies now — in sharp contrast to its early years in Britain when the field was heavily influenced by the British new social and cultural history that emerged in the 1960s. Moreover, the teaching of many topics of popular culture in a globalizing world cannot take place without being severely flawed, if not set within a world-historical context (e.g., Hopkins, 2002). Only in this way can one truly counter tendencies of Euro-American-centrism in which the allegedly exceptional history of modernity and postmodernity of the North Atlantic world is commonly taken for granted (Morley, 1996, 349–352). Herein lie ripe opportunities for combating latter-day forms of Western cultural imperialism as well of orientalism (Said, 1978; Hourani, 1992; Hodgson, 1992) that tenaciously persist in the current, so-called postcolonial era.

A Popular Culture Program from a Critical-Emancipatory Perspective

In line with my programmatic statements above, I suggest that, ideally, teaching popular culture could be divided into five areas of interest and associated analytical frameworks, based on the existing practices of research of culture: (1) the political economy and institutional structures of culture; (2) cultural history and the persistence of cultual patterns; (3) the production and distribution of culture; (4) the societal effects and reception of culture; (5) meaning systems and social actions in relation to the reproduction and change of institutionalized culture (J.R. Hall and Neitz, 1993, 17–19). These frameworks define the focus and boundaries or subject matter of the field of culture. A given analytical framework brings into focus particular aspects of phenomena in the social world that are relatively distinct from those highlighted by other analytical frames. In practice, two or more areas of interest are sometimes dealt with simultaneously. One must also acknowledge that some disagreements about (popular) culture come about because analysts use different frames to define the field. Nevertheless, the analytical distinctions just outlined will be expedient in structuring the curriculum and division of labor among staff. Further, whenever appropriate with regard to the problems of interest, popular culture should be taught in tandem with elite culture, as well as from a comparative perspective, depending on the chosen topics, questions, and methodological approaches. The five major areas of interest can further be characterized as follows:

1. *Political economy and institutional structures of culture.* This concerns first of all the sociopolitical context such as existing property relations and production systems, technological infrastructure and material resources, demographic structure, class and status relations, as well as overarching patterns of material and symbolic culture as represented in various social institutions such as work and family, language, prevailing ideologies, collective representations, and value orientations. This area of interest also includes the more specific economic–institutional circumstances under which the production of culture proper takes place: economic property patterns, market relations, and the management strategies of specific commercial enterprises as well as the patronage systems of private agencies and persons, and the regulatory and funding practices of governments with regard to the private, semi-private or governmental institutions that are directly involved in the production of culture.

2. *Cultural history and the persistence of cultural forms.* Many contemporary cultural phenomena have parallels in cultural practices and processes at other times and places. All societies have basic cultural processes in common, but cultural objects and practices have also spread through imitation, diffusion, and selective borrowing. In the

cultural legacy of preindustrial societies one can find the origins of current forms of popular culture; therefore, past folk culture is of relevance for understanding the cultures of contemporary societies. This also pertains to older cultural customs that have been transplanted abroad; take, for example, the four different British "folkways" that formed the basis for the everyday cultures as these developed in four distinctive cultural areas in the United States from colonial times onwards (Hackett Fisher, 1984). However, in searching for forms of folk culture, one must always remain aware that they renew and adapt themselves to changing circumstances, in which "invented traditions" and practices of fabricated and staged authenticity (Peterson, 1997, 207, 212, 220; MacCannell, 1992, 18) are at stake. Consequently, this area of interest necessarily encompasses phenomena of "folklorization," which refers to a specific historical development in people's dealing with passed-down traditions in the cultural shaping of their social life when a custom or ritual is on the verge of disappearing. Certain influential groups then reappropriate the cultural phenomenon in question, thereby strengthening its representative or demonstrative features in order to make it much easier to put on, thus insuring its survival/revival, albeit in adapted form. As a result, the social function that the cultural phenomenon fulfills for the people involved changes drastically (Nissen, 1994, 10–14). Next to relations between popular and folk culture, this area of interest also entails the development of modern mass popular culture as it came into being, along with the arrival of industrial society in the course of the 19th century (for the United States, see Kammen, 2000), with clear foreshadowings in 18th-century England (Maase, 1997). Last but not least, transcultural, world-historical, or globalizing approaches of popular culture are an integral part of this field of interest.

3. *The production and social distribution of culture.* All culture is not equally accessible to all members of a society. Instead, cultural forms and objects tend to be received and appropriated differently by various social strata and groups on the basis of socially organized production and distribution of culture. The stocks of culture acquired by different social strata and groups are crucial conduits through which social differentiation and association occur on the basis of class, gender, ethnic, and other distinctions. These are not natural occurrences per se but rather the consequences of how culture is distributed. Relevant here too are the ownership and control of cultural distribution, as well as the content of what is distributed, which, in turn, raises questions about the

relationship between culture and power. The cultural forms that are distributed are produced through social action, often in organized form, through the operations of cultural entrepreneurs, cultural industries and art worlds (both popular and elitist). This third area of interest posits the centrality of the processes, resources, actors, roles, activities, organizations, genres, conventions, and recipes through which production and distribution of culture take place.

4. *Societal effects and reception of culture.* Strictly speaking, the word *effect* is not pertinent here, because the consumers of culture are not passive receptacles of culture, but are actively involved in the reception process. They borrow selectively from cultural offerings and appropriate these in ways that are sometimes more, sometimes less creative, but seldom merely passive (although, as we know, the proverbial couch potato does exist). This area of interest encompasses the study not only of the reception of various cultural forms and objects by different audiences or publics but also the wider social and ideological ramifications of popular culture and mass communication that cannot be derived directly from findings in audience response and reception studies.

5. *Meaning systems and social actions.* Instead of analyzing the reception of specific cultural objects by actors, this framework concentrates on how actors draw from among their cultural repertoires in actual conduct, and how these processes reproduce or change a given institutionalized culture. If this area of interest is neglected, popular culture students will be more inclined to accept the existing institutional structures more or less as a given point from where to begin and end their cultural analyses, thus perhaps unwittingly reaffirming an undesirable situation. The area includes social and religious movements and tendencies, subcultures, and countercultures of multifarious kinds that aim for cultural change, along with movements and subcultures with a vested interest in the status quo or that want to turn the clock even further back.

Developing and Discussing Evaluative Judgments

In addition to teaching the theorical frameworks and empirical contents of these five areas of interest, there is also a need to reflect upon appraisals of popular culture. Within the British cultural studies movement there has been a tendency to see culture as more or less synonymous with ideology (Carey, 1996, 65), thereby focusing on political aspects.[34]

This led to the neglect of aesthetics, that is, questions about the quality of form and style in terms of intrinsic beauty, its degree of approximation to the sublime, which is not so surprising, given the fact that cultural studies emerged from disciplines in which issues of taste and judgment are kept away from academic analysis and assessment. The dominant strain of the PCA movement, too, has eschewed aesthetic judgments[35] because of its antielitist position and likewise the considerable influence of a literary studies tradition that refrains from making such evaluations. As Barbara Herrnstein Smith has reminded us, "evaluation" was long ago banned from literary criticism, and is not yet admitted to studies of popular culture (Herrnstein Smith quoted in Frith, 1998, 571). One might add here the "value-free" orientation of the mainstream social sciences, at least to the extent that cultural studies was influenced by the field — a weak influence at best. The "new criticism" of postwar literary studies in America did make critical evaluations though, but these remained confined to "technical," formal judgments of the intrinsic literary qualities of canonical texts, with high modernist poetry as the privileged literary form and stories and novels relegated to a secondary place. The focus was particularly on the elements of a poem's construction and its aesthetic dimension in a narrow sense, eschewing its historical context, social function, or political significance (Aronowitz, 1993, 223–225).

There is a major exception to the general trend, however, and that was the elitist cultural program of the Leavisite tradition organized around the magazine *Scrutiny* in Britain, which made critical judgments in terms of binary oppositions such as Culture versus *kitsch* or mass culture. The leftist variant of this tradition with a more nuanced view of popular culture in its relation to high culture — as practiced by Hoggart and Williams, among others — had a distinctive impact on British cultural studies in its formative years but then moved to the background and ultimately disappeared completely. The Leavisites created in Britain "an educational space for the study of popular culture. Both Hoggart and Williams occupy this space in ways that challenge many of the basic assumptions of Leavisism, while also sharing some of these assumptions," according to John Storey. Because of "this contradictory mixture — looking back to the 'culture and civilization' tradition, while at the same time moving forward to culturalism" and laying the foundations of cultural studies, Hoggart's *The Uses of Literacy* (1957), and Williams's *Culture and Society* (1963) and *The Long Revolution* (1965) can be considered as both texts of the break with Leavisism and examples of left–Leavisism (Storey, 1998, 45).[36] The latter strain also had some influence among literary and cultural critics within the tradition of the cultural front in America.

In order to help redress the overall imbalance I would recommend (when possible) fostering classroom discussions about aesthetic judgments of culture informed by insights from the sociology of art regarding social influences both on the production of culture and subsequent aesthetic evaluations (Wolff, 1981, 1993). In seeking to defend popular culture against uncritical cultural populism, as I attempt here, Simon Frith (1991) has argued that "the essence of cultural practice is making judgments and assessing differences ... there is no reason to believe *a priori* that such judgment processes work differently in different cultural spheres" (574). The foundation of this argument becomes stronger when we acknowledge that the conventional distinction between form (high culture) and function (low culture) is no longer tenable, even when conceptualized as a contrast between the realm of quality and aesthetics on the one hand, and relevance and productivity on the other.

Just like popular culture, high culture is fully absorbed within commodity production; according to John Frow (1995), it is a *pocket* within commodity culture. High culture's primary relationship is with the intelligentsia — also called the "category of cultural workers" or "new middle class" (not identical to the ruling class, however) — and with the education system, "the system which is the locus of their power and the generative point for most high-culture practices" (Frow, 1995, 86).[37] Like popular culture, elite culture can incorporate any number of diverse aesthetic texts. However, the fact that the categorical distinction between high and popular culture has become blurred, does not mean that no critical judgments are possible or necessary anymore. Frow suggested that the analysis of cultural texts should occur in relation to what he describes as "the institutionalized regimes of values that sustain them and that organize them in relations of difference and distinction" (87). These regimes, and their accompanying semiotic codes, are relatively independent of, and bear no immediate relation to class, gender, ethnicity, age.

The notion of "regime of values" enables us to reflect critically upon the relationship between canonical high culture and popular culture outside the canon, and to conceive of these as evaluative practices rather than as collections of texts with a necessary internal coherence. Thus it is possible, for example, that a graffiti text can figure just as prominently within a high culture regime as a popular culture one. In the end, one does not fall back on the use of these categories as substantive or internally coherent categories, but merely accepts the fact that the concepts of high and popular culture continue to rule the cultural field and work to bring about ideological effects of cultural distinction (150–151).

With the benefit of hindsight, we can see that the aim of British cultural studies to broaden culture beyond an aesthetic canon based upon an established distinction between "high" and "low" culture shifted from an oppositional project in the 1960s and 1970s to an affirmative interest in cultural consumption during the 1980s, so that almost everything became "culture" under the equivalence of exchange value (Savage and Frith, 1993). In America, cultural studies imported from Britain largely became even more affirmative, according to several observers (but which conclusion has been contested by at least one other, well-informed analyst, as noted earlier). Notwithstanding its radical rhetorics—or perhaps even contrary to its original intentions—cultural studies converged de facto, willingly or unwillingly, toward the market populism advocated by neoconservatives of the corporate right. It seems to me now that this holds only true for the majoritarian cultural studies in America, whereas there is another stream of U.S. cultural studies—weaker in terms of numbers of participants—that cultivates a critical new leftist orientation, especially organized around a counter public sphere of new "little magazines." This is qua setup (but not ideologically) similar to the tradition of the "New York intellectuals" of the 1930s and 1940s. Popular culture studies in the United States, as practiced by members of the Popular Culture Association (PCA) and others in the same vein, was never characterized by a politically oppositional goal, but was from the outset a quintessential American grassroots movement within academia — antielitist and populist in its aims. PCA's inclusiveness and liberality have always been two of its major assets, but the other side of the coin tends to be a dearth of critical theorizing and assessments of popular culture forms.[38] Overall, there is clearly a need for redress, indicated by several leading U.S. scholars of cultural studies, including, during the 1990s, Andrew Ross, Stanley Aronowitz, Douglas Kellner, Gary Nelson, and Michael Bérubé (Frank, 2000, 294). I too added my voice to the chorus a few years ago in a sympathetic yet critical overview of the PCA and popular culture studies in the United States (van Elteren, 2001).

It is my opinion that a curriculum of popular culture should include discussions of mass-mediated cultural stereotypes about sex and gender, race and ethnicity, class, religion, and the like (Hall and Neitz, 1993, 7). The negative aspects of popular culture should also be addressed; take, for example, the modeling of violent behavior as a means of conflict resolution (whereas other methods may be preferable from a humanitarian standpoint) in specific action films or video and computer games, or forms of U.S. popular culture that entail various kinds of conspiracy theories to explain ordinary people's problems. Most importantly, recent diagnoses of the decline of American culture — and by implication of other cultures involved in capitalist globalization, spearheaded by the United States, which threatens the humanistic Enlightenment culture by corporate consumer culture (Berman, 2000)— must be taken seriously, and their implications for the study of popular culture explored further. Obviously, this can only be done by bringing value judgments into the field, which is acceptable if these are then subjected to public discussion and criticism.

Maintaining some notion of distinction in teaching popular culture can also function as a healthy self-reflexive device for cultural scholars themselves. The Norwegian cultural studies proponent Jostein Gripsrud — referring to the basic truth that the ability "to take part in both high and and low culture's codes and practices is a class privilege"— has argued that "[h]igh culture remains a sphere worth conquering with those who now are excluded from it, not least because of the critical potential of its meta-language" (Gripsrud, 1989, 204). The potential of this metalanguage refers to the opportunity to take a critical distance from everyday reality and to create mental degrees of freedom, for oneself or the social group one belongs to. Gripsrud saw it as a significant task for critical intellectuals "to draw on this potential in order to turn [their] inescapable social distance from other categories of people into a critical one, serving an 'emancipatory knowledge-interest'"[39] (204). He asserted that this is the very reason why the traditional distributive idea of cultural politics favored by the social-democratic movements retains some relevance. Gripsrud is correct, I believe. We also have to recognize that this cultural ideal was at one time more widely shared, and included other leftist groupings, progressive-liberal, and Christian-democratic movements in Europe and the United States too.

Likewise, I want to add that popular culture may just as well contain such a critical potential if read properly, as for example, in the case of collective memories engrained in the signifying practices of U.S. popular television, music, film and novels (Lipsitz, 1990). Herein lies a major task for critical intellectuals who teach popular culture courses and take part in public debates on the societal implications of popular culture. But in order to prevent indoctrination by intellectuals who think they more or less have a monopoly on truth-claims and are able to uncover the "false consciousness" of their audiences on this basis, a didactic approach is needed in which there is a genuine two-way communication and dialogue between teacher-scholar and students (critic and audience respectively), with an open-minded approach and active involvement on both sides. Only then can we speak of communicative action as an intersubjective accomplishment of both parties. Despite the fact that a truly balanced dialogue is never easy to achieve, it is something to at least strive for. This aim implies speaking and writing in language accessible to a wider audience (avoiding technical academic jargon) but without dumbing down content.

As I see it, attempting to unleash the critical potential of popular culture also involves recent calls for the revision of the public sphere in the field of culture, aimed at creating better conditions for practicing citizenship in a civil society (Goldfarb, 1991, 143–151; McGuigan, 1996, 135–153, 176–190). These claims recognize a pluralistic public sphere or even competing public spheres in contemporary democracies, evoking the normative values of rational-critical debate and take class, gender, and ethnic differences into account, as well as opportunities and constraints of transnational popular culture forms and new communication technologies (Fraser, 1992; Baynes, 1994). As yet these attempts at recovering this "civil" citizenship are made primarily within a national framework, but there is also a need to rethink citizenship in terms of human rights on a transnational basis in today's globalizing world (since the nation-state may no longer be the most suitable political framework for securing citizenship rights). According to some observers, one might expect a convergence between the idea of global human rights and a concept of late-modern cultural complexity that acknowledges the incommensurability of worldviews, the fragmentation of political discourse, and multicultural citizenship beyond the sphere of the nation-state.[40] Needless to say, this offers great, in some cases almost insurmountable problems for communicative action in educational practices, but even so I would still uphold the ideal of an open discussion about the critical charges and appraisals of the cultural forms concerned.

Of course, I am the first to admit that the teaching of popular culture as outlined here makes great demands on both teachers and students alike. Yet if we take our field seriously, and also seek to have some influence both in academia and the world of politics, there is, in my opinion, no other viable alternative except to set high standards for ourselves. Popular culture is too important a business to be left exclusively to the cultural industries and their uncritical champions.

Notes

[1]Whether this expansion was always positive for the quality of education and research at these institutions, is a question I will address later in this essay.

[2]The continuous attacks on this movement in the media, especially in the Springer press, evoked numerous demonstrations in front of Springer buildings. Even more importantly, the mass media in general, and Springer in particular, were held responsible for the fact that the "masses" did not join the students in the street. In this context the Frankfurt School's critique on the cultural industries could be used as a rationale for the frustrating state of affairs: blinded by ideology (or a "false consciousness"), imposed upon them by the media, the "masses" acted against their own

interests by staying at home (in front of their television sets). The movement's leaders did not analyze the historical origins of Adorno/Horkheimer's perspective, and merely used the latter's theory as a convenient "explanation" why revolution did not come about. Many of them acquired leading positions in academia in the 1970s, as well as strategic positions in the media, the rest of the educational system, and other important areas of social life. To the extent that they kept their political beliefs, they tended to hang onto an overdetermined version of the all-pervasive power of the culture industries, and the Frankfurt School's distinction between "good" high culture (i.e., selected works of modernism) and "bad" mass culture, ignoring the fact that since the time of Adorno and Horkheimer the good/bad dichotomy had been modified and made more complex by members of the neo–Frankfurt School (Kreutner, 1989, 246–247).

[3]Compare, for instance, Mark Twain's well-planned and carefully cultivated appearances in public life and his obsessive focus on the clever trick, the skillful manipulation in this writings; he was one the first real stars of American literary culture in the modern sense of the word (Fluck, 1994). Another good example is, of course, Ernest Hemingway.

[4]In associating cultural mandarins with popular culture — albeit it of a certain kind: niches within mass-mediated culture for intellectual debates — Agger (1982) offers a paradoxical word combination or oxymoron, of course. He gives the example of a Habermas essay on the reunification of the two Germanies in a West German magazine (before the reunification) which would have much greater credibility than a similar essay by Galbraith (let alone Jameson) in an American magazine (Agger, 176). However, Agger exaggerates the difference, in my opinion. There are still publication outlets for critical intellectuals in the United States, although both their number and reach have diminished significantly, and public intellectuals are increasingly becoming marginalized; in this the further deregulation of the media landscape by the Federal Communications Commission (FCC), which allows an even heavier concentration of media-owning corporations than before, certainly does not help either. Agger also does not recognize that in Europe the space for critical intellectual debate is diminishing as well and that, on the other hand, Europeans take notice of the writings of critical American intellectuals, directly or as filtered through translations or summaries in European publications.

[5]According to Pine and Gilmore (1999), as a consequence of mass customization, commodities change into goods, goods tend to change into services, and services are said to change into experiences. Commodities are interchangeable because they have not yet undergone any treatment. Goods made out of commodities are material or tangible. Services, consisting of a number of immaterial activities carried out for a client and often at the client's request, are generally higher priced than goods. Although experiences are intangible, people may attach great value to them because they are memorable, so they are willing to pay substantial amounts in some cases. Pine and Gilmore depict experiences as the fourth economic type of supply; different from services as services are from goods. While experiences as economic commodities are nothing new — think of the Disney empire — they have long been neglected and perceived as similar to everything else supplied in the service sector. However, according to Pine and Gilmore, they have now been discovered as the way for producers to survive in the ever more competitive future.

[6]A frightening example is the use of popular music genres (including so-called "turbo folk," rock, punk, "global beat," and dance) by Serbs and Croats for purposes of ethnic exclusion of "the other," only weakly countered by among other things cosmopolitan Yugo-rock in the Bosnian capital of Sarajevo in former Yugoslavia (Barber-Kersovan, 2001).

[7]By the 1960s, most of them had backed away from their earlier Marxism and toned down their criticisms of capitalism and mainstream American culture under the exigencies of cold war anticommunism. Like the elitist cultural conservatives, they now tended to hold the masses themselves, rather than the cultural industries, responsible for their ignorance (Lazere, 1997, 7).

[8]Mills's (1963) view was bleaker than that of Trilling, Greenberg, and Warshow, however. He saw no place for the autonomous avant-garde or intellectual. But neither did 1987 the hold the rank and file and stars of the cultural industries responsible for the then-existing political situation in the United States, which he considered oppressive from his New Left perspective. Rather, Mills saw both the hacks and the stars as possible agents of change, and called on "cultural workmen" to "repossess" the cultural apparatus, based on an ideal of workers' control (Mills, 1963, 418–419; Denning, 1996, 112–113).

[9]Next to Stuart Hall's stronghold, the legendary Centre for Contemporary Cultural Studies (CCCS) in Birmingham, there were other institutions and intellectual projects involved in the early development of cultural studies in the UK — in particular the Society for Education in Film and Television (SEFT) should be mentioned here (Bennett, 1998 43–44).

[10]This is probably due to the fact that cultural studies had relatively more to offer in terms of theoretical frameworks, and with regard to areas of interest such as ideology and the politics of the popular, working-class culture, youth subcultures, "race"/ethnicity, cultural globalization and cultural policy-making.

[11]In this view of a fair society, the notion of equity is one that promotes opportunity for all but that is indifferent to the preexisting and resulting distribution of risks and rewards. Consequently there is little inclination to use governmental power to equalize chances at the starting point, or to improve the circumstances of those at the starting line if they are unlucky or simply fail. For the same reason trade unions and notions of social partnership are regarded with deep suspicion. In this worldview, business should have as much room to maneuver as possible to pursue its interests. This makes it very difficult to develop and wield countervailing powers against the status quo.

[12]This is a major reason why a small number of articles by Stuart Hall drew disproportionate attention among American cultural studies practitioners.

[13]There have been some countertendencies, which distinguished themselves in this regard, however, including a group of British expatriates at the University of Minnesota; members of the Department of Communication at the University of Massachusetts, Amherst; the Mass Communications Program at the University of California, San Diego; the Departments of Sociology at the City University of New York and the University of New York at Buffalo, New York; the Unit for Criticism and Interpretative Theory at the University of Illinois, Urbana-Champaign (Lazere, 1987; Nelson, 1998 and Grossberg, 1982; Angus and Jhally, 1992; Agger, 1989; Ross, 1993; Aronowitz). Also relevant is the East-West Center in Honolulu, Hawaii, with its Program for Cultural Studies, that plays an intermediary role between Western (mostly Anglo-American) cultural studies and an emerging field of international, non–Western dominated cultural studies. Paradoxically, Australian cultural studies scholars (including immigrant Ien Ang from Holland) have been major instigators of this attempt to develop such international cultural studies (Stratton and Ang, 1996).

[14]The public sphere included in Denning's view three spheres, each with its own professionals, part-timers, clerical workers, and public: "first, the culture industries of film, broadcasting, recording, publishing, education, and journalism," that "serve to regulate and facilitate communication"; "second, the state cultural apparatuses,

including a wide range of local, regional, and national agencies, libraries, museums, and schools; and third, the voluntary associations including unions, political associations, churches, and religious congregations, foundations, 'high culture' proper (privately supported orchestras, opera companies, universities, and historical societies), the world of small alternative businesses (such as independent bookstores), and what remains of folk culture, groups of hobbyists and enthusiasts" (Denning, 1992, 31).

[15]Yet at a subterranean level, British cultural studies retained some critical elements of its leftist heritage.

[16]Although McGuigan's critique was widely acknowledged by cultural studies scholars in the course of the 1990s, this seems to have had hardly any impact on the actual development of the field, and critics continued to attack cultural studies on these grounds.

[17]The latter even included Martin Jacques, former editor of *Marxism Today* who, in 1993, helped found the London think tank Demos connected with the "Third Way" of "New Labour," and became its director. Jointly with British cultural studies' figurehead, Stuart Hall, he edited the seminal 1989 collection of essays *New Times* that marked the tradition to "post–Marxism" of this group of British intellectuals. Two other former contributers to *Marxism Today*, Geoff Mulgan and Charles Leadbeater, also joined the new strain and fueled New Labour's ideological thinking and were even directly involved in the development of policies by Blair's administration in the late 1990s (for further details, see Frank, 2000, 347–353).

[18]For a similar critical view on excessive identity politics in the form of "culture wars" and the fragmentation of the left in America in the past decades, see Jacoby (1994); Gitlin, (1995).

[19]For this reason also an overt hostility toward sociology can be found among many poststructuralist and postmodernist thinkers. On the other hand sociology is also one of the few academic fields in the United States (and possible even more elsewhere) that have hardly been susceptible to postmodern tendencies (Rosenau, 1991).

[20]Such scholastic visibility can be obtained through cultural radicalization which allows and encourages strong statements; another strategy is highly ideosyncratic "theorization" to acquire and maintain professional distinctiveness, which have both become endemic in literary and cultural studies (Fluck, 1990, 14).

[21]However, the usage of the concept of alienation with regard to "the condition of postmodernity" (Harvey, 1989) is not without its problems. "The trouble with alienation ... is that it refers to problems of identity derived from production, whereas postmodernity is best understood with regard to consumption and consuming identities in a global marketplace, which may or may not be a problem depending on where you stand with respect to postmodern discourse" (McGuigan, 1997, 208). Nonetheless, I argue that labor and the workplace still have a significant influence on people's identities and ways of life in this globalizing, late-modern world, and are not replaced by consumption and membership of a consumer society as the sole determinants of people's identities and stances in life. In this regard the concept of alienation can still be used, albeit with some obvious modifications concerning the changed nature of much of work (due especially to incorporation of modern computer and communications technologies), and the greater impact of consumerism on many people's everday life.

[22]Yet in structural functionalism the major emphasis was on structural influences on cultural beliefs and values. The same applies to conflict sociology. More generally, European classical sociology was very selectively absorbed into American sociology at the expense of cultural sociology. For example, Weber's historical studies of the influence of religious values on social and economic institutions were highly influential in American sociology but relegated to the sociology of religion, which obtained

a privileged position vis-à-vis cultural sociology, and Durkheim's work on social structure — a major influence on structural functionalism — was privileged above his interest in culture, which was at least as important. In the history of American sociology
it were mostly proponents of symbolic interactionism who assigned a signficant role
to cultural meanings in influencing human behavior (Crane, 1994, 1–2).

[23]This situation remained unchanged until at least the mid–1980s. Craig Calhoun
has pointed out how most American introductory textbooks showed vestiges of this
tendency, in that culture was compartmentalized as the topic of a single chapter, and
hardly mentioned elsewhere in the text. Religion, for instance, was usually discussed
with little or no connection to the concepts introduced in the culture chapter, whereas
culture and religion are integrally related, as most classical sociologists recognized. Also
worrisome was that such culture chapters were largely based on the work of Kroeber,
Linton, Mead, and others, whose works were those of anthropologists of two of three
generations past. No leading contemporary cultural anthropologists were mentioned,
let alone recent works in literary criticism, philosophy, and history that are central to
social studies of culture. Calhoun added, however, that textbooks are usually lagging
behind intellectual changes in the discipline, and that these books are also biased indi-
cators because they generally avoid theoretical complexity (Calhoun, 1989, 1–2).

[24]Another important carrier of U.S. cultural influence abroad, which is often over-
looked, is evangelical Protestantism, particularly its Pentecostal variant (Brouwer et
al., 1996; Schaefer, 2004).

[25]Interesting comparisons have been made between the Americanization of former West Germany and the "Sovietization" of former East Germany (Jarausch and
Siegrist, 1997).

[26]Of course, I am aware that national identity is not necessarily identical with
intellectual *habitus*, since we do have American citizens who work within European
intellectual traditions and vice versa. What I mean here, are the dominant approaches
in U.S. academia. The predominance of American popular cultural analysts is also
understandable given the relative larger number of U.S. practitioners than those from
other countries, and the strong global impact of U.S. culture.

[27]Winfried Fluck employed the term *Americanization* in this context, to refer to
"developments that have either already taken place in the United States or are in a state
of advanced development there, so that they can serve as models, or, where still contested, at least indicate some of the problems and consequences connected with them"
(Fluck, 1990, 9). More specifically with regard to literary and cultural studies this meaning of the term *Americanization* concerns "an advanced stage of professionalization
developed most clearly and strongly in the United States, but setting new standards
for scholarship in the humanities all over the world" (Fluck, 1998, 67 n 6). This
advancement in American scholarship has next to positive, also clearly negative implications. It entails an institutional dominance of American scholarship "in which the
professional pressure to be different and 'original' at all costs has become overpower-
ing.... It has transformed the humanities into a professional practice in which the pressures of the academic market fuel a race for constant product innovation which, in turn,
nourishes an escalating logic of overstatement designed primarily to gain professional
visibility" (Fluck, 2000, 154). From this Tocquevilleanlike perspective, the development hinted at is most advanced in the United States, but is taking shape in Europe
as well, as Fluck pointed out, "not because Americans have found a way to skilfully
lure or pressure us into that direction but the inner logic of a growing professionalization under market conditions leaves very little choice in the matter" (Fluck, 1990,
9) thus referring to the growing influence of capitalist globalization in this domain as
well.

[28]This also holds true for a too heavy reliance on British cultural studies by international scholars, since the American dominance in cultural studies is, for the time being, to a great extent a derived hegemony of British cultural studies, which situation has especially been contested by Australian practitioners of cultural studies (Davies, 1995, 162–163; Morris, 1992, 471; Stratton and Ang, 1996).

[29]Egalitarian liberalism is necessary here to build "an infrastructure of justice," as Hutton called it (96, 2003), and he saw shades of this all over Europe, referring to the legacies of social democracy and social Catholicism that form the foundation of the European welfare state. "The call to abandon this moral world view by Europeans openly admiring of the US, and to follow the doctrines of multiculturalism in the name of diversity to reproduce America's approach to recognising minority groups is a calamitous mistake. Once group politics trumps the politics of social solidarity, the foundations of further injustice are laid for everyone. Massive inequality and falling social mobility result as it becomes impossible to articulate any sense of a social contract or common purpose once group rights overwhelm the believe in collective efforts and collective responsibilities" (96).

[30]Yet, as all comparative cultural analysts know full well, it is no small feat to get rid of one's own cultural biases and prejudices and attain truly accurate perceptions and judgments, because with intercultural comparisons one immediately faces a basic methodological problem, which has been poignantly called "mental colonialism" (Pinxten, 1999, 50). This problem becomes evident when the basis of comparison is too exclusively Western to enable the researcher to get to a sensible comparison. Phenomena in other cultures are then exclusively appraised on the basis of characteristics of one other culture, that is of one's own, in this case, Western culture, which is taken as the basic yardstick. Anthropologists have tried to overcome such ethnocentrism by immersing themselves for a longer period in the indigenous cultures concerned, thus trying through participant observation to understand the life-world of locals from their own perspective (the so-called *emic* approach). Whenever possible, the "others" are then also approached as competent actors and involved in the process of comparison through attempts at a dialogical approach in which genuine two-way communication takes place. In the literature we find examples of successful practices of this kind, albeit with their inevitable limitations because of the fundamental nature of the exchange process that entails power imbalances between the ethnographer and his or her research object (Pinxten, 43–67).

[31]This tradition emerged from the intellectual concerns of a group of French historians gathered around the journal *Annales: Economies, Sociétés, Civilisations*, who aimed for an integral, "totalizing" historiography by means of an analytical framework consisting of various interdependent layers of historical reality (the physical-geographical, economic-technological, social-structural, and mental-cultural level respectively), thereby employing theories and methods borrowed from the social sciences.

[32]That is, an exclusive focus on the present and neglect of the past.

[33]This is not the case in its various structuralist variants. For a good overview of current historical sociology that does take culture into account, see Morawska and Crane, (1994); and regarding various cultures of inquiry in sociohistorical research, see J.R. Hall, (1992, 1999).

[34]Admittedly, ideology is a crucial concept in the study of popular culture. Graeme Turner called it "the most important conceptual category in cultural studies" (Turner, 1996: 182). In much cultural analysis in the British tradition of cultural studies, the concept of ideology has been used interchangeably with culture itself, and especially popular culture. However, the terms are not quite synonymous. As Stuart Hall suggested, "Something is left over when one says 'ideology' and something is not present

when one says 'culture'" (Hall, 1978, 23). Here Hall referred, of course, to politics (Storey, 1997, 2–3).

[35]Some of PCA's leading figures think differently; for example John G. Cawelti. As Stephen Tatum pointed out, "Cawelti has argued throughout his career that teachers and sympathetic critics of popular culture not reject out-of-hand 'high' cultural or serious artistic traditions, and he has reminded those defenders of the traditional canon about the very historicity and fluidity of cultural boundaries, defining the divide between so-called serious and formulaic literature" (Tatum, 1991, 81).

[36]In the same vein, Stuart Hall decoupled the question of intrinsic literary and cultural merits of specific texts from its moorings in the practice of cultural classification. He did not see popular culture in terms of fixed qualities of given content but in relational terms; that is, as those cultural forms and practices that deviated from the established canon and were kept away from it by symbolic practices of screening and exclusion. Crucial in his eyes was how "high culture" at any given time in history was defined in relation to "low culture" (Hall, 1996, 293–294). The book on the "popular arts" by Hall and Whannel (1964) can be seen as a classic left–Leavisite approach of popular culture forms such as Hollywood westerns and pop songs, trying to discriminate between what is good and what is bad *within* popular culture (Storey, 1998, 46, 63–70).

[37]Frow made a necessary distinction between practices that are still quite closely tied to the status and family life of the upper class, such as ballet, opera, and perhaps also the theater, and the more "rootless" practices of art, literature, and film. In this he came close to Bourdieu's approach in terms of cultural *habitus* that takes place for a significant part through socialization within families and class-bound cultures.

[38]In the late 1980s, an analyst of the reception of U.S. popular culture in New Zealand, mentioned his debts to both British cultural studies and (PCA-style) American perspectives of popular culture studies, emphasizing that he still felt drawn to the latter for their "generosity of spirit and enthusiasm," but also conceding that the American popular culture studies "frequently lack intellectual rigour or fail to acknowledge the self-interest of the culture industry." He also criticized the then prevalent definition of culture as ideology within British cultural studies, as being "too limiting because of its inability to adequately explain mainstream popular culture and its subsequent romanticising of subcultural activity. It remains fixated with the idea of the production and consumption of popular culture as a predetermined political process. There is always a sense that popular culture is something that happens to other people, whereas we are all intimately involved." A strategy he suggested was to try to marry "some of the theoretical seriousness of British Cultural Studies to the enthusiasm and openness of American Popular Cultural Studies" (Lealand 11–12). Although in the meantime things have changed to some extent both in cultural studies and popular cultural studies, these still remain different traditions and further attempts at a dialogue between the two should be endorsed.

[39]See Habermas (1968); Calhoun, (1992); for a well-balanced critique of Habermas's theory of communicative action and notion of "the ideal speech situation," or unconstrained, open debate among equals, see Baert (2001) 90–92.

[40]For an interesting yet speculative view on this topic, see B.S. Turner, (1993, 1994).

References

Agger, Ben. *Cultural Studies as Critical Theory*. Washington, DC.: Falmer P, 1992.

Angus, Ian, and Sut Jhally, Editors. *Cultural Politics in Contemporary America*. New York: Routledge, 1982.

Aronowitz, Stanley. *Roll Over, Beethoven: The Return of Cultural Strife*. New York: Westview, 1993.

Baert, Patrick. "Jürgen Habermas." In Anthony Elliott and Bryan S. Turner, Editors, *Profiles in Contemporary Social Theory*. London: Sage, 2001, 84–93.

Barker, Chris. *Cultural Studies: Theory and Practice*. London: Sage, 2000.

Barber-Kersovan, Alenka. "Popular Music in ex–Yugoslavia between Global Participation and Provincial Seclusion." Andreas Gebesmair and Alfred Smudits, Editors, *Global Repertoires: Popular Music Within and Beyond the Transnational Music Industry*. Aldershot, UK: Ashgate, 2001, pp. 73–87.

Baynes, Kenneth. "Communicative Ethics, the Public Sphere and Communication Media." *Critical Studies in Mass Communication*, 11 (1994): 315–326.

Becker, Howard S. *Art Worlds*. Berkeley : University of California Press, 1982.

Bennett, Tony. *Culture: A Reformer's Science*. London: Sage, 1998.

Berman, Morris. *The Twilight of American Culture*. New York: Norton, 2000.

Bérubé, Michael. *Public Access: Literary Theory and American Cultural Politics*. New York: Verso, 1994.

Bettig, Roland V. *Copyrighting Culture: The Political Economy of Intellectual Property*. Boulder, CO: Westview, 1996.

Bijsterveld, Arnoud-Jan. *Het Maakbare Verleden: Regionale Geschiedenis en Etnologie in Brabant op de Drempel van de Eenentwintigste Eeuw*. Inaugurele rede aan de Katholieke Universiteit Brabant, February 11, 2000.

Blundell, Valda, Shepherd, John, and Ian Taylor. *Relocating Cultural Studies: Developments in Theory and Research*. New York: Routledge, 1993.

Brouwer, Steve, Paul Gifford, and Susan D. Rose. *Exporting the American Gospel: Global Christian Fundamentalism*. New York: Routledge, 1996.

Browne, Ray B. "The Dynamics of Popular Culture Studies." In Peter Freese and Michael Porsche, Editors, *Popular Culture in the United States*. Essen: Verlag die Blaue Eule, 1994, pp. 31–48.

Budd, Mike, Entman, Robert C., and Clay Steinman. "The Affirmative Character of U.S. Cultural Studies." *Critical Studies in Mass Communications*, 7 (1990): 169–184.

Calhoun, Craig, Editor. *Comparative Social Research. A Research Annual*, Vol. 1. Greenwich,of CT: JAIP, 1989.

Calhoun, Craig, Editor. *Habermas and the Public Sphere*. Cambridge, MA: MIT Press, 1992.

Carey, James W. "Overcoming Resistance to Cultural Studies." In John Storey, Editor, *What is Cultural Studies?: A Reader*. London: Edward Arnold, 1996, pp. 61–74.

Clifford, James, and George Marcus, Editors. *Writing Culture. The Poetics and Politics of Ethnography*. Berkeley, CA: University of California Press, 1986.

Crane, Diana. *The Production of Culture: Media and the Urban Arts*. Newbury Park, CA: Sage, 1992.

Crane, Diana, Editor. *The Sociology of Culture: Emerging Theoretical Perspectives*. Oxford, UK: Blackwell, 1994.

Davies, Ioan. *Cultural Studies and Beyond: Fragments of Empire*. New York: Routledge, 1995.

de Certeau, Michel. *The Practice of Everyday Life*. Berkeley: University of California Press, 1984.

Dekker, Ton, Herman Roodenburg, and Gerard Rooijakkers, Editors. *Volkscultuur: Een Inleiding in de Nederlandse Etnologie*. Nijmegen: SUN, 2000.

Denning, Michael. "The Academic Left and the Rise of Culture Studies." *Radical History Review*, 54 (1992): 21–47.

Denning, Michael. *The Cultural Front: The Left and American Culture in the Age of the CIO*. New York: Verso, 1996a.

Denning, Michael. "Culture and the Crisis: The Political and Intellectual Origins of Cultural Studies in the United States," In Cary Nelson and Dilip Parameshwar Gaonkar, Editors, *Disciplinarity and Dissent in Cultural Studies*. New York: Routledge, 1996b, pp. 265–286.

Ehrenreich, Barbara. "The Challenge for the Left." *Democratic Left*, July–August (1991): 3–4.

Epstein, Barbara . "Why Poststructuralism is a Dead End for Progressive Thought." *Socialist Review*, 25 (1995), 2: 83–119.

Eskola, Katarina, and Erkki Vainikkala. "Nordic Cultural Studies— An Introduction." *Cultural Studies* 8.2 (1992): 191–197.

Ferguson, Marjorie, and Peter Golding, Editors. *Cultural Studies in Question*. London: Sage, 1997.

Fisher, Philip. "Appearing and Disappearing in Public Social Space in Late-Nineteenth-Century Literature and Culture." Sacvan Bercovitch, Editor, *Reconstructing American Literary History*. Cambridge, MA: Harvard University Press, 1986. 155–158.

Fiske, John. *Understanding Popular Culture*. Boston: Unwyn Hyman, 1989.

Fiske, John. "Popular Discrimination." *Modernity and Mass Culture*. Ed. James Naremore and Patrick Brantlinger. Bloomington: Indiana UP, 1991.

Fiske, John. *Power Plays, Power Works*. New York: Verso, 1993.

Fluck, Winfried. *Populäre Kultur. Ein Studienbuch zur Funktionsbestimmung und Interpretation populärer Kultur*. Stuttgart: Metzler.

Fluck, Winfried. "The Americanization of Literary Studies." *American Studies International* 28.2 (1990): 9–22.

Fluck, Winfried. "Emergence or Collapse of Cultural Hierarchy? Popular Culture Seen from Abroad." In Peter Freese and Michael Porsche, Editors, *Popular Culture in the United States*. Essen: Verlag die Blaue Eule, 1994, pp. 49–74.

Fluck, Winfried. "The Humanities in the Age of Expressive Individualism and Cultural Radicalism." *Cultural Critique*, 40 (1998): 49–71.

Fluck, Winfried. "Internationalizing American Studies: Do We Need an International American Studies Association and What Should Be Its Goals?" *European Journal of American Culture*, 19.3 (2000): 148–155.

Frank, Thomas. *The Conquest of Cool: Business Culture, Counterculture, and the Rise of Hip Consumerism*. Chicago: University of Chicago Press, 1997.

Frank, Thomas. *One Market Under God: Extreme Capitalism, Market Populism, and the End of Economic Democracy*. New York: Anchor Books, 2000.

Fraser, Nancy. "Rethinking the Public Sphere. A Contribution to the Critique of Actually Existing Democracy." In Craig Calhoun, Editor, *Habermas and the Public Sphere*. Cambridge, MA: MIT Press, 1992, pp. 109–142.

Friedman, Jonathan. *Cultural Identity and Global Process*. London: Sage, 1994.

Frith, Simon. "The Good, the Bad, and the Indifferent: Defending Popular Culture from the Populists." *Diacritics* 21 (1991) 4: 102–115. Reproduced in John Storey, Editor, *Cultural Theory and Popular Culture. A Reader*. 2nd ed. London: Prentice Hall, 1998, pp. 570–586.

Frow, John. *Cultural Studies and Cultural Value*. Oxford: Clarendon Press, 1995.

Gans, Herbert. *Popular Culture and High Culture: An Analysis and Evaluation of Taste*. New York: Basic Books, 1974.

Gans, Herbert. "American Popular Culture and High Culture in a Changing Class Structure." *Prospects: An Annual of American Cultural Studies*, 10 (1985): 17–37.

Garnham, Nicholas. "Political Economy and the Practice of Cultural Studies." In Marjorie Ferguson and Peter Golding, Editors, *Cultural Studies in Question*. Ed. Marjorie Ferguson and Peter Golding. London: Sage, 1997, pp. 56–73.

German Matters in Popular Culture. Guest Editor Christoph Lorey and John L. Plews. Theme issue *Journal of Popular Culture* 34. (2000) 3.

Gitlin, Todd. *The Twilight of Common Dreams: Why America Is Wracked by Culture Wars*. New York: Metropolitan Books Henry Holt, 1995.

Gitlin, Todd. "The Anti-Political Populism of Cultural Studies." In Marjorie Ferguson and Peter Golding, Editors, *Cultural Studies in Question*. London: Sage, 1997, pp. 25–38.

Goldfarb, Jeffrey C. *The Cynical Society: The Culture of Politics and the Politics of Culture in American Life*. Chicago: University of Chicago Press, 1991.

Gripsrud, Jostein. "'High Culture' Revisited." *Cultural Studies* 3.2 (1989): 194–207.

Habermas, Jürgen. *Technik und Wissenschaft als "Ideologie."* Frankfurt: Suhrkamp Verlag, 1968.

Habermas, Jürgen. *Knowledge and Human Interest*. London: Heinemann, 1972.

Habermas, Jürgen. *The Structural Transformation of the Public Sphere: An Enquiry into a Category of Bourgeois Society*. Cambridge: Polity P, 1989 (original German publication 1962).

Habermas, Jürgen. *The Theory of Communicative Action*, Vol. 1. Cambridge, UK: Polity Press, 1991a.

Habermas, Jürgen. *The Theory of Communicative Action*, Vol. 2. Cambridge, UK: Polity Press, 1991b.

Hackett Fisher, David. *His Albion's Seed: Four British Folkways in America*. New York: Oxford University Press, 1989.

Hall, John R. "Where History and Sociology Meet: Forms of Discourse and Sociohistorical Inquiry." *Sociological Theory*, 10.2 (1992): 164–193.

Hall, John R. *Cultures of Inquiry: From Epistemology to Discourse in Sociohistorical Research*. Cambridge: Cambridge University Press, 1999.

Hall, John R., and Mary Jo Neitz. *Culture: Sociological Perspectives*. Englewood Cliffs, NJ: Prentice-Hall, 1993.

Hall, Stuart. "Some Paradigms in Cultural Studies." *Annali* 3 (1978).

Hall, Stuart. "The Formation of a Diasporic Intellectual. An Interview with Stuart Hall by Kuan-Hsing Chen." In David Morley and Kuan-Hsing Chen, Editors, *Stuart Hall: Critical Dialogues in Cultural Studies*. New York: Routledge, 1996, pp. 484–503.

Hall, Stuart. "Notes on Deconstructing 'The Popular.'" In Raphael Samuel, Editor, *People's History and Socialist History*. London: Routledge, 1981. 227–240. Rep. in John Storey, Editor, *Cultural Theory and Popular Culture: A Reader*. London: Prentice Hall, 1997, pp. 442–453.

Hall, Stuart, and Martin Jacques, Editors. *New Times: The Changing Face of Politics in the 1990s*. London: Verso, 1989.

Hall, Stuart, and Paddy Whannel. *The Popular Arts*. London: Hutchinson, 1964.

Hannerz, Ulf. *Cultural Complexity: Studies in the Social Organization of Meaning*. New York: Columbia University Press, 1992.

Harvey, David. *The Condition of Postmodernity*. Oxford: Blackwell, 1989.

Hesmondhalgh, David. *The Cultural Industries*. London: Sage, 2002.

Hodgson, M.G.S. *Rethinking World History: Essays on Europe, Islam and World History*. Cambridge, UK: Cambridge University Press, 1992

Hoggart, Richard. *The Uses of Literacy: Aspects of Working-Class Life with Special Reference to Publications and Entertainments*. London: Chatto & Windus, 1957.

Hoggart, Richard. *The Way We Live Now*. London: Chatto and Windus, 1995.

Hopkins, A.G., Editor. *Globalization in World History*. London: Pimlico, 2002.

Hourani, Albert H. *Islam in European Thought*. Cambridge: Cambridge University Press, 1992.

Howe, Irving. "The Value of the Canon." *New Republic* (18 February 1991): 42.

Hutton, Will. *The World We're In*. London: Abacus, 2003.

Jacoby, Russell. *Dogmatic Wisdom: How the Culture Wars Divert Education and Distract America*. New York: Doubleday, 1994.

James, Allison, Jenny Hockey, and Andres Dawson. *After Writing Culture: Epistemology and Praxis in Contemporary Anthropology*. New York: Routledge, 1997.

Jarausch, Konrad, and Hannes Siegrist, Editors. *Amerikanisierung und Sowjetisierung in Deutschland, 1945–1970*. Frankfurt: Campus, 1997.

Jensen, Joli. "An Interpretative Approach to Cultural Production." In W. Roland and B. Watkins, Editors, *Interpreting Television*. London: Sage, 1984, pp. 98–118.

Kammen, Michael. *American Culture American Tastes: Social Change and the 20th Century*. New York: Knopf, 2000.

Kellner, Douglas. "Critical Theory and Cultural Studies: The Missed Articulation." In Jim McGuigan, Editor, *Cultural Methodologies*. London: Sage, 1997, pp. 12–41.

Kreutzner, Gabriele. "On Doing Cultural Studies in West Germany." *Cultural Studies* 3.2 (1989): 240–249.

Lazere, Donald, Editor. *American Media and Mass Culture: Left Perspectives*. Berkeley: University of California Press, 1987.

Lealand, Geoff. *A Foreign Egg in Our Nest? American Popular Culture in New Zealand*. Wellington: Victoria University Press, 1988.

Lipset, Seymour Martin, and Gary Marks. *It Didn't Happen Here: Why Socialism Failed in the United States*. New York: Norton, 2000.

Lipsitz, George. *Time Passages: Collective Memory and American Popular Culture*. Minneapolis: University of Minnesota Press, 1990.

Maase, Kaspar. *Grenzenloses Vergnügen: Der Aufstieg der Massenkultur 1850–1870*. Frankfurt am Main: Fischer, 1997.

MacCannell, Dean. *Empty Meeting Grounds*. London: Routledge, 1992.

McChesney, Robert W. *Rich Media Poor Democracy: Communication Politics in Dubious Times*. New York: New Press, 2000. (orig. Urbana: University of Illinois Press, 1999).

McGuigan, Jim. *Cultural Populism*. New York: Routledge, 1992.

McGuigan, Jim. *Culture and the Public Sphere*. New York: Routledge, 1996.

McGuigan, Jim. "Cultural Populism Revisited." In Marjorie Ferguson and Peter Golding, Editors, *Cultural Studies in Question*. London: Sage, 1997, pp. 138–154.

Mattelart, Armand, and Michèle Mattelart. *Theories of Communication: A Short Introduction*. London: Sage, 1998.

Mills, C. Wright. "The Cultural Apparatus." In Irving Louis Horowitz, Editor, *Power, Politics, and People: The Collected Essays of C. Wright Mills*. New York: Ballantine, 1963, pp. 406–420.

Morawska, Eva, and Wilfried Spohn. "'Cultural Pluralism' in Historical Sociology: Recent Theoretical Directions." In Diana Crane, Editor, *The Sociology of Culture: Emerging Theoretical Perspectives*. Oxford, UK: Blackwell, 1994, pp. 45–90.

Morley, David. "EurAm, Modernity, Reason and Alternity or Postmodernism, the Highest Stage of Cultural Imperialism?" In David Morley and Kuan-Hsing Chen, Editors, *Stuart Hall: Critical Dialogues in Cultural Studies*. London and New York: Routledge, 1996, pp. 326–360.

Morley, David. "Theoretical Orthodoxies: Textualism, Constructivism and the 'New Ethnography' in Cultural Studies." In Marjorie Ferguson and Peter Golding, Editors, *Cultural Studies in Question*. London: Sage, 1997, pp. 121–137.

Morris, Meaghan. "Afterthoughts on 'Australianism.'" *Cultural Studies*, 6.3 (1992): 468–475.

Negus, Keith. "The Production of Culture." In Paul du Gay, Editor, *Production of Culture/Cultures of Production*. London: Sage, 1997, pp. 67–104.

Nelson, Cary, and Lawrence Grossberg, Editors. *Marxism and the Interpretation of Culture*. London: Macmillan, 1998.

Nissen, Peter. *De Folklorisering van het Onalledaagse*. Tilburg: Tilburg University Press, 1994.

O'Connor, Alan. "The Problem of American Cultural Studies." *Critical Studies in Mass Communication*, 6 (1989): 405–413.

Ostendorf, Berndt. "'Cultural Studies': Post-Political Theory in a Post-Fordist Public Sphere." *Amerikastudien/American Studies*, 40. 1996: 709–724.

Peterson, Richard A., Editor. *The Production of Culture*. Beverly Hills, CA: Sage, 1976.

Peterson, Richard A. "Where the Two Cultures Meet: Popular Culture." *Journal of Popular Culture*, 11 (1977): 385–400.

Peterson, Richard A. "Culture Studies Through the Production Perspective: Progress and Prospects." In Diana Crane, Editor, *The Sociology of Culture: Emerging Theoretical Perspectives* Oxford, UK: Blackwell, 1994, pp. 163–189.

Peterson, Richard A. *Creating Country Music: Fabricating Authenticity*. Chicago: University of Chicago Press, 1997.

Pfister, Joel. "The Americanization of Cultural Studies." In John Storey, Editor, *What is Cultural Studies?: A Reader*, 2nd. London: Arnold, 1997, pp. 287–299.

Pine, Joseph.B., and James H. Gilmore. *The Experience Economy*. Boston, MA: Harvard Business School Press, 1999.

Pinxten, Rik. *Culturen Sterven Langzaam: Over Interculturele Communicatie*. Antwerpen-Baarn: Houtekiet. 3e geactualiseerde druk, 1999.

Rosenau, Pauline Marie. *Post-Modernism and the Social Sciences: Insights, Inroads, and Intrusions*. Princeton, NJ: Princeton University Press, 1991.

Ross, Andrew. *No Respect: Intellectuals and Popular Culture*. New York: Routledge, 1989.

Said, Edward. *Orientalism*. New York: Vintage, 1978.

Said, Edward. *Culture and Imperialism*. New York: Knopf, 1993.

Savage, John, and Simon Frith. "Pearls and Swine — Intellectuals and the Media." *New Left Review*, 198 (March–April 1993): 107–116.

Schaefer, Nancy A. (forthcoming) "Exporting a U.S. Gospel of Health and Wealth: An American Faith Healer in Europe." In Hans Krabbendam and Derek Rubin, Editors, *Religion in America*. Amsterdam: VU University Press 2004, pp. 275–289.

Schlesinger, Philip R. "Europe's Contradictory Communicative Space." *Daedalus*, 132.2 (1994): 25–52.

Schwartz, Stephen Adam. "Everyman an Übermensch: The Culture of Cultural Studies." *SubStance*, 91 (2000): 116–123.

Smelser, Neil J. "Culture: Coherent or Incoherent?" In Richard Münch and Neil J. Smelser, Editors, *Theory of Culture*. Berkeley, CA: University of California Press, 1992, pp. 3–28.

Smith, Barbara Herrnstein. *Contingencies of Value*. Cambridge, MA: Harvard University Press, 1988.

Smith, Philip. "The New American Cultural Sociology: An Introduction." In Philip Smith, Editor, *The New American Cultural Sociology*. Cambridge: Cambridge University Press, 1998, pp. 1–14.

Sreberny-Mohammadi, Annabelle. "The Many Cultural Faces of Imperialism." In Peter Golding and Phil Harris, Editors, *Beyond Cultural Imperialism: Globalization,*

Communication and the New International Order. London: Sage, 1997, pp. 49–68.

Stauth, Georg, and Sami Zubaida, Editors. *Mass Culture, Popular Culture, and Social Life in the Middle East.* Frankfurt am Main: Campus Verlag/Boulder, CO: Westview Press, 1987.

Storey, John. *An Introduction to Cultural Theory and Popular Culture.* 2nd ed. London: Prentice-Hall/Harvester Wheatsheaf, 1997.

Storey, John, Editor. *Cultural Theory and Popular Culture. A Reader.* 2nd ed. London: Prentice-Hall, 1998.

Stratton, Jon, and Ien Ang. "On the Impossibility of a Global Cultural Studies: 'British' Cultural Studies in an 'International' Frame." In David Morley and Kuan-Hsing Chen, Editors, *Stuart Hall: Critical Dialogues in Cultural Studies.* New York: Routledge, 1996, pp. 361–391.

Tatum, Stephen. "John G. Cawelti: Rhetoric of Motives." In Ray B. Browne and Michael T Marsden, Editors, *Pioneers in Popular Culture Studies.* Bowling Green, OH: Bowling Green State University Popular Press, 1999, pp. 67–85.

Tetzlaff, David. "Popular Culture and Social Control in Late Capitalism." In Paddy Scannell, Philip Schlesinger and Colin Sparks, Editors, *Culture and Power. A Media, Culture and Society Reader.* London. Sage, 1992, pp. 48–72.

Tomlinson, John. *Cultural Imperialism: A Critical Introduction.* London: Pinter, 1991.

Tuchman, Gaye. "Conscious Industries and the Production of Culture." *Journal of Communication,* 33 (1983): 330–341.

Turner, Bryan S., Editor. *Citizenship and Social Theory.* Newbury Park: Sage, 1993.

Turner, Bryan S. "Postmodern Culture/Modern Citizens." In Bart van Steenbergen, Editor, *The Condition of Citizenship.* London and Newbury Park: Sage, 1994, pp. 153–168.

Turner, Bryan S. *Classical Sociology.* London: Sage, 1999.

Turner, Bryan S., and Chris Rojek. *Society and Culture: Scarcity and Solidarity.* London: Sage, 2001.

Turner, Graeme. *British Cultural Studies: An Introduction.* 2nd ed. London: Routledge, 1996.

Uricchio, William. "Displacing Culture: Transnational Culture, Regional Elites, and the Challenge to National Cinema." In Annemoon van Hemel, Hans Mommaas and Cas Smithuijsen, Editors, *Trading Culture. GATT, European Cultural Politics and the Transatlantic Market.* Amsterdam: Boekman Foundation, 1996, pp. 67–80.

van Elteren, Mel. "Conceptualizing the Impact of U.S. Popular Culture Globally." *Journal of Popular Culture,* 30.1 (1996a): 47–89.

van Elteren, Mel. "Gatt and Beyond: World Trade, the Arts and American Popular Culture in Western Europe." *Journal of American Culture,* 19.3 (1996): 59–73.

van Elteren, Mel. "The PCA and Popular Culture Studies at the End of the Millennium: *Quo Vadis?* A View from Europe." *Journal of Popular Culture,* 35.1 (2001): 107–143.

van Elteren, Mel. *Cultuurstudies Nader Belicht: Een Kritisch Overzicht van het Terrein.* Tilburg: Faculteit Sociale Wetenschappen — Katholieke Universiteit Brabant, 2001.

van Elteren, Mel. "U.S. Cultural Imperialism Today; Only A Chimera?" *SAIS Review.* Journal of International Affairs associated with Johns Hopkins University's School of Advanced International Studies, Washington, DC, September 2003.

Williams, Raymond. *Culture and Society 1780–1950.* Harmondsworth, UK: Penguin, 1963.

Williams, Raymond. *The Long Revolution.* Harmondsworth, UK: Penguin, 1965.

Williams, Raymond. "The Idea of a Common Culture." Rept. In R. Cable, Editor,

234 Popular Culture Studies Across the Curriculum

Resources of Hope: Culture, Democracy, Socialism. London: Verso, 1968, pp. 32–38.

Willis, Paul. *Common Culture.* Buckingham, UK: Open University Press, 1990.

Wolfe, Alan (1992) "Democracy versus Sociology: Boundaries and Their Political Consequences." In Michèle Lamont and Marcel Fournier, Editors, *Cultivating Differences: Symbolic Boundaries and the Making of Inequality.* Chicago: University of Chicago Press, pp. 309–326.

Wolff, Janet. *The Social Production of Art.* New York: New York University Press, 1981.

Wolff, Janet. *Aesthetics and the Sociology of Culture,* 2nd. ed, London: Macmillan, 1993.

Wuthnow, Robert. "Sociology of Religion." In Neil Smelser, Editor, *Handbook of Sociology.* New York: Sage, 1988, pp. 473–509.

Conclusion

Looking back over the range and the changes to the traditional thinking and canon suggested in these essays, one might be troubled or even a little frightened, for the changes challenge what has traditionally gone on for years in the thinking and teaching. Traditionally, we have walked away from our graduate training glowing with the wisdom of our famous and favorite instructors. To a certain extent this glow is a combination of self-pride and fear. We wear our degrees on our sleeves and in our hearts, display them proudly on our curriculum vita and over our desks (as medical doctors do)— not to say constantly in our conversation. In fact one of the paralyzing restrictions of graduate school is that dictum given us with the degree, that is to go forth, glorify the old alma mater, and conquer the world. Wherever we go thereafter, we never leave the campus from which we graduated. The glory days of our graduate school fill our canons and we never bother to rethink or reload it.

Such an attitude is of course a disservice to our training, ourselves, and our students, and was not intended. School on all levels is supposed to activate the mind, to free it for new ways of thinking instead of training it in the old. Education is supposed to be a journey, not a destination. In our civilization culture changes so rapidly that the mind that has not been freed to accept it is lost. The changes of the new world are frightening or, if you accept them, an open door to development. These challenges make up the new, the popular culture, the "new humanities" of our time.

At the same time that they present a challenge they provide a comfort. In the old educational canons one had to stretch out to comprehend new subjects in new languages. Now the languages are recognizable and the subjects, though startling in their dizzying array of variety are everyday. We are up to our necks in them, but they are our culture. For better or worse, they are our world. You may not care for them and want to become a secular monk or nun, but escape is barely possible. And certainly as an academic and teacher, your colleagues and students are going to lose patience with you unless you keep up with the times.

In these essays there might be some comfort in a side glance at the suggested developments in disciplines other than one's own. For example, though one might see nothing worthwhile in the reforms suggested for his or her discipline, perhaps one might find merit in possibilities for *other* disciplines. Such a crack in *discipline amor* or *discipline defense* is valuable, for it is a first glance at what might become a passionate association. In the study of popular culture as the common unifier in the new humanities, one page in the new book is better than none.

The thesis of this book is that education should explain and drive toward greater democracy in the United States and throughout the world. *Education is too valuable to waste*, and it cannot be found by looking backward. Studies of the past and present are loaded with footnote subjects which do not comment on our world. Popular culture studies blend the past with the present and the future. Increasingly such a goal is the aim of the new humanities. Like it or not, our world consists of its popular culture, and the most useful approach to it is through the new humanities.

About the Contributors

Lynn G. Bartholome   is associate professor of English and philosophy at Monroe Community College, Rochester, New York, where she teaches courses in popular culture, interdisciplinary humanities, literature, writing, and philosophy. She is currently the president of the Popular Culture Association and on the editorial advisory board of *The Journal of Popular Culture*. She is the author of numerous publications, including a forthcoming book on the Jewish community of Rochester, *The Jews of Joseph Avenue*. She is also a volume editor for *The Encyclopedia of World Popular Culture*, a series to be published by Greenwood Press. Her next research project is a cultural history of Jell-O. Dr. Bartholome is a 2004 nominee for a SUNY Chancellor's Award for Excellence in Teaching.

Thomas L. Bell   is professor of geography at the University of Tennessee. He has taught a variety of courses in human geography including economic, urban, and behavioral geography. He has also taught sections of First Year Studies and in the University Honors program, most recently coteaching a freshman seminar with coauthor Margaret M. Gripshover on the geography of utopian communities in the United States. His courses in urban geography are cross-listed with the urban studies program at Tennessee, and his course in the geography of American popular culture is cross-listed in the American Studies program. His current research includes the devolution of specialized agricultural regions, the changing retail structure of small towns, changes in Southern landscapes, and the geography of the modern music industry. He has written a textbook for a course in human geography (*People, Places and Change* for the Annenberg/CPB Project, 1996) and, in collaboration with Dr. Gripshover, has prepared teaching materials for several textbooks in human and regional geography. Dr. Bell is also secretary of the Epsilon of Tennessee chapter of the Phi Beta Kappa Society on campus.

Ray B. Browne   is professor of popular culture, Bowling Green State University, emeritus. He was cofounder of the Popular Culture Association and founder of the American Culture Association and of the *Journal of Popular Culture* and the *Journal of American Culture*, both of which he edited from the beginning to 2002. He has authored and edited over 70 books on all aspects of American and interdisciplinary culture. He is currently working on a book on the Civil War and Reconstruction.

Jane Caputi   is professor of women's studies at Florida Atlantic University. She is the author of several interdisciplinary works: *The Age of Sex Crime, Gossips, Gorgons, and Crones: The Fates of the Earth,* and *Goddesses and Monsters: Women, Myth, Power and Popular Culture.*

Carlnita Greene   is a doctoral candidate in communication studies at the University of Texas at Austin whose specialization lies at the intersection of rhetoric, media, and cultural studies. In her current research, she is exploring the relationship between simulational experiences, politics, and the viability of a public sphere within a hyper-mediated, consumerist society.

Margaret M. Gripshover   is adjunct associate professor of geography at the University of Tennessee. Until 2001, she was associate professor of geography at Marshall University in Huntington, West Virginia. She has taught sections of First Year Studies at Marshall and courses in cultural, rural, Appalachian, economic, gender, medical, and physical geography at Marshall where she has been honored for her outstanding teaching. Since coming to Tennessee she has taught courses in world regional, economic, and cultural geography and workshops for teachers wishing to become highly qualified in geography through the Tennessee Geographic Alliance. She has been involved with medical research on rural Appalachian women through the medical school in Huntington and more recently has been involved in collaborative research with Thomas L. Bell on agricultural and small-town change. She also has done research on improved horse and mule breeding practices and the origin and diffusion of the Tennessee walking horse. She is the author or coauthor of teaching materials for textbooks in world regional geography.

C. Richard King   is associate professor of comparative ethnic studies at Washington State University. His work has appeared a variety of journals, such as *American Indian Culture and Research Journal, Journal of Sport and Social Issues, Public Historian,* and *Qualitative Inquiry.* He is also the author/editor of several books, including *Team Spirits: The Native American Mascot Controversy* (a CHOICE 2001 Outstanding Academic Title), *Postcolonial America,* and most recently *Telling Achievements: Native American Athletes in Modern Sport.* He is presently completing work on a book on race and racism in American popular culture.

David J. Leonard   is an assistant professor in the Department of Comparative Ethnic Studies at Washington State University. His articles have appeared in *American Jewish History, Popmatters, Colorlines,* and at conferences sponsored by Popular Culture Association and Organization of American Historians. He is currently working on a manuscript on race, gender, and national identity within video games, and another examining race and Kobe Bryant.

Katherine Lynde is an English teacher at Blacksburg High School in Montgomery County, Virginia, where she teaches British literature, American literature, and AP language and composition. She received her bachelor's and master's degrees at Virginia Tech. While at Tech, she became acutely interested in using both popular culture and American studies as vehicles for teaching literature and its relevance to students. She currently lives in Blacksburg, Virginia, with her husband, Stuart, and their three children.

Arthur G. Neal is adjunct professor of sociology at Portland State University. His recent books include *National Trauma and Collective Memory* and *Intimacy and Alienation: Forms of Estrangement in Female/Male Relationships*.

Ann Kneavel earned a Ph.D. in British literature from the University of Ottawa. Currently she is head of Arts and Sciences at Goldey-Beacom College, Wilmington, Delaware, focusing her research on the interconnections of film and literature across various humanities disciplines.

Douglas A. Noverr is a professor in the Department of Writing, Rhetoric and American Cultures at Michigan State University and a member of the core faculty in the American studies program. He has published widely on sport history and biography and on sports films. He contributed over 30 articles to the multivolume *Biographical Dictionary of American Sports* and 10 articles on sports figures in the *American National Biography* volumes. He regularly reviews book on sports for a number of journals and is on the Editorial Advisory Board for the *Journal of Popular Culture*.

Raymond Ruble received his Ph.D. in philosophy from the University of Wisconsin in 1970. Since that time he has been teaching philosophy at Appalachian State University in Boone, North Carolina. His teaching and research interests include the history of philosophy, critical thinking, and Greek classics as well as the application of these areas to popular culture. He is currently working on a critical thinking text for high school students.

Michelle Sharkey is a Ph.D. candidate in comparative studies at Florida Atlantic University.

Gregory Thompson received his Ph.D from Florida State University, and is the author of the forthcoming text *Sports Collectibles and the Culture of Fandom*. He is a cultural historian whose scholarly interests range from Shakespeare studies and globalization to the role of the shopping mall in American culture. His eclectic research agenda is a product of an academic background that began with a bachelor's degree in theater performance, was followed by a master's in religious studies and concluded with the Ph.D. in humanities (American studies/American history). "I do not regret that I am sometimes difficult to easily categorize. In fact, my studies reflect questions directed toward the dangers of bureaucracy and technology and the desire to systemize human beings and their roles in society."

Benjamin K. Urish   is a culturologist, meaning he takes a scientific approach to investigating culture, cultures, and cultural phenomena. He specializes in entertainment forms, mass media, humor, and popular culture. He once taught 47 credit hours in one year, with nine different preps, five of them courses he was originating. He is at work on numerous projects including a volume on comedians in American film, and another on American striptease.

Mel van Elteren   is associate professor of social sciences at Tilburg University, the Netherlands. He has written widely on the history of the social and behavioral sciences and in the domains of social history, cultural studies, and American studies. He is currently completing a book that aims to offer an adequate conceptualization of processes of Americanization, at home and abroad, with special emphasis on their relationships to U.S. imperialism, past and present.

Helen Youngelson-Neal   is emeritus professor of economics at Portland State University. She is continuing her research on the globalization of popular culture with a specific focus on the internationalization of popular culture industries.

Index